INDUSTRIAL RELATIONS
IN LATIN AMERICA

INDUSTRIAL RELATIONS IN LATIN AMERICA

A study of the parties involved, the theory and practice of their interactions and procedures in disputes, with special reference to the private sector

Edited by
EFRÉN CÓRDOVA

PRAEGER SPECIAL STUDIES • PRAEGER SCIENTIFIC

New York • Philadelphia • Eastbourne, UK
Toronto • Hong Kong • Tokyo • Sydney

Library of Congress Cataloging in Publication Data

Córdova, Efrén.
    Industrial relations in Latin America.

    1. Industrial relations—Latin America—Addresses,
essays, lectures.   I. Title.
HD8110.5.C67   1984   331'.098   83-24480
ISBN 0-03-070284-4 (alk. paper)

Published in 1984 by Praeger Publishers
CBS Educational and Professional Publishing
a Division of CBS Inc.
521 Fifth Avenue, New York, NY 10175 USA

© 1984 by the International Labour Organisation

456789 052 987654321

Printed in the United States of America
on acid-free paper

8/83 0084T

Preface

This book provides a picture of collective labor relations in the private sector of Latin America at the beginning of the 1980s. It begins with a general description of the existing situation, of which the main feature is the tendency of employers and workers, and of their organizations, to take greater direct responsibility for their relations instead of leaving them, as they had done in the past, to be regulated mainly by the state. The development, structure, and functions of the parties to labor relations (trade union, employers' organizations, and departments of labor) are then considered. Next, the various forms of collective labor relations (collective bargaining, workers' participation in the management of undertakings, other collective relations at the undertaking level, and tripartite cooperation) are examined. The last five chapters deal with the disputes arising from such relations: their classification, ways of settling them, conciliation, arbitration, labor courts, strikes, and lockouts. A short historical introduction shows in what setting each of the institutions considered has evolved.

Besides providing an overview, this work examines the significance of changes in Latin American labor practice over the last few years and highlights their importance: labor relations in Latin America have a long history, and an inventory can now be made of their successes and failures. This book emphasizes that past stereotypes must be left behind, and that the importance of the trend toward voluntarism that seems to be gaining ground in nearly all Latin American countries must be fully recognized.

Also, this work seeks to show the validity of socioinstitutional approaches that combine legal analysis with reference to practice, and particularly to current problems in Latin America. Although the still prominent role of legislation necessarily means that the legal aspect of labor relations must be given due importance, an effort has been made to include statistical references, and to introduce information on why the various institutions exist in different countries, the procedures they have followed, and the forms they have taken in practice.

The International Labour Office (ILO) has already addressed itself on various occasions to certain aspects of labor relations in Latin America. A study examining the role of legislation and collective bargaining in laying down conditions of work and settling labor disputes was prepared for an inter-American study conference on labor-management relations held at Montevideo, Uruguay, in 1960.[1] A comparative study of collective bargaining in Latin America, which included a paper on collective bargaining trends in Venezuela,[2] was published in 1978. More recently interest has been shown in the development of labor relations in state-owned undertakings and the public service.[3] A number of reports to the last three conferences of American states that are members of the ILO have dealt more or less fully with social participation, tripartite cooperation, and the role of departments of labor in labor relations.[4] None of these publications, however, has attempted to cover all the institutions, procedures, and practices in the private sector that comprise what are known as "industrial" or "collective" relations. It is the purpose of this book to fill that gap.

Although it refers to the whole of Latin America, this book does not specifically refer to the present system of labor relations in Cuba, which differs substantially from that in the other countries of the region and therefore cannot be easily included in a comparative study; in any event, the private sector in Cuba is very small.

Efrén Córdova, the editor of this study, who has written nine of the chapters and parts of others, has been assisted by Geraldo von Potobsky, Emilio Morgado, and Arturo S. Bronstein, who, like him, are officials of the International Labour Office. He wishes to express his thanks for assistance received from Professor Oscar Hernández of the University of Barquisimeto, Venezuela, who was on the staff of the ILO in 1980 and cooperated in the research for chapters 9, 10, and 11.

Efrén Córdova
International Labour Office
June 1983

Notes

1. ILO, *Some Aspects of Labour–Management Relations in the American Region,* reports prepared by the International Labour Office for the Inter-American Study Conference on Labor–Management Relations (Montevideo, November 3–12, 1960), Labour–Management Relations Series, no. 11A (Geneva: ILO, 1962).

2. ILO, *La negociación colectiva en América latina* (Geneva: ILO, 1978).

3. See Arturo S. Bronstein, ed., *Las relaciones laborales en las empresas estatales de América latina* (Geneva: ILO, 1981); and Efrén Córdova: "Labour Relations in the Public Service in Latin America," *International Labour Review,* Sept.–Oct. 1980, pp. 579–94.

4. *Participation of Employers' and Workers' Organisations in Economic and Social Development; Role of Other Social Institutions,* Report III, Ninth Conference of American States Members of the International Labour Organisation, Caracas, 1970 (Geneva: ILO, 1970); *Strengthening and Furthering of Tripartite Co-operation,* Report III, Tenth Conference . . . , Mexico City, 1974 (Geneva: ILO, 1974); and *Public Labour Administration and Its Role in Economic and Social Development,* Report II, Eleventh Conference . . . , Medellín, Colombia, 1979 (Geneva: ILO, 1979).

Contents

List of Tables

Introduction

1

The Latin American Picture

by
Efrén Córdova

Every system of labor relations is marked by varying emphases on voluntarism and government intervention, cooperation and conflict, institutional and behavioral aspects, centralization and decentralization. While the relative importance of the particular elements fluctuates according to economic and social conditions, they are always present to some extent.

For many years close government supervision, chronic conflict, legalism, and the adoption of a decentralized model of collective bargaining were distinctive features of the labor relations system in Latin America. It was widely believed that labor relations systems applied only to workers in private enterprises, and that even there they could not be effectively applied except to industrial workers.

These characteristics seemed to foreshadow limited participation of the parties and a growing atrophy of the system, and the likelihood of such an outcome became more pronounced as the hazards affecting freedom of association and the possibilities of collective bargaining increased in frequency. There was also much talk of employers' intransigence and of calls to class struggle by the revolutionary trade union movement that gave rise to the belief that the parties could operate only in a basically conflictual framework. Many studies of labor relations were published that dealt solely with legal matters and ignored practical implications and subtle differences in behavior.

There seemed to be little prospect of any change in this situation, since the above-mentioned characteristics appeared to be firmly rooted in national traditions. Government supervision, for example, stemmed largely from the centralist traditions that have long been typical of Latin American institutions and politics,[1] and from a desire to control the de-

3

velopment of collective relations and supplant the trade unions in taking protective or beneficial action. The conflictual atmosphere was due to economic underdevelopment and the clash between authoritarian patriarchal management and the growing radicalism of the trade union movement. Legalism was the result of national characteristics and the Spanish–Portuguese legacy of Roman law and legal codification. In addition, there was a preference for decentralization in collective bargaining, so as to avoid confrontation on an industrywide or national scale that might affect public order; the government, which controlled the main regulatory function (legislation), preferred to decentralize the regulation, through agreements, of matters of secondary importance.

Four Typical Current Situations

At the beginning of the 1980s certain of these characteristics and trends may require a thorough reappraisal, and others may need to be placed, at least tentatively, under the heading of myth. In reality the pattern of labor relations today is far more varied, more complex, and sometimes more contradictory than the foregoing observations might suggest.

First of all, it is clearly no easy matter to arrive at opinions or give assessments applicable to all the countries of the region or to all the sectors of the economy in a given country. Four separate kinds of national situations should be distinguished and will be referred to repeatedly in the remainder of this book. The first is that of countries where labor relations seem to have reached an appreciable level of development and maturity. In such countries difficult obstacles have been overcome, the most turbulent periods in the history of labor relations have been left behind, and many useful practices have been institutionalized. More important, the foundations have been laid for a relatively normal functioning, particularly at the enterprise level, of the interplay of interests and the balance of power that lie at the core of labor relations. Mexico and Venezuela can be cited as examples of this first group.

A second situation is that prevailing in Argentina, Chile, and Uruguay, which have a long history of labor relations but an institutional framework that has been undergoing profound changes. A third situation is found in Ecuador, Honduras, and the Dominican Republic, where labor relations are still in a formative phase, employers' and workers' organizations are still relatively weak, and collective bargaining can be considered as being in its infancy. Brazil on its own would make up a fourth category, in which the labor relations framework is the closest to the conventional stereotype of Latin American labor relations. Collective bargaining is of little importance, and the Consolidation of Labor Laws and the labor courts play a dominant role that perhaps has no parallel in the other countries.[2]

The other countries of the region display various features of the four situations mentioned. In some of them, moreover, certain sectors of the economy are still marked by a high degree of conflict and confrontation. Mining in Bolivia, the metal trades in Brazil, the public sector in Colombia, and the educational system in Peru are examples of this group.

Common Trends

Many of the characteristics and trends that can be observed in one or another of these groups are not found in the rest, and general comments must be qualified by certain reservations when specific groups of countries are referred to. Even with these reservations, it would be possible to pick out certain characteristics that, although very different from the initial pattern, are common to all the countries of the region or applicable to different groups among them.

One such characteristic is the extension of labor relations to agriculture and the public sector. There are still serious problems in applying legislation and developing collective labor relations outside the towns. In Bolivia, for instance, general labor legislation covers less than 20 percent of the economically active population, but almost everywhere there has been a gradual extension of the general system of labor relations to cover wage-earning agricultural workers. In almost all countries agriculture is no longer excluded from the legislation, and agricultural workers' organizations have grown in strength. In the early 1970s various authors were already remarking that the advent of new organizations, the wider spread of conflicts, and greater awareness among the peasants pointed to the imminent appearance of a new political and social force in the area.[3]

Chapter 2 of this book contains a section on trade unionism in agriculture that confirms this view. The extension of labor relations to the public sector (civil service and nationalized undertakings) is indisputably a current issue; it has already been covered in other ILO publications, and will not be given special treatment here. Neither will this book specifically refer to the extension of labor relations to other sectors or categories of workers (such as supervisors and employees in positions of trust), who in some countries appear to be in an ambiguous situation in regard to freedom of association and their inclusion in collective bargaining.

This chapter will concentrate on the changes that have taken place in the other characteristics and trends, especially the trend toward voluntarism, which is steadily growing in strength and is in contrast with the dependence on state intervention that formerly characterized the system; and the fact that labor relations are conducted within a dual system in which employers and workers often act outside the legal framework set up to regulate collective labor relations. These trends diverge from those that were formerly considered traditional in the region, and demonstrate

the need to make a general reappraisal of labor relations in order to prevent myths from developing and to seek a better balance between legal
standards and reality.

Voluntarism

The word "voluntarism" is used in this context to denote the fact that
employers and workers themselves exercise greater responsibility over
the regulation of their relations and the determination of working conditions. In other words, labor relations reach a certain level of maturity,
making for relative emancipation of management and labor from government supervision. Although this emancipation takes place mainly at the
enterprise level, it undoubtedly means greater freedom of action for the
parties involved and makes for a more dynamic operation of the system in
general. It does not, however, mean that a full voluntarist system has
come into being, since that would be difficult in the Latin American social
context and inappropriate in the present economic situation. I am referring only to a tendency toward greater autonomy and the possibility that
there is now a mixed system with features reflecting both dependence and
autonomy.

The characteristics of the labor relations systems of Latin America
tentatively summarized in this fashion are the fruit of recent developments. In the 1960s collective labor relations were still developing somewhat haltingly and under constant government supervision. For example,
in 1962 an ILO publication reported that, except in a few countries of the
region, collective bargaining was of minor importance and was in many
cases limited to only a few of the larger undertakings.[4] Most agreements
of the time were concluded under the procedure for settling disputes, and
direct dealings were rarely more than mere preliminaries to the next
stage. Several studies on Latin American trade unionism in the 1960s referred to its relatively limited state of development and described it as
being a predominantly revolutionary movement closely bound up with
politics.[5] Still more disquieting was the fact that labor relations at the enterprise level were being conducted in a tense atmosphere that frequently
bordered on the traumatic, and that contacts and discussions at the national level were marked by the absence of a consensus. Strikes were
rarely called to put pressure on the employer, and much more frequently
to bring about government intervention.

Although this situation still tends to persist in some countries and
some sectors, it has undergone a notable change in most of them. What
are the outward signs of such change? There are three main indications of
the trend toward a greater measure of voluntarism: the spread of collec-

tive bargaining, the growing importance of conciliation as a means of solving disputes, and the emergence of new forms of participation.

Collective Bargaining

There is no doubt that collective bargaining has been growing steadily in most of the countries. There is a tendency nowadays for direct negotiation to be used to discuss and settle matters that used to be left to government intervention or to conciliation and arbitration procedures. Admittedly this trend is not yet established in some countries. In Ecuador, for example, the proportion of demands on employers resolved through direct negotiation in 1978 was 46 percent,[6] while in Peru it was no higher than 55 percent of the total.[7] In other countries, however, employers and workers seem more inclined to attach greater importance to dialogue and direct agreement, which they formerly regarded merely as preliminary steps in the procedure for settling disputes.

This new attitude has given rise in nearly every country to increases in the number of agreements concluded each year and in the number of workers covered by such agreements. In this regard it is sufficient to cite the statistics given in an ILO publication showing that in 1972–77 the number of collective agreements rose in 13 of the 14 countries recorded, while the number of workers covered rose in nearly every instance.[8] More recent information in Chapter 5 of this book is similar. It should be added that in Brazil, where collective bargaining used to be very unimportant, a large number of productivity-linked wage negotiations have taken place since 1979 (particularly in the São Paulo area). Table 1.1 gives some indications about the recent evolution of collective bargaining in that country.

Table 1.1. Number of Collective Agreements in Brazil, 1977–81

	Type of Agreement	
Year	Enterprise-Level (acordos colectivos)	Industrywide* (convenções colectivas)
1977	1,100	350
1978	1,046	232
1979	2,105	242
1980	2,221	351
1981	1,616	975

*Includes state and regional agreements applicable to all undertakings in a given branch of the economy.

Source: Centro de Documentação e Informática, Ministerio do Trabalho.

Collective bargaining has been resumed in Chile and Panama after interruptions of seven and two years, respectively (but in Chile is still subject to strict limitations that hamper its functioning at the industry level and render it, to all intents and purposes, impossible in small undertakings). In other countries, where legal restrictions were placed on wage negotiations, discussion of collective agreements continued on other conditions of work, such as paid and unpaid leave, job evaluation, and sickness insurance in Uruguay. Even in countries where labor relations are still in the formative stage, collective bargaining has experienced a substantial development in several sectors. In the sugar industry of the Dominican Republic and Ecuador, for instance, periodic negotiations have normally taken place since the 1960s. The agreements entered into at the Valdez sugar mill (Ecuador) and at La Romana (Dominican Republic) can easily be compared with those concluded in any industrialized country. And the agreements in force at the Tela Railroad Company and the National Electric Corporation of Honduras are detailed and comprehensive documents printed and distributed to all the workers concerned.

Although negotiations are conducted mainly at the enterprise level in Latin America, in Argentina and Brazil they are generally on an industry-wide basis, and in Mexico, Panama, Peru, and Venezuela some agreements cover entire branches of the economy. In Argentina, where the discussion of agreements at the industry level was suspended in 1976, and in Brazil, which also used to prefer that level of bargaining, agreements covering specific undertakings have been proliferating.

At the same time as the quantitative increase, a no less important qualitative transformation has been taking place. Collective bargaining is ceasing to be exclusively a process of confrontation and is becoming a normal mode of communication. Discussions are losing their emotionally traumatic nature and gradually becoming ordinary events that take place periodically and are considered essential. This change is reflected in the nature and scope of agreements, which are ceasing to be merely the result of improvisation or compromise and are becoming complex, extensive documents. In countries where industrial development is less advanced, wage claims continue to monopolize the attention of the parties, but in the others a wide range of demands and contractual clauses can be noted.

Even with respect to wages, it is possible to see how negotiations are assuming growing importance in determining the average wage rates prevailing in the different countries of the region. It is not easy to establish a precise causal connection between collective bargaining and the secular wage rises observed in the region, but the fact that the average wages in the industrial sector are moving further and further from the minimum rates laid down by governments seems to show that these levels have been affected by a factor quite distinct from official action that can hardly be identified with labor market forces.[9] The old dictum that in Latin

America "minimum wages" means "maximum wages" has ceased to be true.

The magnitude and importance of the change in collective bargaining can be seen from its gathering momentum since the early 1960s in spite of the changes in development strategies during that time. It might be argued that the import substitution policy that prevailed until a few years ago favored wage bargaining by inspiring many protectionist measures that ensured a certain profit margin, and therefore some leeway for bargaining; but this policy was limited in scope and could not explain the extension of formal labor relations to sectors of the economy to which protectionist policy did not apply. It is even more notable that these relations were extended later, when policy veered toward entering the world market, which assumes greater price competitiveness and often means reduced protection for domestic production. Together with more recent austerity measures sponsored by the International Monetary Fund, these policies can hardly be regarded as favorable to wage bargaining. There is, however, no doubt that such bargaining continued to flourish even in the countries that most vigorously applied the new development policies.

Various reasons account for this increase in collective bargaining. The first is connected to the fact that labor codes that governed labor relations for so many years are becoming obsolete and fail to take account of all the labor problems in contemporary society. While some codes were so detailed and comprehensive when they first came into force that they made collective bargaining almost pointless—so much so that the earliest agreements simply reproduced certain of the codes' provisions—nowadays, some 30 or 40 years after their promulgation, the capacity of the codes to set effective standards is far from being the same. Thus, collective bargaining emerges as a natural complement to the labor codes and allows a more flexible response to changing labor conditions. In some countries, such as Panama, the government itself recognizes that it is a function of the labor department to promote collective bargaining as a normal means of establishing working conditions.

The second reason has to do with the increase in the number of medium-size and large undertakings that have sprung up as a consequence of advances in industrialization. Higher density of workers employed in the factories and greater complexity of functions have inevitably resulted in a need to lay down ground rules best adapted to the circumstances of each undertaking. This in turn explains the high concentration of collective bargaining in modern industry, plantations and in public undertakings.

The third reason is a sociological one and indicates a change in attitude. Employers and workers both feel more ready to break with paternalistic and individualistic traditions, and to involve their respective organizations in the everyday task of conducting labor relations. Similarly, employers' and workers' organizations are moving from the sidelines to the heart of the labor relations system. The employers' organizations have shifted from a position of almost exclusive concern with economic matters, while the workers' organizations have moved away from the political or sociopolitical arena and toward the sphere of labor.

This convergence of attitudes will have several important consequences. First, employers' organizations, together with individual employers, are integrating themselves into the system, and this is introducing a measure of professionalism into labor relations. In this connection one might mention the studies carried out in 1978 in Colombia and 1977 in Mexico by the National Association of Industrialists (ANDI) and the Confederation of Chambers of Industry (CONCAMIN) on collective bargaining practices in the respective countries.[10] Second, trade union activity is gaining strength because the workers' organizations are showing greater interest in presenting demands and concluding contracts at the enterprise level; this leads them to present a united front, to eliminate competition from nonorganized groups, and to obtain greater support from the rank and file. Third, the reaffirmation of their joint concern with labor problems and the relative rapprochement of both parties at the heart of the system make communication easier and a more independent pattern of development possible.

The parties involved in the system thus show more interest in discussing conditions of work and embarking on a dialogue, and greater ability to do so. On the employers' side this change has also taken place through the rise of a new type of professional management. Where previously obstinacy and negative reactions were the rule, now many managers prefer to approach collective bargaining in a more impersonal and pragmatic manner. Obviously, there are still many exceptions, particularly in the countries where labor relations are still in the formative stage, and there is still a long way to go before bargaining becomes an entirely rational process, but in the modern sector of the large, semi-industrialized countries of the region, individual employers and their organizations now function very differently from the way they did in the 1960s. In fact, this change in attitude is shown not only in greater interest in labor matters but also in greater readiness to shoulder the main responsibilities under the system. In Venezuela, for example, the employers' umbrella organization, FEDECAMARAS, in 1980 expressed its preference for more bargaining and less government intervention, arguing that this change would encourage the adoption of machinery for concerted action at all levels and prevent the government from taking over responsibilities properly belonging to trade unions and employers' organizations.[11]

There have also been deep-rooted changes on the workers' side, and many trade unions and trade union leaders who formerly would have refused to negotiate now do so in a calm manner and on a regular basis. Here, too, of course, there are many exceptions, and in one and the same country it is sometimes possible to see clear differences in position, depending on the ideological stance of the trade union concerned.[12] In Peru, for example, a 1979 study reports that attitudes on collective bargaining varied from one trade union confederation to another. While some regarded negotiation as an effective instrument for a dialogue between workers and employers, others regarded it as a transitory means of pressing workers' demands, and there were many who rejected it as a weapon of the employers. The first two attitudes were those of the majority unions.[13]

This change in attitude is reflected in the content of agreements. Instead of being no more than ad hoc compromises putting an end to differences, agreements have been acquiring the status of minor codes that periodically attempt to regulate production activities to a greater or lesser extent. Another consequence of the change is the greater degree of compliance with the obligations resulting from agreements. A study carried out in Mexico on more than 200 industries emphasized as long ago as 1974 that obligations agreed on were largely respected by both parties in major and medium-size undertakings, and were only occasionally violated in the smaller undertakings included in the sample.[14] Similar studies conducted in Argentina and Venezuela reported a tendency toward greater compliance with obligations entered into. Although in some countries, particularly in those where labor relations are in the formative stage, additional demands are frequently made during the period of validity of a contract or one of the parties calls for certain of its clauses to be amended, it is no less true that in other countries the idea of a peace obligation applicable during the term of the agreement has in practice begun to spread.

In any case, it should be noted that violations of contracts are no longer automatically referred to the labor courts; efforts are made to settle the matter by the parties themselves, using internal joint committees or appeals machinery. In some countries such committees are of long standing. In Uruguay, for example, committees for implementation of contracts and arbitration were initially established for the banking and textile industries by agreements signed in 1963 and 1964, respectively. Although such committees are of more recent date in other countries, their present spread stands in contrast with the provisions of some laws (dating from the 1950s and 1960s) under which the labor department was assigned the tasks of enforcing and administering the agreement in question.

Conciliation

In the past, failure by management and labor to reach agreement during the direct negotiation phase entailed appeals to conciliation and arbitration boards or calling strikes and lockouts. However, the statutory machinery for the peaceful settlement of disputes operated irregularly, and was slow and unnecessarily formalistic; in many cases it was bypassed by the parties; and conflict was open and regularly fell outside the law. A high percentage of strikes were thus declared illegal.

In Chile it was observed in 1969 that "an enormous majority of strikes were illegal and that their number was constantly on the increase."[15] In Colombia in the same year, 68 percent of the strikes called were illegal. In 1971 only 5 of the 233 strikes that took place in Venezuela were considered legal.[16]

Governments could not remain indifferent to this situation, and so an unofficial conciliation system came into being, in some countries conducted by labor inspectors and in others by conciliation officers of the department of labor. This type of conciliation, which might be called administrative, became important because of the opportunities it afforded for flexibility and prompt and effective intervention. In some cases the opportunities offered were in contrast with the ineffectiveness of the boards and their slow, cumbersome, and formalistic legal procedure. In other cases administrative conciliation was used to bring government incomes and wages policies to bear on the settlement of disputes. Whatever the reasons, the advent of administrative conciliation resulted in the attachment of increasing importance to those features of voluntarism that exist in all systems for the settlement of disputes.

The proportion of disputes settled through administrative conciliation was thus rising at a time when those resolved through the decision of a third party were falling. In some countries, such as Venezuela, the predominance of conciliation has relegated arbitration to oblivion for all practical purposes. In Mexico it has been reckoned that for some years now more than 90 percent of collective disputes are settled through the conciliation machinery of the Ministry of Labor.[17] In Argentina, where individual conciliators have always been preferred, the number of agreements obtained by conciliation was already high at the beginning of the 1970s.

Conciliation is gaining ground even in countries where the conciliation and arbitration board procedure continues to be used as well. In Costa Rica, for example, a study carried out in 1976 reported that "disputes are settled mainly by means of conciliation," and went on to list only 6 cases of arbitration out of a total of 293 disputes reported for that year.[18] In Ecuador some 70 percent of collective disputes referred to conciliation and arbitration boards in 1975 were settled by compromise, by waiver, or by default, while only 12 percent of cases were settled in courts of law and the remainder were withdrawn.[19] In Panama the Complaints and Appeals Section of the Ministry of Labor and Social Welfare was involved in more than 1,500 cases of collective mediation in 1974–75, while the total number of arbitration awards made between 1971 and 1976 was no more than ten; although in 1979 there were in that same country about 300 cases of collective bargaining and 32 strikes were called, there was only a single case of compulsory arbitration, and even in that case the parties came to an agreement before an arbitration award was made.

Part III of this book will discuss these changes in greater detail; meanwhile, the above data reveal to what extent parties are more inclined to resort to administrative conciliation procedures as a means of reaching agreement, a fact that shows the interest of employers and workers in not having working conditions regularly fixed by the government and in assuming greater responsibility themselves. Admittedly, the wider use of conciliation machinery in some countries is due to the fact that it is mandatory, but, apart from the fact that such an obligation also existed in the past and was frequently not complied with, it could not on its own explain the higher proportion of cases in which agreements were reached by this means. In any case, the situation has obviously evolved considerably since the 1960s, when some authors were still able to state that Latin American legislation sought the settlement of disputes through voluntary arbitration, except where a strike affected public services, in which case arbitration was compulsory.[20]

Worker Participation

The signs that forms of participation other than collective bargaining are developing are less visible, and might even be disputed in some countries. It has even been assumed by some observers that in Latin America, worker participation in decision making takes place through collective bargaining at the enterprise level and that where this occurs, there is no need to introduce other forms of participation, such as workers' representation on boards of management. There has, moreover, been some resistance to the establishment of joint councils or other bodies designed to foster collaboration or to deal with subjects of mutual interest. Some recent legislative experiments relating to workers' management (Argentina), codetermination (Chile), and labor communities (Peru) have been abandoned, substantially altered, or deprived of their most striking participatory features.

In many countries, however, some participation experiments have been of undeniable importance. In the private sector, for example, certain forms of participation have developed out of collective bargaining, and others have been brought into being by law. The type of participation born of agreements sometimes tries to facilitate their administration by establishing joint or appeals committees, and at other times gives rise to the establishment of joint councils or workers' committees with social welfare functions that often last much longer than the duration of the agreement. Examples of this second type are committees entrusted with the regulation of personnel grading, those handling loans or facilities for housing, education, or social assistance, those encouraging cultural activities, and those dealing with productivity and wage matters.

Alongside such experiments, in some countries (Brazil, Costa Rica, Honduras, and Mexico, for example) accident prevention and safety and health committees have been set up by law, and have to a great extent succeeded in taking root, as have works councils with broad functions in Panama and joint training committees in Mexico. In the public sector there are numerous examples of workers being represented on the management of public undertakings—for example, in Venezuela generally and in other countries in specific undertakings. In the civil service, too, some laws have recognized the right of public servants to be represented on bodies having important labor functions, the Appeals Board in Ecuador being one such example. It should, however, be noted that of the various types of participation mentioned here, the most widespread at present are those provided for under collective agreements. (A fuller description of these and other forms of participation is in Chapter 6.)

A more controversial but somewhat symptomatic form of participation relates to the appearance in Costa Rica since 1980 of the Solidarity Associations composed of workers and representatives of management in each enterprise, which already cover a substantial number of undertakings. These associations decide on the distribution of funds, wage increases, and the improvement of other conditions of employment in a spirit of cooperation and mutual understanding, thus doing away in practice with trade unions, government intervention, and collective bargaining. Although these associations constitute a deceptive and dangerous form of participation intended to leave aside trade unions, their rapid spread in Costa Rica and their similarities to the objectives of the "independent" unions of Monterrey, Mexico, and a few other experiments point to a certain interest in exploring collaborative forms of relationships within enterprises.

While there is not yet a great deal of worker participation in the management of undertakings, participation by employers' and workers' organizations in official bodies dealing with labor matters is considerable. The responsibilities of these bodies cover many fields, including consultative, quasi-judicial, management, supervisory, and standard-setting functions. The tripartite bodies were first set up to deal with minimum wages, settlement of labor disputes, and social security. Tripartite cooperation has expanded into many other activities, including economic and social planning. Even in countries such as Brazil, where trade unions are of relatively little significance at the enterprise level, social policy has nonetheless led to their representation at the state or federal level in bodies with functions as diverse as the National Council for Wages Policy, the regional and higher labor courts, the Permanent Commission on Social Law, the National Occupational Safety and Health and Industrial Medicine Foundation, the Executive Council for the Length-of-Service Guarantee Fund, and the Supervisory Council of the National Institute for Social Welfare.

As was stated in an ILO report presented to the Eleventh Conference of American States Members of the International Labour Organisation, tripartism has flourished in the region, in line with the interests and needs of departments of labor and other parties to labor relations systems.[21] However, it should be noted that most of the tripartite cooperation bodies were not provided for in the labor codes, but were set up by subsequent laws recognizing the importance of employers' and workers' organizations. Experience also shows that not all tripartite cooperation experiments have been successful; only those that faithfully reflect the representativeness of the organizations themselves or that deal with crucial questions and provide real scope for action have succeeded in becoming working components of the labor relations system. (Chapter 8 offers an inventory of this variant of the trend toward participation at the national level or in individual branches of the economy.)

Growth of Parallel Systems

The trend toward autonomy has been largely spontaneous in its growth or has had very little outside help. Its development has been due largely to factors inherent in the dynamics of collective labor relations and to the natural growth of the system. In almost no country has it been the outcome of a labor policy conceived and brought into being to promote collective labor relations. Unlike individual labor relations, whose regulation in Latin America has reached appreciable levels of sophistication, collective relations have often achieved their present degree of development outside the sphere of state regulation, and in some cases despite it. Unlike Spain, where the 1980 Workers' Statute clearly heralded a shift from outside regulation to voluntary arrangements, Latin America offers no example of legislation that similarly foreshadows the shift toward autonomy.

Labor policies continue to adhere, on paper, to the principles that inspired the promulgation of labor codes under which government regulation of collective labor relations was based on the assumption that industrial relations were a manifestation of class struggle, which, it was feared, would have repercussions on society as a whole. Government intervention was thus seen both as a means of moving toward a comprehensive official regulation of conditions of work, so as to make trade union action unnecessary, and as a way of inducing employers and workers to seek the settlement of their disputes through the government. Thus the government had the basic functions of dispenser of rights and of regulator, conciliator, and arbitrator of disputes. Although it was recognized that collective interaction existed, it was not supposed to be of prime importance.

While some constitutions and basic laws confirm the principles of freedom of association, collective bargaining, and the right to strike, those principles have not been properly developed in implementing legislation. The Constitution of Venezuela, for example, states that laws shall be passed to encourage the development of collective labor–management relations and establish adequate regulation of collective bargaining and the peaceful solution of disputes. However, the relevant implementing legislation has not yet been adopted; the Act of 1936, which devotes only a few sections to collective bargaining, remains in force (with some amendments). When an act was passed in Venezuela (1958) making provision for industrywide collective bargaining, the government continued to arrogate key functions to itself. In other countries, such as Ecuador and Uruguay, the constitutions are silent on the promotion of collective bargaining, although they refer to related subjects such as the rights of association and participation, and labor disputes.

Apart from constitutional texts, the standards for promoting and regulating collective labor relations were frequently insufficient. Although the codes and the legislation in general made a significant contribution to other aspects of setting standards, their treatment of collective labor relations was not of equal quality. For example, the Labor Act of Bolivia devoted only six sections to workers' and employers' organizations, and nine to the peaceful settlement of labor disputes. In Peru the act of 1971 concerning collective bargaining tried to speed up the process of negotiation, but the procedure as a whole seems to have been thought up in relation to the final phase, that of administrative solutions. It is interesting to note that the section of this act relating to collective bargaining begins by envisaging the possibility that it may break down. In Uruguay, where the laws on working conditions and social security go back to the beginning of the century, the regulation of collective labor relations dates back only to 1973, and has been the subject of some controversy. An Ecuadorean expert has described the legal framework for collective bargaining in his country as being complex and confused;[22] and a Chilean author stated in 1974 that in his country labor legislation and the accompanying controls had seriously impeded rapid adjustment to change on the part of management and labor.[23]

The government departments concentrated on settling open conflicts and making good the delays and shortcomings of the judicial machinery in dealing with legal disputes. Nevertheless, the increasing number of economic disputes caused by the decentralization of collective bargaining and the high number of legal disputes calling for attention exceeded the capacity of the departments concerned. Small wonder, therefore, that they had very little time for encouraging collective bargaining, preventing disputes, or upgrading the labor relations skills of employers and workers.

In many cases political problems restricted the exercise of freedom of association and resulted in the adoption of regulations refusing recognition to certain organizations, preventing the free election of officers, or otherwise affecting the premises on which collective bargaining is based. Although in some cases more liberal regulations were introduced, recognizing certain aspects of militancy and class struggle in labor relations, no general framework was drawn up for the strengthening and institutionalization of collective labor relations.

The approach of many of the labor codes to collective labor relations presupposed that every negotiation was a conflict and that every conflict ended in a strike. To have a strike classified as legal or illegal thus seemed more important than to settle the substance of the dispute. To embark on conciliation and arbitration procedures seemed more urgent than to encourage direct negotiations. Moreover, in some countries direct negotiations were discouraged, in that participants were denied the protection afforded in the case of claims settled by a dispute procedure, since only signatories of the records embodying a settlement under such a procedure enjoyed trade union immunity from dismissal.

In other countries the confusion between the bargaining process and the settlement of disputes is reflected in legal doctrine.[24] In Panama the parties may initiate conciliation proceedings without attempting direct negotiations, and in Ecuador there is provision for the constitution of a conciliation and arbitration board when the employer fails to reply to a statement of claims or rejects it outright. In other cases it is the bilateral nature of negotiations that is placed in doubt, as happens in Colombia when the employer makes counterproposals (contrapliegos) on receiving demands by the trade union.

Direct negotiation was not given proper guarantees or facilities. In Argentina, Chile, the Dominican Republic, and Panama the unfair labor practices system was introduced, but failed to receive the necessary support or could not take root in practice. In Argentina the National Council for Labor Relations was set up to ensure the prohibition of such practices, but it was dissolved in 1979. In Panama the number of unfair practices registered by the Ministry of Labor and Social Welfare in 1974–75 was five. In the Dominican Republic the ban on unfair practices remains largely a dead letter. The result of all the foregoing is that failure to comply with the obligation to negotiate does not result in penalties and in many countries the obligation cannot be effectively enforced without a strike.

The same discrepancy between law and practice can be seen in other institutions. The procedure of extending agreements to third parties, including enterprises that were not signatories of the agreement (known in

Mexico as the "generally binding collective agreement" or *contrato-ley*), is rarely used in practice. In Ecuador, more than 40 years after the procedure was introduced in the Labor Code, not a single such collective agreement had been signed. In Venezuela relatively few collective agreements of this kind are extended. Only in Mexico has the principle succeeded in acquiring any importance, and this is due to the fact that the Act of 1970, "recognizing a reality that made the old formula obsolete," allowed direct conclusion of binding collective contracts for an entire branch of industry, as well as maintaining the procedure for extending one or more existing contracts to third parties. This last procedure is, however, considered "outdated and pointless."[25]

The provisions included in some labor codes on the effects of agreements were not entirely satisfactory. In Ecuador doubts as to the binding nature of agreements still exist, and it is thought that compliance with them can be required only by means of strikes; current regulations confuse agreements with contracts, and require agreements to be suspended or terminated in circumstances that would be applicable only to collective contracts.

In Bolivia, Chile, and Colombia (in some cases) the scope of agreements has been limited to workers who are trade union members. This system may have induced nonorganized workers to join a union, but has weakened the concept of the agreement as a universal standard. Everywhere the procedure for the approval of agreements was hedged about with strict formalities not always connected with checking their legality, and in some cases conferring discretionary power on the labor authority to approve or reject clauses of an agreement that were contrary to government policy.

To these restrictions were added more recent ones created by concern over inflation and development problems. First to suffer were wage negotiations, as a consequence of government policies to slow inflation through periodic adjustments in remuneration or in the light of changes in the cost of living or through total control over wage movements. Later, in some countries, other subjects for negotiation, such as dismissals, working hours, or rest periods, came to be excluded from the scope of agreements. In yet other countries the entire bargaining system was restricted by the introduction of development projects and labor plans to promote investment, stimulate capital formation, and speed up economic growth. The repercussions of this new type of state interventionism or autonomy of action are obvious. Not only was the institutional framework for bargaining adversely affected, but the very substance of collective bargaining was restricted.

The machinery for settling disputes has not proved auspicious for the development of autonomy. Everywhere provision was made for the settlement of disputes by the parties themselves, but this remained subject to excessively formal and legalistic procedures under which a conciliation meeting was regarded as a mere formality paving the way for other action of greater importance. The prevailing system in most Latin American countries entrusted the settlement of disputes to tripartite boards or tribunals that were sometimes permanent and sometimes ad hoc. The boards held formal hearings that had little in common with conciliation. They were slow and hampered by procedural formalities. Employers' and workers' representatives on them systematically voted for their own side, and both the conciliation proceedings and the final decision devolved upon the chairman, who was often a labor inspector or a member of the judiciary.

Experience with conciliation boards was not very convincing, and in some countries it even came to be considered a failure.[26] It did not take governments long to realize that conciliation could be brought about much more effectively by an administrative officer than by a collegiate body or a member of the judiciary. Administrative conciliation did not, however, supersede the old system of conciliation boards, but was superimposed upon or preceded it. In only a few countries (for example, Chile in 1979 and Panama since 1972) have specialized conciliation officers from the department of labor and panels of possible independent arbitrators been substituted for tripartite boards. In the other countries two systems exist side by side: the unofficial system of conciliation by officers of the department of labor and the system of conciliation boards that can also arbitrate disputes. Even in Argentina, where the system of individual conciliators is used, the parties frequently refuse to recognize the settlement procedures and immediately resort to direct action.[27]

Retention of the system of conciliation and arbitration boards is probably due to the fact that they can also be used to pronounce on the lawfulness of strikes. However, since the procedure was slow and the requirements hard to meet, there were few trade unions prepared to follow the course of action laid down by law, which explains the great number of illegal strikes. In the Dominican Republic a confederation asserted in 1975 that it had organized 100 strikes since it was founded, all of them illegal; an ILO study of the same year suggested that this was because of the practical difficulties in exercising the right to strike.[28]

State regulation of strikes, moreover, was ambivalent. On the one hand, in many countries limitations on the exercise of the right to strike were laid down—linked, for example, with prior definition of a strike as lawful, the requirement that it have the support of the majority of the workers concerned, the need to give notice, or the maximum duration of the work stoppage. On the other hand, efforts were made to provide legal strikers with advantages that do not exist in other countries—for example, a prohibition of the employment of other workers or attempts to continue operations, obligations on employers to continue paying wages during the strike, inclusion of days not worked by strikers in qualifying periods for holidays, and permission for sympathy strikes. These guarantees are most conspicuous in Ecuador, where striking workers have the right to occupy the establishment or undertaking even for sympathy strikes.

What has been said so far shows how marked the contrast is between the legislation in force and reality. Although the effectiveness of direct negotiation has been underestimated and it does not enjoy the protection conferred by law on negotiation through procedures for settling disputes, in practice it has been gaining ground. Although administrative conciliation is often conducted *extra legem* (without being expressly authorized by law for the purpose) or without the legal backing given to conciliation boards or tribunals, it has nevertheless become increasingly prevalent as a means of solving conflicts of interest. Moreover, provision has been made for settling legal disputes, both individual and collective, by labor courts, but in practice grievance committees and administrative conciliation systems dispose of most such disputes before they reach the courts. Finally, there are many strikes that are illegal because legal strikes are rather difficult to declare, despite the advantages conferred on them under the laws in force. Thus an ambivalent situation has arisen in which the legislation in force is not totally adhered to and what is done is justified on the grounds of its effectiveness.

This view is generally valid, but not absolutely so. The present analysis may have extrapolated certain specific situations or turned some examples into generalities. No doubt there are some countries where the prevailing practices are sanctioned, or have been encouraged, by legislation. While it would not be appropriate to attribute the impressive growth of collective bargaining to the latter, legislative measures have no doubt influenced the level and form of negotiations. In Argentina, for example, the broad outlines of the system in terms of the level of negotiation and the legal status of the unions are in line with legislation. Something similar can be said for the preference given in other countries to collective bargaining at the enterprise level.

Tripartite cooperation has also been encouraged by government action. But in many countries institutions established as a result of legislation have since been substantially altered or brought into line with reality. In Argentina, for example, the joint committees so important in labor–management relations have been spontaneously broadening their functions and developing in practice into two different types of committees for which there is no provision in law. In other countries many examples can be cited of tripartite cooperation bodies that in practice have moved far from their initial goals or have been falling into disuse. It can therefore be noted that, apart from isolated cases or specific institutions, collective labor relations appear for the time being to be marked by the existence of parallel systems, the one foreseen in the legislation and the other prevailing in practice.

The Picture Reconsidered

The characteristics that can at present be observed in Latin American labor relations do not fit in with the ones traditionally attributed to the region. Above all, there is a noticeable effort to break with the interventionist models that used to govern collective labor relations and to increase the autonomy of management and labor. There is greater dynamism and informality of interactions between them, in contrast with the strictness with which relations are controlled and directed by the labor codes. Despite the continuing influence in the region of such factors as paternalism, dependence, and legalism, collective labor relations are tending naturally toward direct negotiations rather than toward following the more complex triangular worker–government–employer formulas prescribed by law. Latin American experience shows that in the end, and within certain limits, the inherent dynamics of labor relations gain the upper hand in spite of the weight of tradition and interventionist legislative systems.

This situation is in line with the general evolution of labor relations toward less intervention by the labor authorities and a slower pace of legislative change as employers' and workers' organizations consolidate their positions as representative bodies of occupational interests. It does not support a 1972 forecast that Latin American labor relations would evolve more in accordance with the general political system than with their own dynamics.[29] Political factors have exerted a strong influence on Latin American labor relations. Peronism in Argentina determined the shape of trade unions and the level of negotiations; the whole scheme of Brazilian labor relations was modeled on the system conceived by Getúlio Vargas and his minister of labor, Lindolfo Color, during the Estado Novo; and in Chile restrictions on the functioning of unions and collective bargaining were the result of the measures adopted by the military regime of 1973.

But there were other important developments in these same countries. While Argentina suspended collective bargaining in 1976 and prohibited top-level federations in 1979, some forms of wage negotiation have taken place in enterprises and with regard to the revision of industrywide agreements; and the national labor center is de facto recognized. Reference has already been made to the upsurge of collective bargaining in the industrial state of São Paulo, Brazil, in 1978–79, a phenomenon that has continued to be so visible in 1980–83 that growing demands for the modernization and liberalization of the system are now being formulated. In Chile there was the creation, in 1974, of tripartite national commissions in charge of fixing conditions of employment and the reestablishment in 1979 of a limited but active form of collective bargaining.

All this means that labor relations can no longer be explained in terms of their being merely a subsystem of the political system. In the long run, unless in exceptional situations (such as Cuba) or for relatively short periods, politics cannot prevent the natural process of growth and expansion of labor relations that has been so marked since the early 1970s.

The trend toward greater independent-mindedness is emerging in Latin America at a time when a number of countries with a voluntarist tradition, such as the United Kingdom and Sweden, are to some extent retreating from that position and seem to be prepared to accept some government intervention. However, there is no incongruity in these different patterns of evolution. They simply prove that the extremes of rigid government interventionism and outright voluntarism are untenable, and indicate a general trend toward convergence in different parts of the world.[30] In fact, counterbalancing forces can be seen in action: the movement toward greater workers' participation and greater free interplay of the parties, and the recognition of the need to protect the common good. In the final analysis the two forces tend to seek mutual accommodation and to produce a system combining adequate autonomy with the recognition that some government intervention is as essential in labor relations as in other fields.

Notes

1. See Claudio Véliz, *The Centralist Tradition of Latin America* (Princeton: Princeton University Press, 1980).

2. In 1973 a Brazilian author stated: "If there is one institution of labor law that has practically no effect on the life of the community, it is the collective agreement." Evaristo de Moraes Filho, "Evolución del derecho de las convenciones colectivas en el Brasil," in *Estudios sobre la negociación colectiva en memoria de Francisco de Ferraris* (Montevideo: Facultad de Derecho y Ciencias Sociales de Montevideo, 1973), p. 332. However, this observation does not appear to be totally valid at present.

3. See, for instance, Xavier Flores, *Agricultural Organisations and Economic and Social Development in Rural Areas*, Studies and Reports, n.s. no. 77 (Geneva: ILO, 1971); and Almino Affonso et al., *Movimiento campesino chileno*, 2 vols. (Santiago de Chile: ICIRA, 1970).

4. ILO, *Some Aspects of Labour–Management Relations in the American Region*, Labor–Management Relations Series, no. 11A (Geneva: ILO, 1962), pp. 33–34.

5. See Robert J. Alexander, *Organized Labor in Latin America* (New York: The Free Press, 1965); and Miles E. Galvin, *Unionism in Latin America* (Ithaca, N.Y.: New York State School of Industrial and Labor Relations, Cornell University, 1962).

6. See Hugo Valencia Haro, "Ecuador," in R. Blanpain, ed., *International Encyclopaedia for Labour Law and Industrial Relations*, vol. 1 (Deventer, Netherlands: Kluwer, 1979), p. 252.

7. The data on Peru vary considerably according to year and source. A study published in 1973 reported that in the two previous years, 76 and 75 percent, respectively, of grievances were resolved by direct agreement. See J. Rendón Vasquez, "La negociación colectiva en el marco de la nueva economía peruana," in *Estudios sobre la negociación colectiva . . .*, p. 439.

8. ILO, *La negociación colectiva en América latina* (Geneva: ILO, 1978), pp. 8, 9. See also Arturo S. Bronstein, "Collective Bargaining in Latin America: Problems and Trends," in *International Labour Review*, Sept.–Oct. 1978, p. 584.

9. ILO, "Asalariados de bajos ingresos y salarios mínimos en América latina," Working Paper PREALC/170 (Geneva: ILO, 1979), p. 81. (Mimeographed.) It is nevertheless asserted that in some countries, such as Bolivia and Brazil, the proportion of wages and salaries in national income has fallen in the last few years. For Bolivia, see "La nueva política salarial," in *Trabajo* (La Paz), Mar. 1980.

10. For Colombia, see Asociación Nacional de Industriales (ANDI), *Cuadro Comparativo de Convenciones colectivas* (Bogota) 1978; and for Mexico, Confederación de Cámaras Industriales de los Estados Unidos Mexicanos, *Análisis de las cláusulas contenidas en 1,500 convenios* (Mexico City: CONCAMIN, 1977).

11. XXXVI Asamblea Anual de FEDECAMARAS, Maracaibo, 22–28 de junio de 1980, *Tesis del sector empresarial de Venezuela sobre el desarrollo económico y social* (Caracas: FEDECAMARAS, 1980), p. VIII-F-6.

12. Some references to the development of trade unionism on the basis of collective bargaining (not necessarily ruling out a political bent) are in Mark Thompson, "Collective Bargaining in the Mexican Electrical Industry," *British Journal of Industrial Relations*, Mar. 1970, pp. 55–68; and Francisco Zapata, "Action syndicale et comportement politique des mineurs chiliens de Chuquicamata," in *Sociologie du travail*, July–Sept. 1975, pp. 225–42.

13. See "Confederaciones de trabajadores y grupos ultras: Principales indicadores," in *Análisis laboral* (Lima), June 1979, p. 13.

14. Miguel Cantón Moller, *La armonía en las relaciones obreros patronales: Encuesta y análisis de sus factores* (Mexico City: Sociedad Mexicana de Geografía y Estadística, 1974), pp. 36–37.

15. Héctor Humeres Magnan, *Apuntes de derecho del trabajo* (Santiago de Chile: Editorial Jurídica de Chile, 1969), pp. 273–74. See also Jorge Barría Serón, *Las relaciones colectivas del trabajo en Chile* (Santiago de Chile: INSORA, 1967), p. 12.

16. Ministerio del Trabajo de Venezuela, *Memoria*, 1971, p. 126.

17. See "The Settlement of Labour Disputes in Mexico," in *International Labour Review,* May 1971, p. 487.

18. Gerardo Suárez, "Investigación sobre conflictos económicos y convenciones colectivas en Costa Rica" (San José: Cedal-La Catalina, 1976), table 11 and commentary. (Mimeographed.)

19. Hugo Valencia Haro, *Legislación ecuatoriana del trabajo* (Quito: Editorial Universitaria, 1979), p. 504.

20. Guillermo Cabanellas, *Compendio de derecho laboral* (Buenos Aires: Bibliográfica Omeba, 1968), vol. II, p. 410.

21. ILO, *Public Labour Administration and Its Role in Economic and Social Development* (Geneva: ILO, 1979), p. 43.

22. Valencia, "Ecuador," p. 230.

23. Alberto Armstrong, "El sistema de relaciones industriales chileno y la necesidad de cambio," in Universidad de Chile, Facultad de Ciencias Económicas y Administrativas, Departamento de Relaciones del Trabajo y Desarrollo Organizacional, *Symposium sobre el futuro sistema de relaciones industriales en Chile* (Santiago de Chile: DERTO, 1974), p. 18.

24. See, for example, Guillermo Camacho Henríquez, "La negociación colectiva en Colombia," in *Estudios sobre la negociación colectiva . . .*, pp. 351–52; and G. González Charry, "Colombia," R. Blanpain, ed., *International Encyclopaedia for Labour Law and Industrial Relations,* vol. III, p. 108.

25. Néstor de Buen, *Derecho del trabajo* (Mexico City: Editorial Porrúa, 1976), vol. II, p. 699.

26. See Euquerio Guerrero, *Manual de derecho del trabajo* (Mexico City: Tallers Gráficos Galeza, 1962), vol. II.

27. A. J. Ruprecht, "Argentina," in R. Blanpain, ed., *International Encyclopaedia for Labour Law. . .*, vol. II, p. 169.

28. ILO, *Generación de empleo productivo y crecimiento económico: El caso de la República Dominicana* (Geneva: ILO, 1975), p. 226.

29. R. Stavenhagen and F. Zapata, *Future Industrial Relations: Latin America* (Geneva: International Institute for Labour Studies, 1972), p. 18.

30. This conclusion tends to corroborate the theory of the convergence of industrial relations systems implied by John T. Dunlop's analysis. See John T. Dunlop, *Industrial Relations Systems* (New York: Henry Holt and Co., 1958); and Clark Kerr et al., *Industrialism and Industrial Man* (Cambridge, Mass.: Harvard University Press, 1960), pp. 233ff.

Part I: The Actors

2

Trade Unions

by
Geraldo von Potobsky

Differences in the trade union movement necessarily reflect the background against which it operates. Trade union characteristics in a country and region depend on a whole array of economic, social, and political factors, traditions, and historical experience. The political and traditional factors particularly influence the form taken by trade union legislation, which may be constant or change suddenly with the ups and downs of political regimes. However, mere description of the legal framework within which workers' organizations operate would inevitably give only a partial and imperfect picture, and that framework must therefore be related to the changes in the trade union movement itself and in the circumstances in which it operates. Such changes occur in all social institutions, but their pace may become particularly quick because of political vicissitudes in the trade unions of developing countries.

Various authors have been tempted to divide the history of trade union development into stages. Mazzoni[1] has distinguished four such stages, which he derives from European experience: prohibition or repression, tolerance, legal recognition of trade unions, and transformation of trade unions in some countries from private associations into public bodies. The distinguishing feature of trade unions in the last stage, he says, is that they resemble government agencies, are the official representatives of the various occupations, and perform functions of use to the community under delegated authority, while being subject to far-reaching control.

If we transplant these stages to Latin American countries, the characteristics of the third stage become not only mere legal recognition of trade unions but also legislative promotion and subjection to administrative control. The fourth stage might be described as that at which the trade unions act, either in institutionalized fashion or in practice, by virtue of their close relations with the regime. Government control of occupational organizations is particularly important, and constitutes one of the most marked features in the evolution of Latin American trade unionism.

In Latin American trade union history the arduous period of initial repression began in the last third of the nineteenth century, when many trade unions acted as resistance societies; they were composed mainly of artisans and workers in skilled trades, and were inspired by ideologies brought by European immigrants. The tolerance stage followed, quickly in some countries, less quickly in others, and lasted until the 1920s and 1930s, when laws and labor codes for the detailed regulation of trade union organizations began to spread.

In Latin America this third stage has occurred at the time when, between the individualist trend of law relating to freedom of association, which emphasizes the interests of the individual in relation to the association, and the communal trend giving preference to the interests of the organized community (state or association), the latter has begun to weigh heavier in the balance. In countries where the communal trend prevails, the legislatures seek to protect corporate bodies and recognize the organizations as representing the interests of categories or groups of workers. In return, the state subjects this recognition to observance of various requirements.[2] It is important to note that in Latin America this legislative approach is emerging at a time when the workers' movement, weak and deeply divided politically and ideologically, often serves as the instrument of parties and even of government action. Consequently, legislation protecting trade unions is combined with government control in which there is an element of distrust and prevention.

This type of legislation still prevails, but in the meantime the importance of the trade union movement, its participatory role in labor–management relations and relations with the state, and even its independence of parties and governments have substantially increased.[3]

Many attempts have been made to define the characteristics of the Latin American trade union movement. In any exercise of this kind, the major difficulty is clearly that the countries in this region differ greatly from each other in tradition, experience, and degree of economic and social development. Many such attempts were made in the 1960s, in particular, when authors took strongly pessimistic or optimistic views of trade unionism, basing their conclusions largely on comparisons with the workers' movement in Europe or the United States.[4] Sometimes descriptions written in those years appear to be based on myths or preconceived ideas from a dead past.

In any attempt to identify the common features of trade unionism in the majority of Latin American countries, four basic points should be distinguished. First there is the political activism or ideological drive of the trade unions, or at least of their leaders. This politicization is part of the trade union tradition in Latin America, and in certain cases may become extremely virulent and have far-reaching results. Originally this political activity was partly due to the weakness of trade unions in labor relations; but now it acts as a factor of political negotiation with the government that adds to a union's bargaining strength in relation to the employers. In practice, local trade unions are becoming increasingly active in collective labor relations, and that trend is accompanied by political action, sometimes at the local level but more often at the federation and confederation levels. At the undertaking level the trade union is becoming not so much the instrument of protest that it was in the past as a participant in working out and applying agreements; at the national level it works as a pressure group and agent of reform and social change, but also as a participant in tripartite cooperation.

The second feature is trade union multiplicity and pluralism. The extreme fragmentation of the trade union movement is due to survivals of parochial mentality and the predominance of plant unions; pluralism—more marked at the federation and confederation levels than at the undertaking level—is the result of the political and ideological divisions of the labor movement.

Third, there is the detailed regulatory nature of trade union legislation. This is less a result of Roman law traditions than of the educational, protective, and controlling functions of trade union regulation.

The fourth and last consideration is the high degree of government intervention in the affairs of the trade unions, from their foundation throughout their active life; this is often a means of political interference.

Comparison of the present state of the trade union movement with its state in the 1950s and 1960s at once shows the unions' greater numerical and functional importance today. Their participation in all aspects of national life has grown considerably, but in political and economic affairs it has in some cases, over the last few years, provoked opposition and the introduction of severe restrictions on trade union activity.

Roughly speaking, there are countries that since the early 1960s have shown relative stability in the trade union picture (Costa Rica, Ecuador, Mexico, and Venezuela), others in which new organizational trends have appeared in the trade union movement (Colombia, Peru, and the Central American countries), and countries in which for a number of years trade union organizations have been, and mostly still are, subject to serious re-

strictions or have been restructured by legislation after a change of political regime (Argentina, Bolivia, Brazil, Chile, and Uruguay).

Structure

Before proceeding to study trade union structure in Latin America, a
matter of semantics and practical use of terminology has to be made clear.
Legislation frequently defines the types of trade unions, which are generally four in number: enterprise unions, craft unions, industrial unions,
and multicraft unions; but these terms may vary in meaning. In Chile, for
example, the type of trade union called an industrial union in the previous
legislation was an enterprise-based union of manual workers. In Colombia and Honduras an enterprise union is called a "basic" trade union (sindicato de base). In Ecuador the works committee is virtually an enterprise
union, and craft associations are commonly of salaried employees, as craft
unions used to be in Chile. In Venezuela the craft union is in reality an
industrial union.

Generally speaking, the term "craft union" is not in practice given to
horizontal organizations on the United States or British model, formed of
skilled workers in clearly defined trades. The meaning of the term is
wider, varies according to country, and can even be confused with true
vertical industrial trade unions or include the liberal professions and artisans.

Multicraft unions have been recognized in some countries to act as
substitute for craft unions when the number of workers in a single trade in
any locality is below the number required to form a union for that particular trade. They are normally of much less importance than other trade
unions.

It has become a matter of tradition to assert that the enterprise union
is the most usual one in Latin America. It is the typical trade union organization in countries such as Bolivia, Chile, Colombia, the Dominican Republic, Honduras, Peru, and Venezuela, and exists in a greater or lesser
degree in nearly all the other countries; but the proportion of trade unions
that cover a whole branch of activity, whether they style themselves craft
or industrial unions, and whether they are confined to a given district or
cover the whole country, has grown steadily. Not only is this the typical
trade union structure in Argentina, Brazil, El Salvador, and Uruguay (before the new trade union law); it has become true of a substantial number
of trade unions in Panama, and is very widespread in countries such as
Colombia, Mexico, and Venezuela. In Ecuador works committees are far
outnumbered by trade unions proper and by craft associations.

According to some authors, enterprise unions are more independent
of the state than industrial trade unions or trade unions by branch of activity, which in some cases have become closely linked to government: since

enterprise union leaders are in closer contact with their members, the union's demands will more fully reflect the workers' requirements and demands, whereas the militancy of industrial trade unions may be mitigated by the political mainstays of the state.[5]

The fact is that in Latin America employers have usually preferred to limit collective labor relations to their own undertaking. Whereas in Europe employers have organized themselves to defend their interests against labor and labor has reacted by forming industrial trade unions, in Latin America employers' associations were not at first concerned with collective labor relations. The employers' relations with trade unions have been marked by a certain amount of paternalism within undertakings. A detailed study of the origin of trade union legislation in Chile shows that its provisions relating to enterprise unions were due to conservative influences, whereas its provisions on craft unions—wider in scope than enterprise unions—were inspired by the liberal school of thought.[6]

If the normal pattern of trade union organization is one of enterprise unions, this may hinder union development because in small undertakings, which play an important part in the economy, it is either difficult or impossible to comply with the legal requirement of a minimum number of workers (generally 20 to 25). The small size of the undertakings means that many enterprise unions are weak and skilled leaders able to run their unions efficiently are hard to find.

Nevertheless, legislation has often encouraged enterprise unions. Thus, in Colombia (until 1966) and Honduras "basic trade unions" were given preference in representing the workers of an undertaking. In Ecuador the works committee is the privileged body in regard to collective bargaining and strikes. In Chile the enterprise union was given special protection, in that all the manual workers were obliged to belong to it once it had been formed by majority decision, and it drew a share of the undertaking's profits.

In some countries new legislative trends now favor enterprise unions. In Chile the Trade Union Act of 1979 allows plant unions, enterprise trade unions, and interenterprise trade unions, but collective bargaining may take place only at the enterprise level. In Uruguay the 1981 Trade Union Act requires that enterprise unions be formed, except when the enterprise employs fewer than 15 workers. In the latter event a trade union may be formed to cover workers belonging to no more than 30 undertakings in a given branch of activity. In Argentina the Trade Union Act of 1979 tends to reduce the scope of action of industrial trade unions to the provincial level.

In contrast with this legislative trend limiting the scope of trade union action there is another, promoted by the government or by the organizations themselves, that favors the development of larger trade unions. This was so in Chile[7] under the Allende government, which encouraged the establishment of a single union for each industry.

In Panama the reform of trade union legislation embodied in the Labor Code of 1972 established that the smallest number of workers able to form a trade union should be 50. In Ecuador works committees, although privileged by legislation on labor relations, are still much less numerous than industrial or craft unions.

It is common practice for individual trade unions to form federations and for these federations to form confederations, although a number of unions do keep themselves independent of any affiliation. With few exceptions (of which Argentina was one) collective labor relations are concentrated in individual trade unions. It is noteworthy that the legislation of various countries restricts the formation of federations and confederations. In some countries a minimum number of trade unions is required to form a federation, and a minimum number of federations is required to form a confederation: in El Salvador ten trade unions are needed to form a federation and three federations to form a confederation; in the Dominican Republic the figures are seven trade unions and four federations; in Peru five trade unions and ten federations; in Chile between three and twenty trade unions are needed to form a federation, and twenty trade unions or federations to form a confederation. In Brazil five trade unions are necessary to form a federation within a state, and Department of Labor approval is required to form a federation covering more than one state. In Argentina the trade union law adopted in 1977 precludes the formation of confederations, and in Brazil the only ones allowed are those permitted by legislation for particular branches of activity.

A few countries restrict the activities of federations and confederations in labor matters. In Chile, Ecuador, and El Salvador they may neither engage in collective bargaining nor call strikes, and in Colombia and Honduras they are denied the right to strike.

Although in some countries national legislation imposes restrictions on federations and confederations, that is the level at which the trade union movement's activities and political divisions are most concentrated; most countries have several trade union confederations, each of them comprising various federations.

Table 2.1 lists the principal national organizations of workers and shows the extent of trade union pluralism in Latin America. It will be observed that pluralism reflects ideological differences everywhere except in Brazil, where it reflects classification by sectors of the economy. Ideological divisions sometimes go farther than confederations. In Mexico, for example, there are, in addition to the big confederations, a number of independent trade unions, among them the railway workers', miners', metalworkers', petroleum industry, and electricians' trade unions, a public service workers' federation (whose membership exceeds 1 million), and the Monterrey group of "independent" trade unions not associated with national federations. In Peru the 60 or so left-wing groups outside the confederations include the National Educational Federation (SUTEP).

Table 2.1.   Main National Workers' Organizations, 1983

Country	Organization
Argentina	Confederación General del Trabajo (CGT)*
Bolivia	Confederación Obrera Boliviana (COB)
Brazil	Confederación Nacional de los Trabajadores de la Agricultura Confederación Nacional de los Trabajadores de la Educación y la Cultura Confederación Nacional de los Trabajadores de la Industria Confederación Nacional de los Trabajadores de las Comunicaciones y Publicidad Confederación Nacional de los Trabajadores del Comercio Confederatión Nacional de los Trabajadores de los Establecimientos de Crédito Confederación Nacional de los Trabajadores de los Transportes Marítimos, Fluviales y Aéreos Confederación Nacional de los Trabajadores de los Transportes Terrestres
Colombia	Confederación de Trabajadores de Colombia (CTC) Confederación General del Trabajo (CGT) Confederación Sindical de Trabajadores de Colombia (CSTC) Unión de Trabajadores de Colombia (UTC)
Costa Rica	Central de Trabajadores Costarricenses (CTC) Central Unitaria de Trabajadores (CUT) Confederación Costarricense de Trabajadores Democráticos (CCTD) Confederación Auténtica de Trabajadores Democráticos (CATD)
Chile	Confederación de Empleados de Industrias y Comercio de Chile
Dominican Republic	Central General de Trabajadores (CGT) Confederación Autónoma Sindical Clasista (CASC) Confederación Nacional de Trabajadores Dominicanos (CNTD) Confederación Unitaria de Trabajadores (CUT)
Ecuador	Central Ecuatoriana de Organizaciones Clasistas (CEDOC) (CLAT) Confederación de Trabajadores del Ecuador (CTE) Confederación Ecuatoriana de Organizaciones Sindicales Libres (CEOSL)
El Salvador	Confederación General de Sindicatos (CGS) Federación de Sindicatos de la Industria de Construcción
Guatemala	Central Nacional de Trabajadores (CNT) Confederación Sindical de Trabajadores de Guatemala (CSTG) Federación Autónoma Sindical Guatemalteca (FASGUA) Confederación de Unidad Sindical de Guatemala (CUSG)

Table 2.1. Continued

Country	Organization
Honduras	Central General de Trabajadores (CGT)
	Confederación de Trabajadores de Honduras (CTH)
	Federación de Unidad Sindical (FUS)
Mexico	Confederación de Trabajadores de México (CTM)
	Confederación General de Trabajadores (CGT)
	Confederación Regional Obrera Mexicana (CROM)
	Confederación Revolucionaria de Obreros y Campesinos (CROC)
	Confederación Revolucionaria de Trabajadores (CRT)
	Frente Auténtico del Trabajo (FAT)
Nicaragua	Central de Trabajadores de Nicaragua (CTN)
	Central Sandinista de Trabajadores (CST)
	Confederación de Unificación Sindical (CUS)
	Frente Obrero (FO)
Panama	Central de Trabajadores de Panamá
	Central Istmeña de Trabajadores (CIT)
	Central Nacional de Trabajadores Panameños (CNTP)
	Confederación de Trabajadores de la República de Panamá (CTRP)
Paraguay	Confederación Nacional de Trabajadores (CNT)
	Confederación Paraguaya de Trabajadores
Peru	Central de Trabajadores de la Revolución Peruana (CTRP)
	Confederación de Trabajadores del Perú (CTP)
	Confederación General de Trabajadores del Perú (CGTP)
	Confederación Nacional de Trabajadores (CNT (CLAT))
	Confederación Nacional de Trabajadores (CNT (ORIT))
Uruguay	Acción Sindical Uruguaya (ASU)
	Confederación General de Trabajadores del Uruguay (CGTU)
Venezuela	Central Unitaria de Trabajadores de Venezuela (CUTV)
	Confederación de Sindicatos Autónomas de Venezuela (CODESA)
	Confederación de Trabajadores de Venezuela (CTV)

*At present divided into two main wings: CGT-Azopardo and CGT-Brasil.
Source: Data available in the ILO documentation service.

The number of confederations has grown in the last few years. In Mexico there are six, in Peru five, in Colombia and Costa Rica four, and in Ecuador and Honduras three. The fact that the trade union movement is divided does not prevent united action, especially protest strikes against the government's economic policy or formation by the confederations of coordinating bodies, such as the Congreso de Trabajo in Mexico, the Consejo Nacional Sindical in Colombia, and the Consejo Nacional de Trabajadores Organizados (CONATO) in Panama.

However, trade union pluralism does not occur at the level of the enterprise; in practice there is no coexistence at that level of trade unions separated by ideological or political differences, rivalry between leaders, or other barriers. Indeed, their coexistence is in many cases prevented by legislation: in Colombia and Honduras there may not be two "basic trade unions"; only the one with the greater membership may subsist. The situation is similar in Panama; if there were two or more trade unions when the 1972 code was introduced, it gave them a year to amalgamate, failing which the minority trade unions had to shut down. In Bolivia, El Salvador, and Peru an enterprise union may not be formed unless it covers more than 50 percent of the workers. In Nicaragua 60 percent coverage was required before the trade union law was amended in 1979. In the Mexican civil service only one trade union for each administrative unit is permitted.

In other countries an attempt is made to maintain trade union unity by resorting to the system of the most representative trade union, which is allowed exclusive bargaining rights as representative of a group or category of workers. This is the case in particular in Argentina and Brazil, where organizations with special trade union status or recognized organizations enjoy special privileges. Recognition of the most representative organization for collective bargaining purposes also exists in Costa Rica and Mexico. Even where the existence of parallel trade unions inside or outside the undertaking cannot be avoided (and in particular when an enterprise union can legally coexist with a craft or industrial union), legislation attempts to settle the problem of workers' representation in collective labor relations in this way, or through preferences for negotiation, or joint representation of trade unions.

National confederations and federations usually affiliate with one of the three international workers' organizations: the International Confederation of Free Trade Unions (ICFTU), the World Federation of Trade Unions (WFTU), or the World Confederation of Labour (WCL) and/or their regional organizations, the Inter-American Regional Organization of Workers (Organización Regional Interamericana de Trabajadores, ORIT), the Congreso Permanente de Unidad Sindical de los Trabajadores de América Latina (CPUSTAL), and the Central Latinoamericana de Trabajadores (CLAT).

ORIT was established in Mexico City in 1951, and its headquarters is still there. Of the three regional organizations it is the only one that includes trade unions from the United States. The main objective of ORIT, as laid down in its Declaration of Principles, is "To establish a powerful and effective international organization, composed of free and democratic trade unions, independent of any external domination and pledged to the task of promoting the interests of working people throughout the world and of enhancing the dignity of labor."

The main Latin American organizations affiliated with ORIT, by country, are the following: Brazil—Confederación Nacional de los Trabajadores de la Industria and Confederación Nacional de los Trabajadores de las Comunicaciones y Publicidad; Colombia—CTC and UTC; Costa Rica—CCTD; Dominican Republic—CNTD; Ecuador—CEOSL; El Salvador—Federación de Sindicatos de la Industria de Construcción; Honduras—CTH; Mexico—CTM; Nicaragua—CUS; Panama—CTRP; Peru—CTP and Confederación Nacional de Trabajadores (CNT); Uruguay—CGTU; Venezuela—CTV.

CPUSTAL was established in Brasília in 1964 and has its headquarters in Mexico City. It is strongly influenced by Communist ideology, and defines itself as an autonomous and independent organization that supports the principles of class struggle and presses the economic, social, and political demands of the workers.

The main affiliates of CPUSTAL are the following: Colombia—CSTC; Costa Rica—CUT; Cuba—Confederación de Trabajadores de Cuba (CTC); Dominican Republic—CGT; Ecuador—Confederación de Trabajadores del Ecuador; Honduras—Federación de Unidad Sindical; Panama—CNTP; Peru—CGTP; Venezuela—CUTV.

CLAT was founded in 1954 as the regional organization of the International Federation of Christian Trade Unions (IFCTU). In 1966 it adopted its present name and omitted any reference to religious allegiance. CLAT rejects the capitalist and Communist ideologies and models. In the preamble of its Declaration of Principles it states the need for "a rapid, radical and global change of the economic, social, cultural and political structures of all countries," and proclaims "the necessity of the social revolution in which the workers must be the vanguard and the most decisive element." The headquarters of CLAT is in Caracas, Venezuela. The main organizations affiliated with the CLAT are Colombia—CGT; Costa Rica—CTC; Dominican Republic—CASC; Ecuador—CEDOC; El Salvador—Confederación General de Sindicatos; Honduras—CGT; Mexico—Frente Auténtico del Trabajo (FAT); Nicaragua—Central de Trabajadores de Nicaragua (CTN); Panama—CIT; Peru—CNT; Uruguay—ASU; Venezuela—CODESA.

Membership and Numbers

Quantitative evaluation of the trade union movement in Latin America not only is materially difficult but also calls for a critical attitude and extreme caution in using and interpreting statistics. For various reasons the result can be only approximate and indicate broad trends; available data are usually incomplete or out of date, come from various sources, and lack a common methodology, so that comparison becomes difficult or impossible. They may originate from government statistics or information from trade union confederations, which generally tend to exaggerate their membership. There is no uniform criterion as to the kind of trade unionist recorded by census—he may be a registered member or a paid-up member; unionization rates are sometimes calculated as a proportion of the economically active population, and sometimes as a proportion of the wage earners; and practice is not uniform as regards the type of organization taken into account.

It is, however, possible to give a broad outline of the situation. Trade union membership rates, however reckoned, differ widely from one country to another. In Argentina, Brazil, Mexico, and Venezuela they fluctuate between 25 and 35 percent (much the same as the rate in more industrialized countries); in other countries they are much lower—between 10 and 17 percent in Colombia, Costa Rica, Ecuador, Panama, and Peru, and under 10 percent in Haiti and Paraguay.

Comparative assessment of these figures is difficult because there may be sharp changes in unionization; at times it may rise or fall very quickly because of, for example, the current political situation or new legislation, and available data are not updated to reflect these changes.

Unionization rates differ according to country and also from one national sector to another, being generally high in mining, manufacturing industry, rail transport, sugarcane and banana plantations, and banking. Workers in commerce, construction, and service are much less organized.

As a general rule the highest unionization rate is found in the sectors of the economy with the highest proportion of wage earners. The occasional flagrant exceptions are due to special circumstances, such as restrictive legislation. Certain sectors amenable to trade union organizations can show notable results; their membership rate approaches 100 percent, as in the state undertakings of Argentina, Costa Rica, Mexico, Peru, and Venezuela, sometimes as a result of union security clauses. This high degree of unionization occurs even in countries where trade unions are (or were) barred from the public sector.

The fact that a concentration of wage earners leads to a higher unionization rate signifies that in any country, that rate depends largely on the size of this category of workers; but the size of the work force in key sectors of the economy, such as mining and manufacturing, although their proportion of wage earners is high, is much smaller than in other activities, such as agriculture and commerce and services in general, where the proportion of wage earners is lower.

It should in any event be made clear that the unionization rate does not reveal the real influence of trade unionism on society and the economy. A high trade union concentration in certain dynamic sectors of the economy may have a multiplier effect on other sectors and push up the general wage level. The support given to trade unions by workers depends less on their membership than on their attitude in disputes. A glaring example of this is the massive strikes in support of wage demands or in protest against government economic policy. The actual participation of trade union organizations in various government bodies, and in economic and social planning and decision making, reflects their influence on national life more exactly than does their membership rate.

Another aspect of quantitative assessment of trade unionism is the number of trade union organizations in existence. It has already been mentioned that trade union multiplicity is one of the characteristics of the Latin American workers' movement. The statistics vary a great deal, have not been updated, and are not based on sufficiently accurate definitions; but it is interesting to see this fragmentation of trade unions in small countries as well as in bigger ones, and in spite of the existence of trade unions covering an entire branch of activity. The number of trade unions in 1980 was 504 in Costa Rica, 124 in El Salvador, 133 in Honduras, and 212 in Panama—as against 7,000 in Brazil, 6,746 in Chile, 3,300 in Ecuador, and 5,800 in Venezuela.

Finally, statistics of the size of each trade union show how small they are, even when they are industrial unions: the average membership of a trade union was 207 in Costa Rica, 340 in Honduras (except for agricultural trade unions, in which it was several thousand), 383 in Panama, 220 in Venezuela, and, in the extreme case of Ecuador, 76 for works committees, 74 for trade unions, and 60 for craft associations. Figures for previous regimes in Chile (the average for the 1950s) were 230 members for enterprise unions and 95 for craft unions; more recently these figures were 128 and 119, respectively. Argentina is an important exception; the average number of members per trade union organization there was 3,515, although, at the two extremes, there were a few trade unions with only a few hundred members, two organizations with about 100,000 members, and another two with more than 200,000 members.[8] In Brazil approximately half of the nonagricultural trade union membership was concentrated in 87 major unions.

Trade Unionism in Agriculture

In spite of the high proportion of agricultural workers in most Latin American countries, they are generally much less organized than industrial workers. Only exceptionally is this a direct consequence of legislation; it is normally due to a combination of socioeconomic characteristics.

The situation cannot be properly understood without reference to plantation workers and to the various categories of persons living and working in traditional agricultural society: the small independent farmers, sharecroppers, tenant farmers, other farmers established on big estates, and wage laborers (some of whom are also independent farmers).

Freedom of association is normally less difficult on the big plantations with a stable labor force. There, labor relations can be similar to those in industry, and in fact large organizations have been formed on sugarcane plantations (in Argentina, Colombia, Mexico, and Peru) and banana plantations (in Costa Rica and Honduras); but even there illiteracy, lack of leaders, and the dependence of workers isolated on enormous establishments with few opportunities and means of communication with the outside world cause problems. Special difficulties arise when trade union leaders are forbidden access to these estates on the pretext of property rights, when the workers' right of assembly in public places is restricted, or when there is intimidation and antiunion discrimination. In such circumstances it is not always easy to get the courts or administrative authorities to intervene or give their protection.

In any event, the situation on large plantations is more propitious to trade unionism than in the more traditional agricultural societies, where legal—and human—relations beween peasants and landowners are different, and where there are the additional difficulties of dispersion, great distances, bad communications, instability, excessive labor turnover, and high unemployment and underemployment. Other factors can also curb or prevent any effective organization of trade unions, including action by government or local authorities, and opposition by the landowners, who refuse to parley with workers because they consider that doing so would impair their traditional authority. Finally, the system of land tenure is an important factor, since in many cases trade union development is impossible without land reform (for instance, in Bolivia, Chile, and Mexico).[9]

The workers in the traditional sector are more numerous than wage earners employed on the plantations. According to statistics for the 1970s, in only 5 (Argentina, Costa Rica, Chile, El Salvador, and Uruguay) of the 18 countries of the region did wage earners number over half the agricultural labor force. In the other countries the proportion of wage earners was between 20 and 50 percent (in increasing order) in Panama, Brazil, Peru, Venezuela, Honduras, the Dominican Republic, Guatemala, Ecuador, Mexico, and Nicaragua, and under 20 percent in Bolivia, Haiti, and Paraguay.[10] It should be noted that a proportion of these wage earners—varying with the degree of agricultural development—belongs to the traditional sector.

Agricultural trade unionism in Latin America began only in the second decade of this century in Argentina, Brazil, and Mexico, and spread after World War II. The first organizations were founded in the nonwage-earning sector; the smallholders, sharecroppers, and farmers of common land were the first to organize themselves to defend their interests. Peasant resistance has left bloody marks on trade union history, mainly in this, the most exploited category of the agricultural population.

The organizational difficulties of agricultural workers are not generally legislative ones. Normally, however, the labor codes exclude persons not in wage employment, with certain exceptions (in Costa Rica, Guatemala, Honduras, and Panama). The Agricultural Trade Union Acts passed in Chile in 1966 to promote rural organizations, and later repealed, included self-employed workers; but even when agricultural workers not in wage employment lack the formal protection of trade union law, this does not in practice prevent them from banding together in associations, such as the peasant leagues or communities, or in actual trade unions, together with agricultural wage earners, as in the National Agrarian Federation (FANAL) in Colombia, the National Federation of Organizations of Peasants (FENOC) in Ecuador, the Peasants' Federation in Venezuela, and the National Peasant Federation (CNC) in Mexico.

Land reform, which gave a strong fillip to trade union organization in some countries, may also restrict it. In Peru, for example, the trade unions lost members and influence when the agrarian organizations were founded in 1972. (These organizations, which are governed by Legislative Decree no. 19400 of 1972, are the bodies representing agricultural workers in dealings with the state, private individuals, and public opinion; their duty is to protect their members' interests, train them, and perform social services. They may be formed by workers who work the land themselves or by wage earners, but may not perform the functions of trade unions.) It may appear absurd for workers who have become members of a cooperative or any other kind of collective farming institution to belong at the same time to trade unions that exist to defend those workers' interests against their own community; but experience shows that an individual member of a big communal establishment may be as unable to defend himself against its collective management as against an employer or administrator of an undertaking in which he might work as an employee. Trade union protection proves equally necessary in either case.

In nearly all countries of Latin America, trade union legislation is the same for agricultural wage earners as for workers in industry, commerce, and services. All are covered by the labor code or general trade union law. Until now the only country in which trade union rights in agriculture have not been regulated is El Salvador. In Uruguay recent trade union legislation includes agricultural workers.

Laws that in the past restricted freedom of association in this sector have been abolished. In the Dominican Republic and Honduras certain provisions survive that prohibit the right to organize in agricultural and stock-raising undertakings with fewer than ten permanent employees.

In general, it may be concluded that the legal situation has steadily progressed in trade union matters but much has yet to be done to obviate the difficulties that still survive. Governments have an important part to play in furthering this progress, but a still more important part falls to the existing organizations, which in Argentina, Bolivia, Brazil, Colombia, Ecuador, Honduras, Mexico, and Venezuela have acquired considerable influence.

Trade Unionism in the Public Sector

Although collective labor relations are examined in this book, with special reference to the private sector, no study of trade union organizations in Latin America can fail to consider trade unionism in the public sector, however superficially. The continued growth of the public sector and the proliferation of state services and undertakings in the region make the matter of working conditions in this vast sector, and participation by officials and other state employees in fixing them through the intermediary of their representatives (in particular of their organizations), especially important. Public officials have always been a race apart in regard to regulation of their labor rights. The right to form trade unions was denied them even after the right to organize had become widely accepted in the private sector. Joseph Barthelemy and other prominent jurists maintained at the beginning of the century that the principle behind trade unionism was resistance to exploitation by capital, and that its purpose was to discuss working conditions with employers; since in the public service those conditions were fixed by law, there was no point in having a trade union. In the course of more detailed inquiry, an attempt was made to distinguish decision-making officials from managing or administrative officials, and civil servants in the strict sense of the term, who were covered by administrative law, from public servants or subordinate employees in independent bodies—and to concede the right to organize themselves into trade unions only to the latter category, who came under the labor laws and therefore had the same rights as other workers.

These controversies are now a thing of the past in most countries, at least as regards the right of civil servants and other state employees to form organizations to further and defend their interests. As far back as the first report[11] prepared by the ILO in connection with the adoption of the Freedom of Association and Protection of the Right to Organize Convention (1948), it was stressed that the guarantee of the right of association should apply to all employers and workers, public or private, and therefore to public servants and officials and to workers in nationalized industries. "It has been considered," states the ILO report, "that it would be inequitable to draw any distinction, as regards freedom of association, between wage earners in private industry and officials in the public services, since persons in either category should be permitted to defend their interests by becoming organized, even if those interests are not always of the same kind."

In Latin America much less progress in this direction has been made. Arguments invoking the principles of hierarchy, fidelity, administrative law relations, and even reverence for the state are still being used. It has been stressed that for civil servants there is no inequality of treatment nor clash of interests, no desire for speculation on the part of the public authorities; and that, since civil servants serve the general interest, their organizations would work against the state itself, to the prejudice of the community.[12]

One of the most effective arguments is that any kind of trade unionism in the civil service would have political influence and connotations. Jiménez de Aréchaga, commenting on the draft of the American Convention on Human Rights, wrote that the draft authorized the restriction of the right of public employees to organize and that the desirability of this restriction could not be "ignored in States in which the overly generalized way" in which this right had been established was "seriously compromising, in some cases, the stability of the State."[13]

So much for the theoretical discussions. In actual fact the position, according to certain sources, is that there are in Latin America 15 million civil servants, of whom about 25 percent are organized. This figure is fairly high in comparison with the general unionization rate and if one bears in mind the special characteristics of civil servants, in particular the attitude of many governments toward trade unionism in the public sector. In half the countries of the region, the civil servants' right to organize is still not recognized, and neither, sometimes, is the right to organize of workers employed in public undertakings or autonomous state agencies. Latin America represents the greatest concentration of countries in a single region in which this right is denied.

Among the countries in which public servants have the right to form trade unions are Argentina, Colombia, Costa Rica, Mexico, and Venezuela. Peru joined this group when it expressly recognized this right in its 1979 constitution. In Venezuela it was officially recognized in 1970, when the Civil Service Career Act was passed.

In the other countries the situation varies. In Chile, where this right was traditionally denied, the denial was breached in 1972, when the right was granted to the teaching profession, and a number of organizations already existing de facto in the public and semipublic sectors were allowed to register. These provisions have been repealed, and the new trade union law is not applicable to officials in state administration, whether centralized or decentralized. In Uruguay the Trade Union Act of 1981 is limited to private activity, but the right of public officials to form associations for the defense of their occupational rights is recognized in the Civil Service Act of 1933. In Brazil the right to organize does not apply to civil servants and workers in state undertakings, but since 1974 workers in mixed undertakings have been recognized as having that right. In the Dominican Republic the only workers in state undertakings who are allowed to belong to trade unions are those doing manual work or work requiring mainly physical effort. In Panama legal personality has been granted to trade unions in certain state undertakings. In Guatemala the Labor Code does not cover workers directly or indirectly employed by the state, but in El Salvador the code expressly includes manual and nonmanual workers in autonomous and semiautonomous official institutions.

Even in Colombia, Mexico, and Peru, which recognize the civil servants' right to organize, directors, supervisors, and holders of positions of trust are excluded from that right.

Although so many countries deny their civil servants, and sometimes other categories of state employees, the right to form trade unions, this has not prevented the actual existence and operation of such organizations. These, indeed, are formed de facto or in accordance with the ordinary provisions of civil law (nominally for mutual benefit or cultural or kindred purposes), but in fact act as trade unions defending their members' occupational rights. Large organizations of central or local government employees and of specific groups such as teachers, employees of public health agencies, official banks, and social insurance funds, exist, whatever the legal system in force. The paradox is that the state as employer recognizes de facto, and even negotiates with, groups that the state as legislator repudiates.

To disregard the law and go unpunished prejudices all legal order; and if current realities cause laws no longer suited to the times to fall into disuse, it is in the general interest to suit lawgiving to the social conditions that must be regulated. This applies not only to recognition of the right of civil servants and other state employees to organize, but also to the whole range of collective labor relations in the public sector. Disputes for which there is no suitable settlement procedure, and militancy frustrated by lack of any institutionalized form of participation, disorganize public administration; they also undermine economic development and are prejudicial to the general interest.

Detailed Legislative Regulation and Administrative Supervision

In most Latin American countries trade union legislation is notoriously meticulous and detailed—not only through petti-foggery but also because it follows the principle of supervision of organizations and their external and internal operations. The legislature has taken a dynamic attitude toward trade union law; it protects association for occupational purposes but tries to make sure that trade unionism conforms to a preestablished pattern, under the supervision of labor officers while respecting the free play of internal democracy in the trade unions.

Administrative supervision of trade union affairs in Latin America is reflected both in legislation and in the functions allotted to departments of labor. A clear formula of this kind is that of the Guatemalan Labor Code, which states that the Department of Labor must exercise the strictest supervision over trade unions to ensure that they operate in the manner prescribed by law. The extent of administrative supervision depends on the situation, traditions, and political problems in each country; but supervision by labor officers in all areas of a trade union is an undisputed constant in the rules governing occupational associations.

Legislation normally starts by fixing the trade unions' structure, and for this purpose defines the various types of trade unions that may be formed and specifies the minimum number of members. When dealing with federations and confederations, the law influences their formation, structure, and development by requirements respecting the number of trade unions or federations forming them, the categories of workers represented (horizontal and vertical organizations), and the functions they may exercise, unless—as happens exceptionally—it completely excludes them from the trade union law.

The constitution of trade unions, including preliminary formal ties and final approval of their statutes, is one of the legislatures' favorite subjects. The grant of legal personality, of recognition (as in Brazil), or of trade union status (as in Argentina) is a cornerstone of the system. In the Dominican Republic, El Salvador, and Peru it is also essential for a notary or a representative of the department of labor to be present at the inaugural general meeting. Legislation specifies the documents and information to be submitted to the authorities responsible for labor matters (the record of foundation, list of members, composition of the executive committee, and statutes).

Experience shows that this stage is especially propitious for all kinds of interference with the exercise of trade union rights. Such interference may come from the employers and consist of acts of discrimination against trade unions—mainly dismissals—and from the department of labor. In some countries the legislation grants founders of trade unions special protection against discriminatory action, thus giving specific legal content to their policy of protecting trade unions. Administrative interference may manage to prevent the grant of legal status or to postpone it indefinitely, mainly for political motives, by devious means or through intricate legal formalities.

The future trade union's affairs will be regulated largely through its constitution, to which national legislatures accordingly pay great attention. A very widespread practice is to list the subjects to be covered by the constitution; a more restrictive practice prefers to specify what the rules on such subjects should be. Even where legislation establishes only in very general terms the rules to be observed by the statutes, there are very often more or less detailed provisions on such matters as meetings, notice of meetings, quorum, requirements to be fulfilled by a would-be leader, election procedure, and the organization's financial system. It is, however, unusual to find a provision like the Brazilian one requiring the constitution to include a declaration that the association will cooperate with the public authorities and other associations by practicing social solidarity and subordinating economic and occupational interests to national interests. To take a more particular aspect, it is also exceptional to prescribe that the agenda of general meetings shall be submitted to the administrative authorities (as in Argentina) or that a representative of those authorities shall be present at such meetings (as in the Dominican Republic).

The question of leadership of the trade union is closely linked to what has just been said. The legal requirements to be fulfilled by leaders generally include ones on age, nationality, and exercise of the occupation represented. This last condition has helped to prevent trade union functions from being discharged by outsiders, which is an acute problem in other parts of the world. It has not, however, lessened the politicization of most leaders, whatever their ideology, in spite of sporadic legal interdicts against trade unionists of certain ideological or party loyalties. The nationality requirement has in certain countries been established in a rigid form that, for example, restricts executive functions to persons who are nationals of the country by birth, or requires a certain number of years to have elapsed since their naturalization.

In Latin America the legislation lays down in detail the requirements to be met by the electoral procedure within the trade unions and the rules applicable to their executives.[14] There are numerous references to the quorum and voting majorities in general meetings or direct elections, the frequency of elections, term of office, numerical composition of executive bodies, and restrictions on reelection of leaders. Brazilian legislation is the most detailed in this respect and also contains requirements not generally found elsewhere: the requirement of seniority in the occupation to qualify

as an elector; the deposit of candidacies supported by good conduct certif-
icates; precise rules on convening meetings, signifying opposition to candidacies, voting papers, the form of ballot, electoral bureaus, and the registration of participants in compulsory voting; the presence of a
supervisor from the Department of Labor at elections; the appointment of
a temporary administrator to hold elections if they are not held within the
required time; approval of results; opposition to results; and invalidation
of votes.

Argentina also has a set of detailed regulations on electoral procedure; inter alia, the law lists the executive posts to be filled, and requires
an electoral delegate to be appointed if the summons to the meeting is not
sent out in time, and a committee of three members to be formed to supervise the elections and accept or reject the lists of candidates to be submitted to compulsory voting.

The administrative authorities of certain countries have the important prerogative of removing trade union leaders from office. Provisions
to that effect exist in Argentina, Brazil, and Colombia, and have been applied especially in the first two on various occasions by means of "inter-
ventions" in the operation of the trade union organizations by government officers in charge of labor matters. In Argentina such officers are
also empowered to disqualify leaders transgressing requirements of the
law or of the constitution of the union.

Another important area of trade union legislation and the powers of
departments of labor relates to trade union funds.[15] In general the intention is to protect members against embezzlement and to ensure that funds
and property are administered in the workers' interests, but legal and administrative requirements are so far-reaching that they raise problems of
undue interference with freedom of trade union action.

It is fairly usual to require that buildings be acquired only to serve as
union offices, for meetings, and as social and educational centers, and to
forbid funds to be used for political purposes. The rules for financial management frequently require that funds shall be deposited in a bank (sometimes a state bank); that not more than a certain amount of cash may be
kept for current expenses; that certain signatures shall be necessary to
withdraw money from the bank; and that expenditure in excess of a certain amount must be authorized by the general meeting. Financial administration is subject to many regulations. It is usual to require executive
bodies to give an account of their administration to the general meeting
and that the general meeting should approve the budget; in addition the
administrative authorities are responsible for outside supervision of that
administration. A general requirement is that a yearly or half-yearly report of receipts and expenditures and a statement of account shall be
made to the authorities, and that accounts shall be kept in the form prescribed by law. In addition, trade unions must at all times hold accounting
documents at the authorities' disposal and submit any required informa-

tion to them. In some countries the administrative authorities are empowered to carry out inspections and investigations whenever they see fit.

Apart from these requirements and practical measures, there are other, less general ones that are peculiar to certain countries. In Brazil, for example, all workers are required to pay trade union dues whether or not they are members of the trade union, and the law specifies how funds are to be distributed and used (on the subject of trade union contributions see Chapter 7). In Argentina the law provides that trade unions may not intervene in the conduct and administration of social welfare. In Colombia the auditor on the executive committee must be a representative of the minority faction elected, and the treasurer must lodge security with the union. In the Dominican Republic the general meeting must appoint from among its members one or more commissioners to audit the funds, and those commissioners may convene the general meeting in an emergency.

In general, it is fair to say that the setting up of trade unions, and the administration and supervision of their property, are the two most common subjects of regulation and administrative supervision.

There remains the question of suspension and dissolution of trade union organizations as a penalty for breaking the law. In most countries this has to be done by the courts, but in a few countries the law delegates such powers to the labor administration authorities, sometimes with the right of appeal to the courts. In Argentina the Department of Labor may suspend the main functions of a trade union or cancel its trade union status or registration; in Colombia the authorities may suspend a trade union, and may go so far as to dissolve it in the event of an illegal strike; in Honduras suspension and dissolution of a trade union may be ordered by the administrative authorities only if the union has taken part in an illegal strike; in Brazil the Department of Labor may suspend a trade union or cancel its certificate of recognition; in El Salvador the department may suspend or dissolve a trade union organization; and in Bolivia a trade union may be dissolved by order of the administrative authorities.

Politicization and Labor Relations

The politicization of Latin American trade unions has often been discussed, but the term covers various circumstances, such as relations between the workers' movement and the parties, governments, or certain ideological factions; trade union reactions to government economic policy; pressure put on the government to pass favorable legislation or settle a collective dispute; strikes to defend the existing institutional structure; or action to overthrow it.

There has always been, and there still is, political action of one kind or another by trade unions in all countries and regions. It has even been maintained that it is in the nature of the working-class movement to defend certain social interests by putting pressure on society as a whole, and to oppose economic power on behalf of specific social interests—those of employed labor.[16]

In Latin America the working-class movement was incubated by the anarchist, anarcho-syndicalist, and socialist ideas brought by European immigrants. It was mainly a movement of artisans and skilled workers that challenged the validity of the existing social order, its anarchist and anarcho-syndicalist members rejecting any participation in conventional politics or political action. With the growing industrialization of the first quarter of the twentieth century, this faction lost ground to the socialists and Communists, whose influence on urban workers was exerted through the corresponding class parties. Diversification of the economy brought with it, however, a middle-class political elite that challenged the primacy of the traditional ruling class based on land ownership, whose members were out of touch with the new power structures and ideas. The social crisis was aggravated by the depression of the 1930s. This situation led to the development of labor and trade union legislation after World War I, largely as the result of new liberal political ideas, and in some cases to intervention by the armed forces.

Much has been written on the period beginning in the 1930s and on the relations established among trade unions, political parties, and governments. The main emphasis has been on trade union dependence on sympathetic political parties and some governments' tutelage of the trade union movement they had created. In fact, the trade union legislation that was passed was intended to give form to a weak movement that continually sought party or government support because it had little weight in collective labor relations. The abundance of labor laws was an incentive to continue political action in search of new legal benefits; and trade union leaders began to take part in political bodies, forging a tradition that only accentuated politicization.

Trade union legislation nevertheless barred the trade unions from all political activity, or at least party politics, thus bringing about a situation that still obtains and in which the legal framework does not reflect reality.

The links forged between the new liberal bourgeois parties and the trade unions did not prevent continuing or resumed relations between other sections of the trade union movement and the socialist and Communist parties, the influence of the Catholic Church on part of the labor movement, or the vigorous populism encouraged by certain governments. This populism managed to maintain the unity of a trade union movement supported by the political party in power, but the other schools of thought increased the congenital pluralism of the labor movement.

The characteristic dependence of trade unions on political parties or governments has already been noted. This situation, caused by the initial weakness of trade unions, has tended to change with their growth since the 1950s and 1960s, as the result of certain circumstances, notably the fall of the governments or parties that supported them, economic difficulties that have led trade unions to assert their independence of friendly governments in response to pressure from their rank and file, and the greater cohesion and fighting powers of trade unions as compared with political parties.

Political action and political alliances have generally been at the apex of the trade union movement. The rank-and-file organizations, whatever their ideological or party affiliations, have never ceased to make work-related demands in whatever way their outlook suggests or their abilities allow. The anarchists continued their philosophical debates on the organization of society and in addition made wage claims and demanded improved working conditions, which they attempted to enforce without discussion by going on strike. The situation tended to change with growing industrialization and the appearance of new schools of trade union thought that increasingly resorted to collective bargaining wherever they were recognized and the employers were willing to negotiate. Legislation offered a means of settling these economic disputes in accordance with the principles of judicial procedure.

Collective labor relations at first developed mainly in undertakings with a high concentration of skilled workers, in mining areas, and on a few plantations. The strength of trade union organizations and their power to press claims encouraged workers to concentrate on work-related grievances, irrespective of, and even in opposition to, any political tendency or alliance.[17] It was observed that "Although in theory the functions of the trade union movement embrace political as well as industrial action, in its daily local practice the industrial aspect tends to predominate."[18] This remark is confirmed by the growing importance of collective bargaining, whatever the ideological or political trend of the trade unions. Only where the trade unions are weak, as when they cover unskilled workers and marginal undertakings and industries, are they obliged to depend mainly on political favors or government intervention to further their demands and obtain satisfaction.

The trade union movement nevertheless continues, at its apex, to defend political attitudes, to react to government action, to consolidate its own place in society, and, depending on its political leanings, to strive for a change in the national economic and social system.

In fact, the trade unions promote the interests of the sector they represent on two planes, occupational and political. They link or separate those planes at will and according to the level at which each union works. The more the union is decentralized, the more it will be concerned with industrial relations and the more autonomous it will be. This does not prevent the trade union movement from taking joint action on the political plane, bringing together opposing factions, even if such action conflicts with its party alliance, to protest government economic policy. Nor does it prevent certain unions or confederations from furthering open conflict on an industrial pretext but in fact for political purposes. This kind of action best reflects what is normally understood by trade union "politicization."

Notes

1. G. Mazzoni, *La conquista della libertà sindacale* (Rome: Edizioni Leonardo, 1947), pp. 72 ff.

2. ILO, *Freedom of Association*, Studies and reports, Series A (Indusrial Relations), no. 28, vol. I, *Comparative Analysis* (Geneva: ILO, 1927), pp. 137–40.

3. See, for instance, F. Zapata, "Las organizaciones sindicales," in R. Katzman and J. L. Reyna, comps., *Fuerza de trabajo y movimientos laborales en América latina* (Mexico City: Colegio de México, 1979).

4. See, for instance, Robert J. Alexander, *Organized Labor in Latin America* (New York: The Free Press, 1965); V. Alba, *Historia del movimiento obrero en América latina* (Mexico City: Libreros Mexicanos Unidos, 1964); Miles E. Galvin, *Unionism in Latin America* (Ithaca, N.Y.: New York State School of Industrial and Labor Relations, Cornell University, 1962); M. Poblete Troncoso and B. G. Burnett, *The Rise of the Latin American Labor Movement* (New York: Bookman Associates, 1960) and "Latin American Labor Unions," in *United States–Latin American Relations*, compilation of studies prepared under the direction of the Subcommittee on American Republics Affairs of the Sub-committee on Foreign Relations, U.S. Senate, 86th Cong., 2nd sess., Document 125, August 31, 1960.

5. See, for instance, Zapata, "Las organizaciones sindicales," pp. 213–15.

6. J. Morris, *Elites, Intellectuals and Consensus, a Study of the Social Question and the Industrial Relations System in Chile* (Ithaca, N.Y.: New York State School of Industrial and Labor Relations, Cornell University, 1966).

7. ILO, *The Trade Union Situation in Chile*, report of the Fact-Finding and Conciliation Commission on Freedom of Association (Geneva: ILO, 1975), paras. 244, 254.

8. Ministerio de Trabajo y Seguridad Social de la Argentina, *Censo nacional de asociaciones profesionales* (Buenos Aires: The Ministry, 1965). Figures from a study on 502 trade unions responding to a questionnaire.

9. Xavier Flores, *Agricultural Organizations and Economic and Social Development in Rural Areas* (Geneva: ILO, 1971), passim.

10. ILO, *Yearbook of Labour Statistics, 1977–80* (Geneva: ILO, 1978–81), Table 2A.

11. ILO, *Freedom of Association and Industrial Relations*, Report VII, International Labour Conference, 30th Session (Geneva: ILO, 1947), pp. 108–09.

12. G. Cabanellas, *Derecho sindical y corporativo* (Buenos Aires: Editorial Bibliográfica Argentina, 1959), p. 420.

13. Organization of American States, Inter-American Commission on Human Rights, 24th Session, *First Report on Trade Union Freedom*, prepared by J. Jiménez de Aréchaga, Document no. OEA/Ser.L/V/II.24 (May 7, 1971), p. 95.

14. See B. Gernigon, *Procedures for the Election and Removal from Office of Trade Union Leaders* (Geneva: ILO, 1977).

15. ILO, *The Public Authorities and the Right to Protection of Trade Union Funds and Property* (Geneva: ILO, 1974).

16. A. Touraine, "Situations ouvrières et types de démocratie économique," in *Revue de l'Institut de sociologie* (Brussels) no. 1-2, (1961) pp. 31-42.

17. F. Bourricaud, "Syndicalisme et politique: Le cas péruvien," *Sociologie du travail* (Paris) (1961): no. 4, pp. 33-49; Mark Thompson, "Collective Bargaining in the Mexican Electrical Industry," *British Journal of Industrial Relations*, March 1970, pp. 55-68; and F. Zapata, *Los mineros de Chuquicamata: Prodoctores o proletarios?*, Cuadernos del CES, no. 13 (Mexico City: Centro de Estudios Sociológicos, Colegio de Mexico, 1975).

18. Ibid., p. 70.

3

Employers' Organizations

by
Arturo S. Bronstein

The abundance of material published on labor relations in Latin America usually concentrates on trade unions or on government policies for protecting labor, but pays virtually no attention to the other party to the labor relations system: the employers and their organizations. The purpose of this chapter is to give a succinct account of employers' organizations in Latin America.

If workers' trade unions and employers' organizations are compared, it will be seen that the latter generally date back further. Their participation in labor relations is, however, much more recent, for various reasons. First, practically no Latin American country except Brazil has real employers' organizations resembling those in other parts of the world. Second, business organizations in Latin America have nearly always been concerned with defending economic interests, promoting trade, or regulating an industry, profession, or trade; only rarely have they also represented the employers' interests in social or labor affairs. Third, the labor relations systems of most countries favor collective bargaining and labor–management contacts at the undertaking level or the establishment of procedures to settle disputes by the government authorities, but does not promote bilateral relations between trade unions and employers' organizations. Employers' organizations had therefore found no domain in which they could play a significant part in labor relations systems.

More recently, however, their participation has been growing to an impressive extent. In some countries it does not yet count for much; but in a fair number of others the weight of employers' organizations in collective bargaining, fixing minimum wages, or settling labor disputes is far from negligible. They also have a marked influence on the personnel and labor relations policies of their members, and in some cases help to draw up social legislation, mainly through their labor affairs committees.

Origin and Development

The remotest antecedents of employers' organizations may be traced back to the colonial period. As early as the end of the eighteenth century *sociedades económicas de amigos del país* were formed in various countries of Latin America; these institutions were largely concerned with the promotion of the public interest, but also represented particular interest groups. It seems more reasonable, however, to date the origin of employers' organizations to the nineteenth century. In 1811 commercial exchanges were founded in Bahia and Rio de Janeiro, Brazil, and subsequently evolved into the first commercial associations. About 1827, also in Rio de Janeiro, a "society for the promotion of national industry" (Sociedad Auxiliadora da Industria Nacional) was founded; this is perhaps the oldest example on the South American continent of an association of industrialists.

For much of the nineteenth century the most vigorous organizations were undoubtedly those of the rural sector. The oldest (and still active) is the Sociedad Nacional de Agricultura, founded in Chile in 1838. A few years later similar associations were formed in other countries: the Sociedad Rural Argentina, formed in 1866; the Sociedad de Agricultores, formed in Colombia in 1871; and the Asociación Rural in Uruguay, also formed in 1871. Sometimes simultaneously, but more often a few years after the agricultural sector because of the precapitalist economic structure of Latin America in the nineteenth century, the employers in other sectors of the economy became organized. Chambers of commerce were founded in Mexico City in 1861, in Montevideo in 1867, in Bogotá in 1878, in Lima in 1888, and in Bolivia in 1890. In 1875 the Club Industrial, later known as the Unión Industrial Argentina, was founded in Buenos Aires. In 1883 an association for the encouragement of manufactures (Sociedad de Fomento Fabril) and a national mining society (Sociedad Nacional de Minería) were founded in Chile. In Peru the Sociedad de Industrias was founded in 1896.

This brings us to the first decades of the twentieth century, when business organizations were formed in increasing numbers. This trend was to a great extent encouraged by the protectionist policy of the state, as shown by its laws founding chambers of commerce and industry (to which the businessmen concerned were obliged to belong) and requiring public registers of firms. This occurred in Colombia, Ecuador, Honduras, Mexico, and Nicaragua, whose legislation granted such chambers a monopoly of functions for the protection of trade and simultaneously established a public law relationship between them and the state. (In Mexico the laws on chambers of commerce and industry passed in 1936 and amended in 1941 granted them the status of independent public institutions having legal personality, formed to represent the general interests of the trades and industries under their jurisdiction and to act as consultative bodies to the state in order to meet the needs of national commerce and industry.)

Governments also encouraged the foundation of voluntary sectoral organizations, some of which represented manufacturing industry and others branches of economic activity such as construction, finance, and insurance. This process became very active in the 1930s and gathered momentum in the following decade, presumably as a direct result of the drastic political and economic changes at that time. For example, in 1936 the Confederación de la Producción y del Comercio was founded in Chile, and in Mexico the above-mentioned legislation was passed, giving chambers of commerce and industry their present form; in 1944 the Asociación Nacional de Industriales was founded in Colombia, during the administration of Alfonso López Pumarejo, largely on his initiative;[1] and in Brazil the present pattern of trade unions and employers' organizations was established during President Vargas' Estado Novo. In Venezuela the Federation of Chambers and Associations of Commerce and Production (FEDE-CAMARAS) was formed in 1944; and in Argentina the General Economic Confederation (now dissolved) was formed in 1950 and reached its zenith during the Perón administration.

The most recent change began in 1950, and here there may be a relation of cause and effect with the introduction of economic development strategies and the appearance of the various systems of regional economic integration, such as the Latin American Free Trade Association (ALALC) and the Central American Common Market. The Inter-American Council of Commerce and Production (CICYP) and the Association of Latin American Industrialists (AILA) brought employers' organizations in the various countries closer together and doubtless helped to consolidate them. Not unconnected with this is the formation of confederations of employers' organizations, particularly in Central America.

Nature and Structure

In most Latin American countries there are no employers' organizations in the strict sense of the term. The only important exception is Brazil, because of the great influence of the laws passed in the 1930s by the Getúlio Vargas regime and later codified in the 1943 Consolidation of Labor

Laws. The trade union structure in the Consolidation most probably represents the last vestige of the corporative systems inspired by Italy's Rocco Act of 1925. Under the Brazilian system there is no integration of workers and employers into a single organization; instead, the principle of a parallel structure has been adopted, so that each workers' trade union representing an "occupational category" is paralleled by an employers' union representing an "economic category." At the national level the National Confederation of Industry is the employers' counterpart of the National Confederation of Industrial Workers, just as the National Confederation of Commerce is the national counterpart of the National Confederation of Commercial Workers and the National Confederation of Agriculture is the counterpart of the National Confederation of Agricultural Workers.

A peculiarity of the Brazilian system is that the law has established a compulsory "trade union contribution" for all workers, payable to their trade unions, and for all employers, payable to their organizations. The employers' organizations in industry and commerce also administer the resources of various important social services: industry (SESI), commerce (SESC), industrial vocational training (including apprenticeship) (SENAI), and commercial vocational training (SENAC). These funds represent 2.5 percent of the total wage bill.

Except in Brazil, the "employers' trade union" is an expression that exists in several labor codes but has been very little used in practice. In Mexico the Employers' Confederation of the Mexican Republic (COPARMEX) has been formed in accordance with the Federal Labor Law, but it is not the sole employers' organization competent in labor questions. The situation is somewhat similar in Panama, where the Industrialists' Union is not the only organization representing the employers in labor matters. In nearly all countries the most usual kinds of organizations are chambers of commerce or chambers of industry and associations formed under civil law (as distinct from commercial law). Some of the chambers are institutions of public law founded in accordance with special legislation, particularly in Colombia, Ecuador, Honduras, and Mexico; the membership of others is voluntary, as in Argentina, Bolivia, Costa Rica, Panama, and Venezuela, and they are more akin to the associations formed under civil law. Associations of the latter type have been formed mainly in agriculture, but also in industry, and include the Unión Industrial Argentina, the Sociedad de Fomento Fabril in Chile, the National Association of Industrialists in Colombia and Honduras, and the Sociedad de Industrias in Peru.

The difference between the chambers and the associations is that the chambers are concerned mainly with rendering general services. The official chambers often keep the public commercial register; in addition they carry out trade regulatory functions such as certifying invoices or export promotion. Other functions may include commercial arbitration, expert investigations, holding fairs and exhibitions, and appointing representatives to various state bodies. The civil associations were formed to advise their members rather than to render services, but above all to defend principles; in practice this distinction may become blurred, since the chambers also usually act as bodies representing interests and the associations render services to their members.

Like the workers' organizations, the structure of employers' organizations varies a great deal in complexity and sophistication from one country to another. The chambers frequently have a pyramidal structure that includes local, regional or provincial, and national levels. They may also be grouped under confederations or federations of industries. The same sort of variety exists among civil associations, but their names do not always show whether they represent individual groups of employers directly or indirectly, or whether they are federations or confederations. It is often observed that some of the so-called federations in fact function as confederations and vice versa; in other cases their structures are hybrid ones.

For example, the Federation of Chambers and Associations of Commerce and Production (FEDECAMARAS) of Venezuela is in reality a confederation. The Confederation of Chambers of Industry of the United Mexican States (CONCAMIN) has as its direct members 35 single national chambers; 4 other national chambers, each of which functions side by side with 2 regional chambers in the same branch; 8 other regional chambers without any corresponding national chamber; a national chamber; 2 regional chambers of manufacturing industry; and 14 industrial associations.[2] The Employers' Confederations of the Mexican Republic (COPARMEX) is an organization of employers' associations. The Sociedad de Fomento Fabril in Chile has individual members, affiliated associations (on a provincial or regional basis), and trade union associations by branch of industry. In spite of its name, the members of the Employers' Confederation of the Dominican Republic are individual firms or employers.

In any event, what matters is not the structure of the organization but whether that structure reflects the various views of employers as a whole and enables them to express their views through a single competent spokesman. This can be done either by an umbrella organization (or confederation) or by an association of individual employers, provided the latter is sufficiently representative. In Latin America there are examples of both extremes. The typical umbrella organization is the Confederation of

Production and Commerce of Chile, which has "branches" representing industry, commerce, agriculture, mining, and construction. A representative organization of the other kind—representative, if not of all employers, at least of a particularly large proportion of them—is the National Association of Industrialists (ANDI) of Colombia, which, although it has only about 800 members, represents 75 percent of national industrial production.

There are quite a number of countries in which it has not been possible to build up an umbrella organization, or confederation, of employers, although a trend in that direction is emerging. In Central America coordinating boards have been founded that are virtually confederations representing practically all sectors of the economy. The oldest of these is the Coordinating Committee of Agricultural, Commercial, Industrial, and Financial Associations (CACIF) of Guatemala, founded in 1947. In other countries these coordinating bodies were founded much more recently, and generally in connection with the Central American Common Market. They exist in all the countries of Central America: the Union of Chambers and Associations of Private Enterprise in Costa Rica, the National Association of Private Enterprises (ANEP) in El Salvador, the Honduran Private Enterprises Board (COHEP) in Honduras, the Higher Council for Private Enterprises (COSEP) in Nicaragua, and the National Council of Private Enterprise (CONEP) in Panama.

In other countries the situation varies. In some of them there is a true confederation, as in Chile, Venezuela (FEDECAMARAS), and, to some extent, Bolivia (Confederation of Private Employers). In other countries coordinating bodies have been founded that operate more or less informally. They include the Employers' Coordinating Committee in Mexico and the National Council of Heads of Undertakings in the Dominican Republic. In still other countries a confederation is being formed—for instance, the Union of Private Employers in Peru (whose greatest difficulty appears to be to cover all employers, in particular the national mining company).

A fourth situation is that of confederations that have lost some of their most important branches—for example, the Federation of Production, Industry, and Commerce (FEPRINCO) of Paraguay, from which the Industrial Union of Paraguay withdrew. The situation is different in Argentina, where under the Perón regime the various employers' organizations were brought together in the General Economic Confederation; but this was due more to political action than to the employers' wishes, and the experiment accordingly did not survive the regime. There are also countries, such as Colombia and Uruguay, where nobody seems interested in forming any such organization, and Ecuador, where the greatest obstacle appears to be regional loyalties. In Brazil legislation does not allow the formation of umbrella organizations or overall confederations, either of employers' organizations or of trade unions; but few countries have reached the general level of organization found in Brazil, where in 1977 about 800,000 employers were affiliated to 2,596 local organizations, 82 federations, and 4 confederations.[3] Table 3.1 shows the principal national organizations of employers in Latin America.

Table 3.1. Main National Employers' Organizations in Latin America, 1983

Country	Organization
Argentina	Cámara Argentina de Comercio
	Cámara Argentina de Sociedades Anónimas
	Comisión Coordinadora Patronal de Actividades Mercantiles
	Confederación de Asociaciones Rurales de Buenos Aires y La Pampa
	Confederaciones Rurales Argentinas
	Federación Agraria Argentina
	Sociedad Rural Argentina
	Unión Comercial Argentina
	Unión Industrial Argentina
Bolivia	Confederación de Empresarios Privados de Bolivia
Brazil	Confederación Nacional de la Agricultura
	Confederación Nacional de la Industria
	Confederación Nacional del Comercio
	Confederación Nacional de los Transportes Terrestres
Colombia	Asociación Nacional de Industriales (ANDI)
	Federación de Cafeteros de Colombia (FEDECAFE)
	Sociedad de Agricultores de Colombia
Costa Rica	Cámara de Comercio de Costa Rica
	Cámara Nacional de Agricultura
	Cámaras de Industrias de Costa Rica
	Unión Costarricense de Cámaras y Asociaciones de la Empresa Privada
Chile	Cámara Central de Comercio
	Cámara Chilena de la Construcción
	Confederación de la Producción y del Comercio
	Sociedad de Fomento Fabril (SOFOFA)
	Sociedad Nacional de Agricultura
	Sociedad Nacional de Minería

Table 3.1. Continued

Country	Organization
Dominican Republic	Asociación de Industrias de la República Dominicana Confederación Patronal de la República Dominicana
Ecuador	Consejo Nacional de Cámaras y Asociaciones de la Producción Federación Nacional de Cámaras de Industria
El Salvador	Asociación Nacional de la Empresa Privada (ANEP)
Guatemala	Cámara de Comercio de Guatemala Cámara de Industria de Guatemala Cámara del Agro Comité Coordinador de Asociaciones Agrícolas, Comerciales, Industriales y Financieras (CACIF)
Haiti	Chambre de Commerce
Honduras	Consejo Hondureño de la Empresa Privada (COHEP)
Mexico	Cámara Nacional de la Industria de Transformación (CANACINTRA) Confederación de Cámaras Industriales de los Estados Unidos Mexicanos (CONCAMIN) Confederación de Cámaras Nacionales de Comercio (CONCANACO) Confederación Patronal de la República Mexicana (COPARMEX)
Nicaragua	Consejo Superior de la Empresa Privada (COSEP)
Panama	Consejo Nacional de la Empresa Privada (CONEP)
Paraguay	Federación de la Producción, la Industria, y el Comercio (FEPRINCO)
Peru	Federación Nacional de Cámaras de Comercio del Perú Sociedad de Industrias Sociedad Nacional de Minería Unión de Empresarios Privados del Perú
Uruguay	Cámara Nacional de Comercio
Venezuela	Federación de Cámaras y Asociaciones de Comercio y Producción (FEDECAMARAS)

Source: Data available in the ILO documentation service.

Participation in Labor Relations

Generally speaking, employers' organizations always participate in labor relations in some way, but the manner varies greatly from country to country. In Argentina and Brazil such organizations are entitled to participate directly in labor relations, but this is not true of most other countries of Latin America, where they lack the necessary powers, doubtless because by their very nature employers' organizations are not unions of employers. This is clear from their constitutions. For example, the constitution of the Confederation of Private Employers of Bolivia states that its aims are the following: "*(a)* to coordinate the interests and objectives of the private sector in general, in order to encourage private investment . . . *(d)* to direct its activities toward internal and external integration . . . *(f)* to raise the technical standard of management. . . ."

The aims of the ANDI of Colombia form what is virtually a political program: "*(a)* to disseminate and further the political, economic, and social principles of a sound system of free enterprise based on human dignity, political democracy, social justice, private property, and freedom . . . *(f)* to press the legislative and executive branches of government to pass laws and make regulations favorable to the objects of the Association . . . *(g)* to cooperate . . . for the introduction and pursuit of a realistic policy of social justice to meet national needs . . . *(k)* to carry out ideological campaigns to explain to the country the merits of political and economic democracy and the advantages of a free competitive market."

Investigation of other employers' organizations would show that labor relations are hardly ever specifically listed among the organizations' purposes in their constitutions; at most there may be vague allusions, such as the "purpose of encouraging industrial training," "further the use of the arbitration system for the settlement of industrial disputes," or "promote harmonious relations between labor and management."

To sum up, in most Latin American countries the functions of employers' organizations do not normally include participation in labor relations. This arises from what could be called a "historic rejection" that was a prevailing characteristic at least until the 1940s, and in many countries until the 1960s, but is now a thing of the past. Employers' organizations first of all toned down their historic rejection, went on to accept the principle of limited participation, and ended in many cases by recognizing that participation in labor relations was or should be part of their normal functions.

Study of the circumstances in which this change took place show that it was not due to a change in the mandate of the employers' organizations, nor to their adopting a new philosophy; it was, much more simply, something that arose out of the natural course of events. Independently of any standard or principle, the employers' organizations began to concern themselves with labor relations when necessary, and took no part in them when the necessity did not arise. For example, as far back as 1906 the Graphic Arts Section of the Argentina Industrial Union entered into a collective labor agreement with the workers of a number of printing works in Buenos Aires who had gone on strike. At that time the employers' organization concerned had no specific mandate to negotiate a labor agreement, nor was there any law regulating collective agreements and their legal effects; what took place was simply due to the intrinsic momentum of events. On the other hand, in 1927, when the government of Venezuela decided to send a tripartite delegation to the International Labor Conference, the Chamber of Commerce of Venezuela showed no interest whatsoever in appointing the employers' representatives, and since there were no other organizations, the government had to consult two banks and various spinning and weaving mills before selecting the employers' delegate to the conference.[4]

This suggests that in labor relations the employers' organizations are much more likely to react to developments than to take the initiative. The workers' trade unions were formed to take part in labor relations and above all to promote them; but the employers' organizations take part in labor relations only because such relations have become important, and even then only to the extent that they have to. The most striking illustration is the situation just before COPARMEX was formed: the Convention of Chambers of Industry met in 1929 in Mexico and discussed the special and difficult problem of "federalization" of the labor laws. The federal labor law already drafted so impressed many delegates to the convention that they decided in 1930 to set up a separate organization to defend the interests of Mexican employers. This was COPARMEX.[5]

Very possibly one of the first points of contact of employers' organizations with labor relations was the need for employers' representation on the national tripartite delegations to sessions of the International Labor Conference. The lists of Latin American delegations to those meetings show that in 1925, of the 11 Latin American delegations, only those of Argentina, Brazil and Cuba included employers' representatives. In 1930, 4 of the 14 delegations were tripartite: the Brazilian delegation included representatives of the Central Association of Industrialists and the Rio de Janeiro Chamber of Commerce, the Chilean one consisted of a representative of the National Chamber of Commerce, and the Cuban one of a representative of the National Association of Industrialists, and the Uruguayan, which did not indicate any specific employers' organization. In 1935 there were 11 delegations, but only those of Argentina, Brazil, Cuba, and Mexico included employers' representatives. In 1939, at the last session of the conference before World War II, for the first time over half of the delegations—7 out of 13—included employers' representatives (although the list of delegations shows that the employers' delegate accredited by Venezuela was the "representative of the Ministry of the Interior on the Children's Welfare Council").

The situation changed drastically at the sessions held after the war: in 1950, 13 Latin American delegations came to Geneva, and 10 (those of Argentina, Bolivia, Brazil, Chile, Colombia, Cuba, the Dominican Republic, Mexico, Uruguay, and Venezuela) were tripartite. In 1960 only 5—those of Bolivia, Costa Rica, Ecuador, Nicaragua, and Uruguay—of the 17 Latin American delegations attending did not include employers' representatives. Their absence from the Uruguayan delegation appears to have been fortuitous, since its employers' representatives had been present on many previous occasions; but apart from Uruguay all these countries were remarkable for their embryonic system of labor relations, generally confined almost entirely to a few undertakings, so that there was very little participation, or desire for it, by the employers' organizations.

The foregoing account shows that the chambers and civil associations of employers did not come into being to deal with labor problems. Their absence for many years from the labor–management scene demonstrates that they were neither interested in nor obliged to deal with such problems. However, there came a time when this reluctance had to yield to a different attitude, first because the inherent dynamics of labor relations made their presence essential to support individual employers or coordinate the action of several, and second because the employers' unions that should have dealt with these matters were seldom or never formed. This also explains why at the present time the extent to which business organizations intervene in labor matters differs according to the characteristics of the relevant sector of the economy. The rural producers' associations hardly ever intervene to any great extent, for the simple reason that in many countries a substantial proportion of the rural sector is still precapitalist and the rural workers' organizations are relatively weak. At the very most, those associations take part in the proceedings of boards fixing minimum wages, because it is in their interest to be consulted on agricultural wage levels. For similar reasons organizations of commercial employers are not very active in labor relations; in any case their activity is not comparable with that of the industrial organizations, which are undoubtedly the principal representatives of the employers.

When the hub of the labor relations system is the undertaking, employers' organizations take second place to individual employers and confine themselves to giving information or advice. But if the hub of that system is an entire branch of economic activity, they are much more active, because they normally have to take part in negotiating sectoral collective agreements. If the system relies on consultation or tripartite negotiation, the central national organizations or, in their absence, the principal sectoral organizations, are generally recognized as representing the employers. Even when the system is basically state-regulated, the employers' organizations do their best to exert some influence, so that they can propose the broad lines of the labor legislation to be adopted or bring pressure to bear for the laws in force to be amended. In practice all these kinds of participation occur.

The two situations in which employers' organizations have to take a more prominent part in labor relations are central national negotiations and the negotiation of sectoral collective agreements. The first of these is almost unknown in Latin America; practically the only important example is the national compromise agreement (Acta del Compromiso Nacional) of 1973, made for political rather than strictly labor reasons between the General Economic Confederation and the General Confederation of Labor (CGT) of Argentina. A few employers' organizations, in particular ANDI of Colombia and FEDECAMARAS of Venezuela, have shown interest in negotiating agreements of this kind, probably because of the traditional contacts that Latin America maintains with Spain and the good results obtained in Spain by the Spanish Confederation of Employers' Organizations through the Interconfederal Framework Agreement of January 1980 with the General Union of Workers (UGT).

It is much more usual for employers' organizations to negotiate sectoral collective agreements, although except in Argentina and Brazil, this is still the exception rather than the rule. In Venezuela the employers' organizations in various sectors, especially textiles and construction, have for some years been negotiating collective agreements covering a branch of industry. In Mexico a number of chambers, especially that for the sugar industry, negotiate the relevant *contrato-ley* (generally binding collective agreement) on behalf of their members. In Peru the banks association concludes the sectoral collective agreement for banking and the Textile Committee of the Sociedad de Industrias negotiates the collective agreement for the textile industry.

In Chile for more than 20 years the Chamber of Leather and Footwear negotiated the collective contract for that industry and took part in administering its indemnity fund, just as the corresponding body for the construction industry used to negotiate the "single rate" scale for that industry; but the new legislation prohibits sectoral collective bargaining, thus limiting participation by employers' organizations. In Bolivia, Panama, and Uruguay there are also examples of sectoral collective bargaining by employers' organizations acting as their members' representatives, but these talks are usually of limited scope. To sum up, generally speaking, negotiation of collective agreements by employers' organizations is a firmly established practice in Argentina and Brazil, is beginning to gain ground in Venezuela, and takes place in a number of other countries, but elsewhere has hardly begun. In any event, the greatest restriction is not so much that the employers' organizations are not willing or competent to carry out collective bargaining as that collective bargaining by industry is still unusual.

In addition to collective bargaining, employers' organizations may avail themselves of various other ways of participating in the labor relations system. The best-known, because the most striking, consists in submitting studies or petitions, or publishing employers' declarations or manifestos, when the government or legislature contemplates amending the labor laws. These submissions are generally accompanied by strong pressure, often including resort to the mass media. It is undoubtedly in the interests of employers' organizations in such cases to act as a brake on measures that will add to the financial burdens of undertakings or undermine the employers' prerogatives. Consequently the submissions are generally supported by technical studies showing that the proposed labor laws will adversely affect the smooth running of undertakings and ultimately harm the economy in general.

The fate of the submissions depends less on whether their arguments are sound or weak than on the ability of the employers' organizations to bring pressure to bear and, above all, on the political background of the labor measures the government proposes to adopt. The employers' organizations occasionally manage to prevail on the government to postpone such measures, or to introduce alterations of form or substance into them; but they cannot always be successful. The government usually moves very cautiously in such matters, and the measures, whether progressive or retrogressive (which is usually a matter of individual opinion) are frequently taken much more for the government's own reasons than on account of any pressure brought to bear by management or labor.

Another form of participation is that exercised through the more or less permanent tripartite bodies that have been springing up in Latin America. (These are extremely numerous, as will be seen in Chapter 8.) Moreover, in various countries the employers' organizations have been represented on the tripartite ad hoc committees that have studied the reform of the labor laws. There is also a trend toward participation in the tripartite advisory bodies whose terms of reference cover labor questions in general, such as the National Labor Council in Colombia and the National Labor Commission in Panama.

Finally, there is the kind of participation that consists in elaborating and putting forward labor relations guidelines and policies for the use of the organization's members. Some organizations have social or labor committees, or a secretariat able to carry out economic and labor studies, that often do valuable work of this kind. Their purpose is to put forward codes of good practice in labor relations matters or suitable personnel policies, bearing in mind trends in labor relations; their functions are, accordingly, to advise and guide, and often they also provide management with training in labor relations.

It is hardly necessary to emphasize how important the latter function can be, particularly its potential effect on labor relations; but it still is not as important as it should be. As already stated in this chapter, in the field of labor relations employers' organizations tend to react to developments rather than to take the initiative; but policy making is the result of a programming or prospective function whose results are not usually immediate but long-term, and employers and their organizations are not yet sufficiently concerned with long-term results.

Present And Future Importance

The chambers of commerce or industry and civil associations have in fact become employers' organizations. As such, they take part in the labor relations systems of most, if not all, Latin American countries, and are proving to be valid bargaining partners of trade union organizations and the government. Their participation varies widely in degree and method from one country to another: it is greater in Argentina and Brazil; not unimportant in Chile, Colombia, Mexico, and Venezuela; and less in the remaining countries.

It seems reasonable to suppose that the more voluntaristic and independent the labor relations system becomes, the more the employers' organizations will participate in it. It is, for example, conceivable that they will take a greater part in collective bargaining and the settlement of disputes; they may also be required to take part in central national negotiations if these are eventually introduced, or in tripartite discussions on social and labor policy. It is also probable that they will have to formulate guidelines and strategies, or to propose the general principles of their members' labor policies. In any event, they are now an accepted part of the labor relations system. Sometimes their opinions carry great weight and sometimes they are less important, but they are never as negligible as they were only a little while ago. In no country of Latin America can any investigation of labor relations now afford to ignore the existence of employers' organizations and the role they are playing in labor relations systems.

Notes

1. See L.F. Cuervo, Asociación Nacional de Industriales (ANDI) (Colombia), in ILO, *Papel de las organizaciones de empleadores en América latina,* Labor-Management Relations Series, no. 51 (Geneva: ILO, 1976).

2. See Marco Antonio Alcázar, *Las agrupaciones patronales en México* (Mexico City: Colegio de México, 1977), pp. 22–23.

3. U.S. Department of Labor, Bureau of International Labor Affairs, *Country Labor Profile: Brazil* (Washington, D.C.: U.S. Government Printing Office, 1980), p. 3.

4. ILO, *Papel de las organizaciones de empleadores en América latina,* p. 11.

5. See A. Escobedo Salgado, "Confederación Patronal de la República Mexicana (COPARMEX)," in ibid., p. 184.

4

Departments of Labor

by
Efrén Córdova

History

The first labor administration bodies appeared in 1907, in Argentina and Chile. Mexico set up a Department of Labor in 1912, and Bolivia and Guatemala did so in 1925. At that time these were units with a small staff and scanty funds, and were generally engaged in compiling a few statistics, carrying out inspections and settling labor disputes.

At their origin the present departments of labor were merely sections or divisions of other departments, generally those of industry and trade, agriculture, home affairs, or public health and social assistance. Occasionally in a particular country the unit in charge of labor matters changed its parent department to suit current opinion of what were potentially the most critical areas or the most suitable means of overcoming problems. For example, in Brazil the Department of Labor was first part of the Department of Agriculture and then moved to the Department of Industry and Commerce. In Peru it was at first assigned to the Department of Home Affairs and Police, was transferred to the Department of Public Works, and then to the Department of Public Health before becoming independent in 1949. It was doubtless considered in Peru that labor matters at first raised a problem of law and order, and later that they could be settled by protection and welfare services, such as housing or social security.

Gradually the statistical or inspection services grew and extended their scope so that other units were formed to deal with the increasing complexity of labor matters by providing placement services, registering trade unions and giving them technical assistance, preventing and settling disputes, protecting women and children, organizing vocational training, and administering social insurance. This trend reached its peak with the appearance of a separate department of labor reporting to a minister or a secretary of state and responsible for elaborating and implementing the government's labor policy.

In most countries of Latin America this consolidation of agencies concerned with labor matters ended in the 1930s and 1940s, but in others went on until recently. In Honduras, for example, it ended in 1959, and in Panama in 1971.

When this second stage in the development of departments of labor at last came to an end, and their place in the government organization was recognized, their scope combined labor affairs with related subjects like assistance to specific groups or social welfare. The titles of Latin American departments of labor still associate them with other affairs, and they also deal in principle with the following: social welfare in Ecuador, Haiti, and Panama; social insurance in Brazil, Chile, El Salvador, Guatemala, Honduras, and Mexico; and social security in Colombia, Costa Rica, and Uruguay. In Peru the Department of Labor was until recently in charge of Indian affairs, and is still responsible for promoting equality of opportunity (promoción social); in Paraguay it is still associated with the Department of Justice.

By 1970 it appeared that departments of labor were finally empowered to play a leading role in the application of social policy and to take on all the problems usually covered by the term "social question," including the planning of social development. In practice, however, they have progressively lost many of the welfare and social security functions formerly assigned to them; in some countries the departments of health, welfare boards, and departments of social welfare have taken over many of those responsibilities. The only country in the region (apart from Cuba) where social security is still administered directly by a ministry of labor is Uruguay. In others social security has been transferred to independent institutes or semipublic bodies seldom supervised by the department of labor. Other departments, too, have taken over the department of labor's responsibilities for labor-related matters such as cooperatives and migration.

A third stage in the development of departments of labor—restriction of their scope to strictly labor matters—is beginning. In a sense they may be said to be returning to their original state, again concentrating more on the problems of employed persons and abandoning any claims on social development as a whole. As the Inter-American Center for Labor Administration points out in a study on the Andean nations, this completes a process of evolution in several stages: departments of labor were at first part of the traditional administrative structure; then of a mixed character (simultaneously labor administration and welfare bodies); later they were concerned with social welfare in a wide sense; and finally solely with labor administration.[1] The last stage is not, however, firmly established everywhere, and in countries like Colombia attempts have been made in recent years to reassert the position of the department of labor as the hub of a broad social sector that includes the cooperatives and social insurance.[2] This has led some authors to believe that labor administration is in a state of constant flux and is torn between the changes of social policy in a modern state and the never-ending reforms of the entire range of public administration.[3]

The restriction of the responsibilities of departments of labor would not do too much harm if it enabled them to concentrate on labor relations problems in the strict sense of the term; but in some countries this erosion of their responsibilities has gone farther than would have been desirable, even depriving them of some of their powers and responsibilities in wage policy; these have been transferred to the department of economic affairs or to independent bodies such as the Brazilian National Council for Wages Policy or to appendages of other departments, such as the Productivity, Incomes, and Wages Commission in Uruguay, which comes under the Department of Industry and Energy.

Characteristics and Limitations

The first impression produced by labor administration in Latin America is that it is highly fragmented. Side by side with departments of labor in the strict sense of the term a host of autonomous bodies specializing in various matters provide public labor administration in its wider sense. This situation is not peculiar to Latin America but is part of a worldwide diversification of social policy, geographical decentralization, and functional "deconcentration." What is characteristic of many countries in Latin America is that the department of labor is not always the key institution in the labor administration system. Decentralized or parastatal institutions often operate in de facto independence and the department is at best confined to the somewhat remote duties of top-level supervision.

Admittedly, laws concerning the organization of departments of labor continue to give them responsibility for many of these subjects, but the effect of the institutional division of duties applied to the new centers, institutes, or boards has been to remove them from the department's orbit. This decentralization is observed principally in vocational training, social security, and productivity centers. However, in Latin America there are hardly any decentralized or autonomous bodies responsible for collective labor relations; even the Mexican conciliation and arbitration boards and the defunct National Industrial Relations Court in Argentina were linked administratively to the department of labor. The only exception is the Brazilian labor courts, which form part of the judiciary and intervene in collective disputes.

Departments of labor generally lack the organization and modern dynamic approach characteristic of the autonomous bodies. The departments grew up in the static administrative system of a laissez-faire state whose functions were limited to maintaining order and protecting private property, and their action was basically to redress wrongs actually committed.[4] In spite of the administrative reforms of the past few years, the style and operations of departments of labor (and of government departments in general) are still strongly marked by that tradition and by the civil service laws passed in the first decades of the twentieth century. Although a few countries carried out drastic reforms and managed to streamline procedure, in other countries it remained largely inefficient.

Public administration handbooks, reports by commissions for administrative reform, and development plans have repeatedly pointed out the weak points of government administration. These apply also to departments of labor. They are that a career in government administration is still far from being a firmly based institution; promotion by merit is frequently unknown; budgetary allocations do not cover the needs of the service; action veers between routine and excessive complexity, and planning is defective; supervisory systems pay too much attention to formalities and not enough to efficiency; and output is low, and suffers from lack of motivation and too little devotion to duty or respect for the importance of public service.[5]

Some of these problems are especially acute in departments of labor. The worst problem is that of funds, which is at the root of other problems. In spite of the important functions of departments of labor, their budgetary allocations are invariably among the lowest in the civil service. As Table 4.1 shows, in five countries of Latin America the budgets of the departments of labor do not exceed 0.5 percent of the national budget, and in five others they vary between 0.5 percent and 1 percent. The general average for the region is 1.3 percent of the national budget, and the median is 0.8 percent.[6]

This lack of resources is of course reflected in the departments' staff establishments, the level of technical skills, and the number of decentralized offices. A Latin American expert estimates that departments of labor in the region have a staff of about 30,000, whereas social security and vocational training personnel number more than 300,000.[7] Other consequences of this lack of resources are low salary scales, high staff turnover, long delays, and poor-quality services. The Venezuelan Department of Labor report for 1976 stressed that shortcomings in implementing the labor relations program were largely due to the financial difficulties in engaging

Table 4.1. Budgetary Allocations to Departments of Labor in Latin America

Country	Year	Total of National Budget	Department of Labor Budget	Percentage Total Budget
Argentina[1]	1974	65,347,297	386,261	0.6
Bolivia[2]	1975	26,742,172,500	22,933,800	0.1
Brazil[2]	1975	113,396,375,000	395,402,600	0.3
Colombia[2]	1974	29,422,228,722	941,762,913	3.2
Costa Rica[2]	1975	2,375,087,476	117,049,969	4.9
Dominican Republic[2]	1974	383,366,924	880,518	0.2
Ecuador[2]	1980	—	119,699,000	—
El Salvador[2]	1974	616,831,606	4,867,534	0.8
Guatemala[2]	1974	355,597,706	2,024,479	0.6
Haiti[2]	1973/74	166,377,000	1,826,060	1.1
Honduras[1]	1980	1,136,765,818	26,396,426	2.3
Mexico[1]	1980	1,683,432,000,000	1,918,146,000	0.1
Nicaragua[2]	1974	1,710,394,000[3]	12,988,000	0.8
Panama[2]	1980	851,828,000	6,796,480	0.8
Paraguay[2]	1980	6,425,920,000	219,000,000	3.4
Peru[1]	1980	967,171,200,000	1,110,500,000	1.1
Uruguay[2]	1978	4,844,292,522	26,084,621	0.5
Venezuela[2]	1980	—	82,320,000	—

[1] In thousands of units of local currency.
[2] In units of local currency.
[3] Excluding independent agencies.

Source: Jorge A. Difrieri, *La administracion del trabajo en América latina,* p. 42.

staff and obtaining equipment.[8] In Colombia a Department of Labor document of 1979 stated that one of the main problems of labor administration affecting collective bargaining was "insufficient staff."[9]

In such circumstances the problems caused by insufficient application of the rules governing a career in the civil service are particularly acute. The department as a whole has not, in many countries, any real body of specialist officials formed on the basis of merit and enjoying adequate guarantees of employment security.[10] In its work on collective labor relations there is often a lack of the technical knowledge, and consequent support, that should be the hallmark of its operations. In most countries there is a mixture of experienced officials who are either veterans of the civil service or former trade unionists, and officials who owe their appointment to political influence and acquire their training in the course of their work. The result is that much of the work is done in a rather improvised way and under the pressure of events, without the advantage of previous study, the official concerned being guided by his own intuition or practical experience.

These limitations are fairly general but are not characteristic of all countries. To cite only one example, in 1979 the Mexican Department of Labor and Social Insurance increased its budget by 7 percent and introduced the fifth stage of its administrative reform, consisting of personnel improvement and development; in 1974 it had founded the National Institute for Labor Studies (INET), which was active in research, training, and dissemination of information.

Another characteristic not applicable to Mexico (or to Brazil and Paraguay) is fairly evident in other departments of labor in Latin America: lack of continuity in top management. Whether because of political upheavals or the close relation between labor problems and the electoral pressures of the government parties, ministers of labor tend not to hold the post for very long; for example, Colombia had five ministers of labor from 1976 to 1981, Venezuela had seven in the decade from 1970 to 1980, and Bolivia had six from 1978 to 1982. When ministers change so quickly, there are also changes in the top reaches of the administrative hierarchy; and the continuity of programs, and even the objectives of labor policy, are affected.

A further characteristic related to the central theme of this study is of more general significance in Latin American departments of labor. This is the "participatory" movement, the tendency for the department of labor to become increasingly an instrument of participation that by design reflects the tripartite character of the labor relations system and conducts its operations in an atmosphere of shared responsibility and understanding. An ILO report, noting that this trend had become general, said that it was due both to the need for more efficient labor administration and to the advisability of promoting closer relations with employers' and workers' organizations.[11] An additional factor is the wish to involve the parties in providing services, to reduce the cost of the services, and to promote the parties' democratic control. These aims have not invariably been achieved in practice, but continue to be invoked in the preambles of relevant instruments (see Chapter 8).

Role in Labor Relations

Departments of labor were first led to intervene in labor relations by labor disputes. In 1964 the ILO observed that the settlement of labor disputes was "one of the most important traditional functions" of a department of labor.[12] The fact is that although many Latin American countries have had labor courts and conciliation and arbitration boards for years, departments of labor have always played a vital role in this area. In some cases departmental action was a forerunner of the judicial or tripartite bodies that were set up to settle disputes. Elsewhere, in cases where the legal framework for conciliation and arbitration boards existed from an early date, the departments gradually embarked upon parallel conciliation activities that have grown significantly over the years.

Labor inspectors were the first representatives of the administration to be involved in labor relations. The very nature of their work, their direct contact with the parties concerned, and the lack of any other specialized services meant that they were directly involved in the settlement of disputes. Later this situation was given legal force and, in addition to the enforcement of labor provisions, the inspectors were given conciliation functions. Although this double function may sometimes entail a contradiction between the duty of conciliation and that of enforcing the law, it still prevails in certain countries. In support of this practice, it is argued that the inspectors themselves feel that they are best placed to settle disputes on the spot, that there is a shortage of personnel, and that the workers prefer to solve their problems in this way.

It is also clear that in distant parts of the provinces, labor inspectors are the only labor authorities available, and accordingly have no choice but to carry out these dual functions. Thus, in Haiti labor inspectors try to obtain out-of-court settlements of labor disputes; when they fail, they turn the case over to an arbitration court or committee. In Venezuela the inspectors are not only involved in the settlement process but actually preside over sessions of the conciliation and arbitration boards. In Guatemala they are obliged to take action on labor–management disputes, and once they have been approved by the inspector-general, any direct and conciliatory arrangements reached acquire the force of law. In Ecuador the Labor Code provides that the inspector shall hear the complaints of employers and workers, and act as a mediator in individual disputes and as chairman of the conciliation and arbitration tribunal in collective disputes.

Special labor relations services were first set up outside the inspection system because of the pressing need for the government to provide proper channels for the settlement of economic disputes so as to avoid public disturbances. Even where conciliation and arbitration committees or boards existed, the procedure was too slow and cumbersome, and was not always able to bring about an urgently needed settlement. What was necessary was a more flexible, speedy, and informal type of machinery that could intervene at any moment on its own initiative or at the request of the parties involved.

In almost every country this machinery has taken the form of conciliation officials. Originally the latter were merely expected to participate in the settlement of disputes; subsequently, however, they became involved in the entire negotiation process and, in some cases, even presided over the negotiations. In Colombia, Chile, and other countries negotiation was part and parcel of the settlement of disputes; elsewhere the conciliation official could later act as the arbitrator. For some governments, giving conciliators this role was not only the fastest way of settling disputes but also a means of ensuring that the agreements or decisions to some extent reflected current labor policies, including employment and incomes policies.

Departments also sometimes found themselves obliged to enforce legal provisions that were normally dealt with by labor tribunals. Here again it was for reasons of expediency that the departments encouraged the parties to reach some kind of informal agreement or compromise on matters that could well have been described as disputes over rights whose adjudication was the responsibility of the judiciary. The intention was to prevent the slowness of judicial proceedings and the unfavorable repercussions on public order or economic development frequently associated with certain legal disputes (for example, collective dismissals).

In some countries individual workers had the right to submit complaints to the inspector, who would then hear the employer, in an attempt at conciliation. This was very common practice, and was usually a voluntary procedure in which the department of labor acted as a kind of friendly counselor. In other countries the participation of the department was more or less compulsory. In Uruguay, for instance, a worker had to go through the administrative conciliation board before he could appeal to the labor tribunal. Finally, there were a number of countries, such as Peru, where the department of labor had judicial or quasi-judicial powers (see Chapter 12).

Gradually, therefore, the administrative services came to provide an alternative—and very often a preliminary or preferential—method of settling disputes over interests and of taking rapid action to prevent rights disputes from becoming more serious. In both cases the intention was originally to take conciliatory action "after the event." Subsequent social developments, however, affected the role of the administration in labor relations, which came to be seen in some countries in an entirely new light, so that it did not stop at settling labor disputes, but could even take preventive action. Departments of labor were forced, by the growth of collective bargaining and the development of employers' and workers' organizations, to look upon labor relations as a continuous process—in other words, as meriting the special attention of the authorities from the outset, and not just when a dispute arose.

Structure

This variety of functions explains the growth of administrative bodies responsible for labor relations. In many countries small units dealing with particular aspects of the subject have become directorates or divisions comprising several units. There is no standard type of labor relations machinery, however, and there are still countries, even those where labor relations are developed, that continue to make collective relations or certain aspects of them the responsibility of the labor inspectorate. Neither is there unanimity of opinion regarding the importance or place in the hierarchy of the body dealing with labor relations; in most countries it is a division or department, in Peru it is a subdirectorate, and in Argentina it is a national directorate. Where labor relations are not considered important enough to warrant a national directorate, they nearly always come under the director-general of labor or, often, under the director of labor administration or of labor inspection. The inclusion of labor relations among the responsibilities of the director-general of labor sometimes implies that they are connected with very dissimilar matters (occupational safety and health, for example); and labor relations are increasingly being recognized as a distinct subject, at least at the departmental level.

The internal organization chart of these divisions also shows the integration that has occurred in recent times. More and more countries are including in their labor relations division a section dealing with collective bargaining, and another for settling disputes. The names given vary from country to country; the collective bargaining section may be called the labor relations service, the collective bargaining service, or the service for assistance in the discussion of agreements. Some countries prefer to highlight the function of settling disputes by using a title that refers to the specific procedure preferably employed for a peaceful settlement of the dispute, as in the Mexican General Directorate of Conciliation and the Ecuadorian National Directorate for Labor Mediation. Other countries distinguish between the settlement of individual and collective disputes, while still others speak more generally of complaints or grievances. Argentina is peculiar in having a structure based on division by economic sectors (metallurgy, meat works, and so on) rather than by subject matter. In Bolivia, the Dominican Republic, and Ecuador the departments of labor still have no services for the encouragement or promotion of collective bargaining.

Nevertheless, the idea of an administrative organization that distinguishes the functions of promoting bargaining (by strengthening trade unions, workers' education, investigation and analysis of bargaining trends, and official approval and registration of agreements) from those of intervention (by means of conciliation, mediation, and arbitration) when bargaining is broken off has slowly been gaining ground in the region. In Costa Rica, for example, the functions of the Labor Relations Division are divided between the Collective Relations Service (comprising the Collective Agreements Section and the Conciliation Section) and the Individual Complaints Service (comprising the Relations Section, the Grievance Section, and the Works Rules Service). In Mexico there is the director-general of conciliation and the Collective Agreements Division directly responsible to the secretary of state for labor. In Panama the Labor Relations Division includes a unit for collective bargaining and another for works rules, plus a complaints unit and a conciliation unit.

This distinction is certainly an advance on previous organization charts. In some countries another distinction has been added that at first sight attempts to distinguish matters of substance or labor economics from functional or operational matters. It is considered that promoting labor relations and settling disputes are not just a matter of training a team of conciliators or mediators, but also of setting up technical units capable of providing these officials and the representatives of the parties concerned with logistic support. Such support is particularly necessary when the department has to propose or decide between solutions that will have financial repercussions on the profitability of the enterprise and the purchasing power of the workers, or on the national rate of inflation. Deciding the extent to which an undertaking can bear heavier financial burdens, or fixing the minimum wage rates or benefits to be granted to the workers so as to improve or at least maintain their level of living, is increasingly regarded as a complex problem calling for a high degree of responsibility and technical knowledge.

Consequently, it has sometimes been found desirable to set up an economic research unit within the department of labor to assess the cost of workers' demands and the economic ability of enterprises to meet them. In Colombia this is done by the Economic Labor Studies Section of the Office of Planning and Labor Economy, which is responsible for making the economic studies on which mediators rely to do their work properly, and in Peru by the National Wages Directorate. Although in other countries the wage divisions are principally concerned with the investigations necessary for fixing and revising minimum wages, they occasionally give technical support to conciliators as well.

Functions

It is often said that in public administration, whenever there is a function to perform, a special unit is set up to deal with it, and the unit in question then further develops the function. This saying is only partially verifiable in Latin America. Admittedly the new structures have given a more complete view of what departments of labor can achieve in labor relations; but enunciation of some of these powers has gone too far, and a great discrepancy has arisen between the powers and responsibilities of the ministers in charge and the material resources allocated to their departments.

In some cases the department has been authorized to exercise virtual control of collective labor relations at all stages and levels. In Argentina a decree of 1963 went so far as to empower the department to direct the collective bargaining process, and various laws authorize it to oversee and control the development of employers' and workers' organizations, including in those powers that of auditing union accounts and supervising union elections. The law respecting the Department of Labor of Costa Rica authorizes it to prepare "model" contracts or collective agreements; that of El Salvador requires that national Labor Relations Division to promote and develop collective agreements, encourage the formation of trade unions, federations, and confederations, and cooperate in developing them; in Peru the Department of Labor takes part in collective labor relations from the direct negotiations stage until the agreement is approved or the dispute is settled, and the basic law establishing the department states that the department's duty is to regulate, direct, and supervise labor relations. Some of these functions are only halfheartedly performed or have fallen into disuse, but in countries where labor relations are still in the formative stages, they are indisputably significant. The department's role is, of course, more marked in countries that are in the throes of political or economic crisis or have inflation problems.

Even where the department's functions are stated soberly and without exaggeration, its labor relations activities are considerable and may extend to regulation, promotion, social harmonization, and quasi-judicial and enforcement work, as well as routine administration. Its regulatory functions are exercised under the regulatory powers of the executive branch of government, and therefore should not infringe upon or go beyond the substance of the laws (although this restriction is not always respected in practice). Quasi-judicial functions are frequently performed de facto and with the parties' tacit consent, even though they encroach on the preserves of the judiciary and undermine the constitutional principle of separation of powers (particularly where administrative decisions have the force of law). The other functions—promotion, social harmonization, prevention, administration, and supervising labor legislation—are part of the governing, administrative, and directive functions normally exercised by the president of the republic through the various departments of government.

In nearly all countries the department of labor is involved in the actual functioning of trade unions because it keeps a record of occupational organizations, ensures that they conform to the law before approving their registration, and settles interunion disputes, particularly in matters of recognition and representativeness. The departments of labor also act as intermediaries between the governments and workers' organizations; as a rule union petitions to the government are channeled through the department of labor and the department acts as the government's spokesman in relation to the unions.

As far as the promotion of collective bargaining is concerned, departments of labor confine themselves to granting official approval to agreements, registering them, and supervising their implementation; others also take part in extending certain agreements to third parties, and a few in preparing handbooks and teaching material, running courses in collective bargaining, and issuing information. It is unusual for permanent machinery to be set up to channel discussions, although there are a few examples of this in countries where bargaining is by branch of activity (as in Argentina) or where such machinery is set up when the bargaining process is suspended (as occurred in Chile with the tripartite commissions). Some departments have issued instructions on the conduct of trade union affairs and bargaining; these relate to the reckoning of majorities, recognition of the trade union, and the conduct of trade union meetings. They have also issued instructions on basic issues for specially weak sectors in which bargaining has not caught on.

The spread of departmental conciliation and mediation in the settlement of disputes has already been mentioned. Sometimes these facilities exist side by side with conciliation by labor courts or conciliation boards; at other times they are a substitute for it. Departments also play a part in arbitration, either by providing facilities for the constitution of the court and preparation of the case for submission to arbitration, or by appointing an official to act as chairman or supplying the sole arbitrator. As will be seen in Chapter 12, in some countries the department of labor adjudicates in individual or collective disputes over rights. This practice of carrying out a multiplicity of dispute settlement functions led Rafael Guzmán to describe the department of labor in Venezuela as "an agency that centralizes settlement of disputes but lacks the means and creative ability to make anything more than temporary settlements."[13]

The departments that used to play—or still play—a key part in settling labor disputes still have not adapted to what should now be one of their most important functions, the promotional one; they are still far more active in labor relations as regulators, composers of differences, and arbitrators than in promoting collective bargaining and preventing disputes.

They may carry out their regulatory and promotional functions either as neutrals or with a view to favoring the growth of one of the parties—the party judged to be particulary weak. The neutral approach also varies, according to whether its emphasis is on regulating labor relations (as in Venezuela), ensuring harmonious labor–management relations and preventing and settling labor disputes (as in Peru), maintaining normality in the production process (as in the Dominican Republic), or promoting and facilitating collective bargaining (as in Argentina). The intention to aid or promote one of the parties largely depends on the government's political options and the stage of development of the trade union movement. It was used in the past in Bolivia, where even the Department of Labor's title included labor development and trade union affairs, and in Colombia, where the Department of Labor regards the promotion of trade unionism as one of its principal aims. Obviously, whatever decision is taken on the purpose and intention of the department's regulatory, promotion, and administrative functions may affect the acceptance and effectiveness of the other functions.

Clearly, the department of labor's role in labor relations is manifold and increasingly important. Accordingly, labor administration cannot be regarded merely as an isolated segment of a general function; it must be looked upon as part of a comprehensive scheme of action for implementing government social policy, since any approach to labor relations is closely connected with other aspects of labor policy and has to be in harmony with economic and social planning. Promoting sound relations between employers and workers, and encouraging both parties to cooperate with the authorities, are advisable not only for their own sake but also to promote productive activity and investment and to increase employment.

The resources available to labor relations divisions to cope with this wide range of duties are usually very limited. Only since 1976 has the

Colombian Collective Labor Relations Division been given adequate resources for the compilation of statistics on collective agreements, and
there are still no such statistics in other countries of Latin America. Also in
Colombia, only six mediators (members of the bar) and one chief mediator were responsible in the early 1980s for the peaceful settlement of disputes. In Ecuador the National Directorate for Labor Mediation comprises
its chief plus three mediators. In Peru the Negotiation Subdirectorate has
two divisions, each composed of only three specialized conciliators.

The problem is not only lack of staff, but also of their quality and
ability. Some countries have built up a corps of specialized officials to settle disputes, such as the labor relations secretaries in Argentina and the
conciliation officers in Mexico; but six countries (Bolivia, Colombia, Ecuador, Guatemala, Haiti, and Venezuela) still give responsibility for settling
collective disputes to labor inspectors whose number, pay, training, and
other duties are in many cases incompatible with the dispute settlement
demands made on them. A distinction has neverless been made in Venezuela between the factory inspectors and other inspectors who specialize
in labor relations and are in fact more concerned with conciliation and
promotion than with inspection in the strict sense of the word. As will be
seen in Chapter 13, in some of these countries (such as Colombia and Venezuela) the statistics on strikes and lockouts are curiously low in spite of
the deficiencies.

Everywhere there is a host of lawyers who occupy most of the mana-
gerial posts and work on assistance and dispute settlement. While the predominance of officials with exclusively legal training is in line with the
legalistic tradition of Latin America and may help in the settlement of
some kinds of disputes, their activities should be coupled with those of
experts in other disciplines who could contribute new ideas, so that the
best-qualified mediator can be chosen for each kind of dispute. It is not
enough to set up economic research services, generally outside the labor
relations division; there must also be a multi-disciplinary approach and
greater specialization within the division. This of course would entail rais-
ing salary scales to make them competitive with those of the public and
private undertakings that at present attract most labor relations experts.

Lawyers also staff legal adviser's offices that are of particular importance in Latin America, and express their views on the interpretation of
labor laws, regulations, and decrees, thus bringing about, in many cases,
the emergence of an extensive body of administrative rulings that has
been a highly important source of labor law.[14]

Not only should their staffs be increased and diversified, but the aims
and functions of departments of labor should be revised in the light of
present trends in labor relations. The trend toward voluntarism has already influenced certain aspects of the structure of such departments

(which have had to accommodate themselves to growing numbers of tripartite cooperation bodies) as well as their functions (which have favored conciliation), but this influence has been limited and at times ephemeral; so far it has been impossible to change the departments' basically interventionist and tutelary approach.

Notes

1. Centro Interamericano de Administración del Trabajo; "Desarrollo institucional de los ministerios de trabajo de los países andinos" (Lima: the Center, 1975, p. 43a.) (Mimeographed.)

2. See Ministerio del Trabajo de Colombia, "Reforma administrativa del Ministerio de Trabajo y Seguridad Social: Texto del decreto num. 062 del 16 de enero de 1976" (Bogotá: the Ministry, 1976), p. 1. (Mineographed)

3. Ernesto Krotoschin, *Tratado práctico de derecho del trabajo* (Buenos Aires: Ediciones Depalma, 1978), vol. I, p. 551.

4. ILO, *Public Labour Administration and Its Role in Economic and Social Development*, Report II, Eleventh Conference of American States Members of the ILO, Medellín, Colombia, 1979 (Geneva: ILO, 1979), p. 4.

5. See F. Onfray, *Las estructuras administrativas de América latina* (Lima: Centro Interamericano de Administración del Trabajo, 1972), pp. 8–17.

6. Based on Jorge A. Difrieri, *La administración del trabajo en las Américas: Evolución y tendencias* (Lima: Centro Interamericano de Administración del Trabajo, 1981), p. 41.

7. Ibid, p. 43.

8. Ministerio del Trabajo de Venezuela, *Memoria y cuenta, 1976* (Caracas: the Ministry, 1977), ch. II, "Dirección del Trabajo, División de Coordinación de Inspectorías del Trabajo," pp. 89–90.

9. A communication by the Colombian delegation to the Andean subregional seminar on collective bargaining, Bogotá, 1979, p. 17.

10. See, for example, ILO, *Generación de empleo productivo y crecimiento económico: El caso de la República Dominicana,* (Geneva: ILO, 1975), p. 227.

11. ILO, *Labour Administration: Role, Functions and Organisation,* Report V (1), International Labour Conference, 61st session (Geneva: ILO, 1976), p. 21.

12. ILO, "The Role of Labour Ministries in the Improvement of Labour–Management Relations in Latin America," Labour–Management Relations Series, no. 20 (Geneva: ILO, 1964), p. 12. (Mimeographed.)

13. Rafael Alfonso Guzmán, "El derecho del trabajo en Venezuela," in *El derecho del trabajo latinoamericano* (Mexico City: Universidad Nacional Autónoma de México, 1974), vol. II, p. 649.

14. Francisco Walker E., *El papel de la administración del trabajo en materia de relaciones de trabajo* (Santiago de Chile: DERTO, 1976), p. 14.

Part II: Theory and Practice of Collective Labor Relations

5

Collective Bargaining

by
Arturo S. Bronstein
and Efrén Córdova

The importance of collective bargaining in Latin America cannot be ignored but should not be exaggerated. Until the 1950s it had only a limited place in the labor relations system, except in Argentina, Chile, Mexico, and Uruguay, where even at that time it was fairly extensive. In the 1960s and 1970s it began to spread to Colombia, Costa Rica, Panama, Peru, and Venezuela, and finally to many of the remaining countries. Today it is practiced almost everywhere, but to an extent that varies greatly from one country to another, as well as from one sector to another in individual countries. Qualitatively it differs from country to country in such a wide variety of matters as the level of negotiations; the scope, duration, and content of agreements; bargaining procedures; and the parties to bargaining.

The observer may be less surprised to see that collective bargaining is becoming more widespread than to see it spread in spite of the fact that the labor relations system, as originally conceived, does not usually encourage it. To start with, the labor relations system has been, and to a great extent still is, basically regulated by the state—that is, it tends to use a regulatory solution imposed from outside in preference to a freely negotiated bilateral solution arrived at by the parties concerned.

Second, although trade unions have considerably expanded their labor relations activity at the undertaking level, their influence has been most visible outside the undertaking, in the political sphere. Third, some Latin American employers have been unwilling to accept the idea of dialogue, participation, bargaining, or any other of the equivalent ideas in modern business management involving deviation from the paternalist

---

Efrén Córdova wrote the sections on procedure and the duration of agreements.

tradition. Fourth, except in a very few countries the labor relations system has not provided for collective bargaining procedures in the strict sense of the term. Even today it is fairly usual to observe that no real bargaining starts before a dispute arises, whereas logically a dispute should be the result of a breakdown in bargaining rather than the starting point for bargaining. Finally, for many years trade union organizations have not been strong enough to negotiate on an equal footing with management.

In spite of these difficulties collective bargaining is tending to gain ground in most countries. It of course has its periods of decline, but these are due less to lack of interest or to rejection by the parties than to political factors or government policies for stabilizing the economy that nearly always impose restrictions on collective bargaining in order to limit the growth of the total wage bill. Generally speaking, these restrictions do not last indefinitely, and once they are over, collective bargaining nearly always resumes more vigorously than before. In any event, its importance should not be exaggerated; workers protected by collective agreements still constitute a minority of wage earners. Collective bargaining is in fact a less important means of fixing working conditions than is legislation, the scope of which is obviously wider; but collective bargaining is no longer exceptional. This chapter will examine its salient features and the problems it raises in practice.

Coverage

Although a few examples of collective agreements can be found in the first two decades of this century, it cannot be said that collective bargaining was then a usual means of fixing wages and working conditions. On the contrary, except in Argentina and Mexico—and to a much smaller extent in Chile, Uruguay, and Venezuela—it was exceptional until 1960, and in many countries even until 1970. Table 5.1 (for which the statistical sources are not all comparable or entirely accurate) provides some indications of its recent development.

Although in most countries collective bargaining did not start to spread before 1960, and more usually 1970, it has since grown very quickly, sometimes to an impressive extent. This is especially evident in Central America, particularly in Honduras and Panama, but it can also be perceived in Ecuador and Peru. In Mexico in 1970 there were at least 50,000 collective agreements, and in 1977 over 60,000, so it may be supposed that practically every undertaking of average importance had its collective labor agreement. The table does not appear to reflect the importance that collective bargaining has had in Argentina, for until it was suspended in 1976, it was practiced basically at the industry level, and collective agreements were therefore extremely wide in scope. The 637 collective agreements and arbitration awards registered in Argentina in

1975 covered nearly all employed persons except those in a few sectors, such as rural undertakings, work at home, and domestic service. Some collective agreements (such as that for workers in commerce) covered over a million workers.

Developments in Chile are worth attention. In September 1973, after the change of regime, collective bargaining was suspended. Years later it was partly resumed by means of a bargaining procedure in tripartite commissions by branch of industry. In 1979 the government adopted a labor plan, and shortly afterward issued a legislative decree reestablishing bargaining, but on a new basis. Bargaining is now permitted only at the undertaking level, and is prohibited on certain subjects that might involve restricting the use of labor or the employer's right to organize, direct, or administer the undertaking. Exercise of the right to strike is prohibited in some undertakings providing essential services, and may not be exercised for more than 60 days in the others. In spite of these restrictions, between August 1979 and May 1980, 2,574 collective agreements covering some 600,000 workers were signed. This represents about 16 percent of the employed population, and certainly 85 percent of unionized workers. Collective bargaining now covers undertakings in the private and public sectors, but not public administration, whether centralized or decentralized, or undertakings over 50 percent of whose budget has been state-financed in the last two years.

The rise of collective bargaining is doubtless partly due to the important changes that have taken place in Latin American economic, political, and trade union structures. For example, the increase in the number of collective agreements since 1960 coincides with the introduction of new economic strategies in this region. There are also obvious causal relations between the growth of unionization, especially in manufacturing industry, and the spread of collective bargaining in the most strongly unionized sectors. Collective bargaining becomes fully developed only when the political atmosphere of labor relations favors it: a study in Venezuela shows that 18,826 of the 21,159 collective agreements concluded there between 1936 and 1975 were made after 1958[1]—once a democratic regime was reestablished. In Panama collective bargaining was practically unknown until 1972, but spread widely once General Torrijos took over. More recently the political changes in the Dominican Republic, Ecuador, and Nicaragua have led to the renewed vitality of collective bargaining.

Conversely, political changes have caused collective bargaining to languish or even disappear for a time, as in Argentina, Chile, and Uruguay. In Brazil the paucity of collective bargaining between 1964 and 1977 paralleled authoritarian policy patterns, while the reopening of bargaining after 1978 kept pace with the new policy of *apertura*, which foresees the full restoration of democracy in that country. In fact, of all the institutions of the labor relations system, collective bargaining is undoubtedly the most sensitive to the political situation.

Table 5.1. Number of Collective Agreements Concluded in 16 Countries, 1972–1981

Country	Previous reference year	1972	1973	1974	1975	1976	1977	1978	1979	1980	1981
Argentina[2]	1960: 302	...	631	...	637	—	—	—	—	—	—
Bolivia[3]	...	47	286	816	291	154	72	108	119	...	...
Brazil[4]	...	...	...	630	1,296	...	1,450	1,278	2,347	2,572	2,591
Colombia[5]	...	...	802	...	982	1,123	1,110	1,018	...	...	...
Costa Rica[6]	1968: 2	27	28	15	42	53	30	40	42	27	33
Chile[7]	1967: 3,763	8,098	...	...	...	...	...	...	2,574	...	1,225
Dominican Rep.[8]	...	...	...	...	...	...	...	...	90	...	...
Ecuador[9]	1966: 32	147	...	183	169	222	194	184	...	...	...
El Salvador	1959: 28	...	227	...	...	...	379	391[10]	...	...	...
Guatemala[11]	...	...	...	...	...	...	...	...	...	...	...
Honduras[12]	1966: 1	18	46	33	29	157	...	59	244	...	...
Mexico[13]	...	...	...	...	...	...	60,813	...	...	125[14]	...
Nicaragua	...	...	...	...	...	...	...	...	...	...	...
Panama[12]	1969: 5	74	162	98	82	108	—	—	16	68	...
Peru[15]	1960: 546	868	1,222	1,355	1,524	1,595	710	1,221	1,327	1,222	1,355
Venezuela[16]	1966: 1,066	1,292	1,401	1,171	1,446	1,754	...	1,681	1,359	...	...

Key: ... not available; — nil.

Table Notes

Note: The number of collective agreements in force is generally higher than that shown for each year, because they are often valid for a period of two or three years, except in Argentina and Peru, where in principle they are valid for one year.

1. Mainly industrial agreements covering wide sectors of activity. Source: Ministerio de Trabajo, Consejo Nacional del Salario Mínimo, Vital y Móvil.

2. Data from Ministerio de Trabajo y Desarrollo Laboral, Dirección General de Trabajo.

3. Data from Getúlio Vargas Foundation. The data for 1980 are from an ILO Department of Labour study on collective bargaining and training of the labor force in Brazil, November 1980, and cover the period January–August 1980.

4. Data from the reports and Specialized Archives of the Ministerio de Trabajo y Seguridad Social.

5. Data from the Instituto Costarricense de la Empresa Privada.

6. Data prior to 1973 are for collective and other agreements deposited with the Department of Labor. The 1979 and 1980 figures are for collective agreements concluded between August 16, 1979, and May 21, 1980. Source: Department of Labor.

7. Data communicated by the delegation to the 1980 session of the International Labour Conference.

8. Department of Labor data. They do not include dispute settlements with the force of collective agreements.

9. Department of Labor data. They do not include "revised" collective agreements, which, if included, would make the number of registered agreements 1,065.

10. Data communicated by the government delegation to the 1980 session of the International Labour Conference.

11. Department of Labor data.

12. Data from a telephone inquiry covering 44 local conciliation and arbitration boards, carried out by the Dirección General de Estudios Económicos y Sociales, Secretaría del Trabajo y Previsión Social. To these figures should be added about 9,000 agreements negotiated under federal jurisdiction.

13. Period 1979–June 1980. Data communicated by the delegation to the 1980 session of the International Labour Conference.

14. Data from Ministerio de Trabajo, Dirección General del Trabajo, Oficina Sectorial de Planificación.

15. Data from *Memorias del Ministerio del Trabajo*.

At best, collective bargaining hardly ever reaches all sectors or all workers; on the contrary, there are many whom it does not cover (such as public administration and, in some countries, public undertakings). Mostly, however, the impossibility is a de facto one—the trade union is weak or the bargaining unit is very small, or both. It is also very difficult for collective bargaining to gain a foothold in the rural sector, except on plantations. Its prospects are no better in small undertakings, and much worse in the minute undertakings of the informal urban sector. All this means that the proportion of the employed population covered by collective bargaining may be large or small, according to country, but that everywhere many groups are excluded. Thus, only in Argentina and Mexico has collective bargaining become really general, but even then not universal. In Venezuela it covers about 33 percent, in Panama a little over 20 percent, and in other countries between 20 and 10 percent or less of the employed labor force. Comparison with other regions of the world shows that its scope is smaller in Latin America than in Western Europe, but that in some countries of the region it compares with that in the United States.

The Parties to Collective Bargaining

Collective bargaining originated in the industrialized countries as a basically bilateral procedure involving two parties, the workers represented by the trade union and the employers either individually, where bargaining is at the undertaking level, or the employers' organization, where bargaining is by industry. In Latin America collective bargaining has followed this general pattern, although in exceptional cases other parties, such as a coalition of nonunionized workers, are involved. Moreover, the department of labor has a vitally important role, since the procedure is nearly always based on the assumption that the department's intervention will be little short of necessary, and often gives it extensive regulatory or protective powers.

The traditional parties to collective bargaining are the workers' trade union and, in most countries, the employer. For many years the trade union was nearly always an enterprise union, except in Argentina and Brazil, but in various countries industrial trade unions are now developing and trying to negotiate for a whole branch of the economy or with each undertaking, establishing or coordinating common bargaining strategies, with the result that workers' demands are beginning to be similar. Of course, this situation does not arise in similar fashion in all countries or branches of industry. In Mexico it occurs above all when enterprise unions function as a section of the national industrial trade union, as in mining and metallurgy. In Colombia it is most noticeable in the construction and cement industries. In Venezuela bargaining is coordinated mainly through the federations, which in that country are constituted on the basis both of the industry and of geographical location (state), and usually act under the supervision of the Venezuelan Confederation of Labor (CTV). In El Salvador and Panama industrial trade unions are fairly well established in nearly all sectors, and therefore generally do the bargaining; but in Ecuador the negotiator is nearly always the works council (equivalent to an enterprise union), and the same is the case in Chile and Peru, except that in Peru bargaining is by industry in a few cases. In Argentina and Brazil bargaining is nearly always carried on by an industrial trade union because the law does not in practice allow enterprise unions.

The usual, if not the only possible, situation in bargaining follows the principle of "only one bargaining unit, one trade union, and one negotiator." This rule reflects the trade union unity that obtains at the establishment level but not at higher levels, where (as shown in Chapter 2) the usual situation in some countries is that the trade union movement is fragmented. In fact, trade union unity in the undertaking (and above all in the establishment) has been imposed by law in Bolivia, Honduras, and Peru, while in Argentina and Brazil the law imposes it at the level of the industry or trade. In other countries the same situation is reached indirectly; in Colombia, for example, it is reached by means of statutory provisions giving the most representative trade union the monopoly of representing the workers for collective bargaining purposes. In Panama it is through the rule that a trade union may not be formed unless the minimum number of workers is 50, a number not easily reached in most small and medium-size undertakings (this may help to explain why the industrial trade union has gained so much ground in that country). In Mexico and Venezuela trade union unity is arrived at by inserting a union security clause in collective agreements, which in practice gives the trade union very close control over the recruitment of staff. The new laws in Chile favor trade union plurality at all levels, but in practice no parallel or rival trade unions have been formed in undertakings.

The employer may refuse to negotiate with the trade union because it does not represent a sufficient number of workers. To get over this difficulty, the law lays down objective standards of representativeness generally based on membership. The minimum rates of membership required vary greatly but are usually high: in the Dominican Republic, to be able to negotiate, the trade union must represent at least 60 percent of the workers in the undertaking, and in other countries at least 50 percent; in Colombia at least 30 percent of the workers in the undertaking must belong to the trade union, but if the proportion is lower, the collective agreement will nevertheless be valid for the union members. In Chile the trade union may negotiate on behalf of its members but not on behalf of other persons. In Argentina bargaining rights are granted to the trade union having the legal status (*personalidad grenial*) granted to the trade union that is sufficiently representative in each branch; at least 10 percent of the workers must belong to a trade union before it can qualify as representative. In Brazil a trade union is not allowed to exist unless its membership covers at least one-third of the workers in the occupational category concerned.

In various countries collective bargaining by nonunionized workers is also allowed, but approaches differ. In Colombia, Peru, and Venezuela it is permitted if there is no trade union in the undertaking, but restricted or even prohibited if there is. In general, bargaining with a group of nonunionized workers is limited to small undertakings in which the trade union is finding difficulty in gaining a foothold or cannot exist because there are not enough workers for it to be legally constituted. In Costa Rica, Chile, and Uruguay, however, the law allows valid negotiation with nonunionized labor even where there is a trade union. In Costa Rica this practice is known as *arreglo directo* (direct arrangement) and has been denounced by the trade unions as an antitrade union maneuver. In Venezuela it is known as *contrato notarial* (contract executed and authenticated by a notary) but is tending to fall into disuse.

The employer's bargaining agent is the employer where bargaining is by undertaking, and the employers' organization when it is by industry. The employer may delegate his powers to his legal advisers, or personnel administration and labor relations officers, in the undertaking if it has sufficiently separated and specialized management functions, but in the small or medium-size undertakings typical of Latin America there is usually no such specialization. The individual employer normally deals directly with the trade union, and at most takes legal advice.

Even in certain larger undertakings personnel and labor relations officers often have only third or fourth rank in the hierarchy and are allowed little freedom to introduce labor policies, and still less to bargain. In the past they did not usually have the specialized knowledge or technical training needed for bargaining, but this state of affairs is changing; nowadays the labor relations officials in many undertakings are specialists in the subject. Another unfavorable influence is the paternalism of some Latin American employers, which prejudices them against bargaining (the same paternalism is found in some public or state enterprises, although in theory these have no "boss"). In any event, the support employers can get from their organizations is not usually very great; the organizations are not accustomed, any more than are the employers, to handling collective bargaining, and only in the last few years have they begun to make any serious effort to meet their members' need for services that will make bargaining easier for them.

The above discussion may help to explain why the employer's bargaining agent may frequently lack the necessary professional touch; and since the same state of affairs may obtain on the trade union side, it is easy to see why collective bargaining is sometimes still regarded as a painful experience. But as it becomes more general, the parties begin to get used to it and the painful experience tends to disappear; at present the pain seems to last until they sign their first collective agreement, after which their relations become more constructive. The situation is of course different when the people around the bargaining table are not the trade union and the boss but the trade union federation (or industrial trade union) and the employers' organization for the branch of activity. The bargainers are then professionals; their relations are impersonal, and this helps to make the bargaining a relatively technical process. But this happens more frequently in industrywide negotiations, which are still exceptional in Latin America except in Argentina, Brazil, and, to a lesser extent, Venezuela.

Role of Departments of Labor

The first thing to be noted with respect to bargaining practices is that intervention by the department of labor in the collective bargaining process is of outstanding importance in Latin America. This state of affairs is partly due to the fact that hardly any of the countries in the region have a well-established procedure for bilateral collective bargaining in the strict sense of the term, and the parties have consequently had to use dispute settlement procedures. Another relevant and perhaps more important factor is the tradition of government interference in labor relations that is still deeply rooted in the mentality of the parties to bargaining and their governments. Governments regard their participation in collective bargaining as part of the tutelage that since 1930 they have nearly always exercised over labor relations, and on many other economic, social, and cultural functions of Latin American society. The parties to bargaining regard the presence of the officers of the department of labor as guaranteeing them a neutral ground for discussion and also a way out, should one be needed, of the deadlocks that are still frequent because of their inexperience.

Be this as it may, participation of the authorities in the bargaining procedure influences the parties' behavior. Collective bargaining often begins with submission of the workers' demands to the management of the undertaking—and, simultaneously, a trade union demonstration outside the department of labor. Often, too, negotiations begin only when a conciliation officer summons the parties to appear before him. In other cases the parties listen to proposals and counterproposals solely through the intermediary of the administration, and usually sign the collective agreement under pressure from the authorities and under the threat that unless they come to an agreement, the question will be submitted to compulsory arbitration. Finally, as an example of the importance that may attend intervention by the public authorities, in most countries the minister of labor, and sometimes even the president of the republic, is personally involved in the most significant collective bargaining negotiations.

The participation of the department of labor in collective bargaining entails two problems: the department has to choose the competent official or body to deal with the matter and to provide the necessary facilities and funds. The first officials given power to take part in collective bargaining were the labor inspectors; this was obviously not an ideal arrangement, since their work is primarily supervisory and should not be confused with conciliation or compromise. In Venezuela and other countries, therefore, a special class of labor inspectors has been formed to deal solely with bargaining and disputes. In other countries corps of conciliators and mediators have been formed from officials of the units (see Chapter 4).

The second problem (also mentioned in Chapter 4) is doubtless the Achilles' heel of the administration, whose resources never grow at anything like the pace of the difficulties it has to cope with. In most Latin American countries the government generally has only a small budget, and departments of labor are usually worse off than others, as is clear from a look at the budgetary allocations for the various departments. The result of this general penury is naturally that there are too few conciliators, they are badly trained, there are few candidates for a career as conciliator, and no resources to improve the conciliation boards' ability to intervene. There is therefore the contradiction that whereas bargaining procedures make it almost inevitable that the department of labor will have to intervene, it is not given the means to intervene effectively. This is perhaps why the number of cases settled by direct negotiation, without its intervening, is on the increase; the parties are beginning to understand that the administration cannot help them very much.

It is nevertheless recognized that the department of labor is still extremely useful in settling certain disputes and should not be dispensed with when they arise; what is necessary is to improve the services it gives. It seems reasonable that the parties should carry out bilateral bargaining without outside help so long as they are not heading for a dispute, and that they should call in the department of labor only when a dispute seems inevitable. The bargaining systems of various countries are tending toward this arrangement; in Venezuela, for instance, where either of the parties or even individual workers can request the presence of an official of the Department of Labor during the bargaining process, it was noted in a 1982 study that private, direct negotiations are becoming customary.[2] However, this practice will not be generally followed until the advent of an independent bargaining procedure unconnected with the settlement of disputes.

Procedures

There are relatively few principles governing the conduct of negotiations. The legal framework has always been more concerned with the regulation of the contents and effects of agreements than with the process leading to their conclusion. In countries where there is provision for the extension of agreements to third parties (Argentina, Ecuador, El Salvador, Honduras, Mexico, and Venezuela), the rules governing such extensions are usually regulated in more detail than the process of negotiation itself. The few existing provisions on the latter are usually found under the heading of direct dealings that the legislature has regarded as spanning a brief period preceding the outbreak of a dispute. Moreover, the practice of basic or framework agreements entered into at the national level, with a view to setting forth the "rules of the game," has never taken root in Latin America.

All this means that in a number of cases, collective bargaining is still carried out in a somewhat improvised or haphazard fashion. There are many instances, however, of established relationships, particularly in large undertakings, under which the negotiating process follows a mutually agreed and orderly procedure. In some countries with developed labor relations, for instance, the chairmanship of the negotiating committee is no longer the automatic perquisite of a government official or of the ranking management representative (as used to be the custom established by paternalistic habits), but rotates among the management and trade union representatives. The same practice is prescribed by law in Peru.

The North American model of collective bargaining, with its emphasis on determination of the appropriate bargaining unit, bargaining in good faith, and prohibition of unfair labor practices, has had no real influence on Latin American law and practice. There are broad references to the duty to bargain either for all enterprises where there are workers affiliated with a union (as in Honduras, Mexico, and Panama) or where the union has the support of a certain proportion of the workers, but nowhere is the principle of bargaining in good faith adequately spelled out. Thus, the employer generally does not incur any particular penalties if he is unwilling to negotiate or if he systematically refuses to agree to anything proposed by the other party. Workers would simply be entitled to declare a legal strike (as in Mexico and Panama) or the department of labor would step in to settle disputes (as happens in most countries).

There are no rules concerning the duty to provide information. The law is silent on this point, which leads to considerable friction and misunderstanding. Meaningful information is for the most part given only during procedures for settling disputes, a fact that obviously operates to the detriment of direct negotiations. Questions relating to the representative character of the union are frequently raised at the first negotiating meeting, but checks on union membership or majority requirements are carried out by government officials without adhering to any specific procedure. While some countries have introduced the concept of unfair labor practices, it does not include refusal to bargain except in Argentina and Chile, and its relevance to the negotiation procedure is almost nil in practice.

However, even if there is no comprehensive framework for the conduct of negotiations, there are nevertheless some provisions that are peculiar to a number of countries. The list of demands is presented through the labor inspector or other official of the department of labor in Bolivia, Ecuador, Haiti, and Venezuela. The negotiating committee may not exceed a certain number of members (three, for instance) in Chile, Haiti, and Venezuela. In Chile the employer is entitled to identify certain periods of the year (not exceeding a total of 60 days) during which collective bargaining may not take place, a provision intended to avoid interruptions during peak periods of economic activity. The periodic provision of information to the rank and file on the development of negotiations is more frequent everywhere than formal ratification of the agreement. Should the union negotiators feel during these contacts with the rank and file that the concessions obtained would not be sufficient to meet their aspirations, they would prefer to turn the negotiation into a dispute and opt for a settlement under government auspices or an arbitration award.

Forms of coalition bargaining involving two or more trade unions are foreseen, inter alia, in Colombia, the Dominican Republic, El Salvador, Mexico, and Panama, but the notion of exclusive bargaining representation for the majority union is gaining momentum elsewhere. Finally, in almost every country there are detailed provisions for the registration of agreements with the department of labor, a requirement that is preceded by a verification of the content of the agreement in relation to minimum standards in the protective labor legislation, and sometimes also in relation to government economic policy.

Faced with a somewhat defective legal framework, the parties have been creating their own bargaining practices, filling the gaps of the law, clarifying its provisions, or establishing their own procedure. They have also been improving their bargaining techniques. As a Mexican author observes, the first rough and sometimes violent tactics gave way to "horse trading" and theatrical approaches that are now being superseded by more rational discussion in which it is not infrequent to use sophisticated and computerized calculations.[3] This, however, is not a universal trend. There are still small and medium-size enterprises, or less advanced countries, in which contract negotiations still take place in an atmosphere of contention and aggression, and in which procedure is improvised and proposals and counterproposals are made in an empirical or rough-and-ready fashion. In such situations it is not uncommon for unions systematically to present excessive demands and employers systematically to refuse most or all of them. Rude verbal exchanges may also characterize the initial rounds of negotiations in some countries.[4]

Levels of Bargaining

For many years the usual, if not the only, bargaining level in all countries except Argentina and Brazil was that of the undertaking. This preference can be explained by economic, historical, and political reasons, such as the exceptional and isolated character of the most dynamic economic units in the first decades of this century; the workers' tendency to set up enterprise unions—a tendency often encouraged by legislation, although in other cases it confined itself to recognizing a de facto situation; the great disparity of undertakings in a given industrial sector, making the adoption of universal standards difficult; and the fact that disputes nearly always came before bargaining or, indeed, the formation of a trade union, and almost invariably took the form of action at undertaking level. It is therefore not surprising that the first collective agreements should have been concluded in individual undertakings, generally after sometimes lengthy disputes. This happened with the miners of Corocoro, in Bolivia, the Barranquilla dockers in Colombia, and the employees of the Great Central Railway in Venezuela (all of whom concluded their first collective agreements before 1920), and with the workers on many banana plantations in Central America (where, practically speaking, the trade union movement and collective bargaining in the countries concerned began in the 1950s and 1960s).

Again for historical and, above all, political reasons, collective bargaining in Argentina and Brazil takes place mainly at the industry level. In Argentina one reason is that the country began to become industrialized at a relatively early date and had few undertakings of exceptional importance. There has also been the special factor that at the beginning of the century, its labor force consisted mainly of Europeans imbued with socialist and anarcho-syndicalist ideology—all of which tended to promote the values of class solidarity. The trend toward trade union action at the industry level was consolidated from the 1940s on, when the Peronist movement encouraged trade union organization at that level. The situation was similar in Brazil from the 1930s on, when Getúlio Vargas began the corporativist experiment whose vestiges remain in the 1943 consolidation of the labor laws. Brazilian trade union structure is based on parallel organizations of employers and workers; the employers' organizations represent the "economic categories," the workers' organizations the "occupational categories," and collective agreements are concluded between two organizations, one of each kind.

More recently there have been some minor, quantitative changes, and there is a tendency to diversify bargaining levels, but there is no reason to believe that any major change will take place in the near future. In some countries there is quite strong pressure on the trade union side for bargaining at the industry level; for example, this was one of the main demands made to the government by the four most important trade union confederations in Colombia in 1977. A similar situation exists in other countries, but strict government control makes it unlikely that bargaining at the industry level will spread in the absence of any official action to encourage it.

This does not mean that bargaining at that level is unknown: in Mexico for some decades *contratos-leyes* (industrywide collective agreements having statutory force) have been negotiated in the textile industry, and the practice has spread to the sugar, alcohol, and rubber industries. The most recent sectoral bargaining has included bottlers of nonalcoholic beverages and broadcasting, and may possibly be extended to cover other industries in which labor standards are controlled by the federal authorities, such as the cement, petrochemical, metal, and iron and steel industries. In Peru there have been negotiations at the sectoral level in some branches of economic activity, particularly the banks, bakeries, service stations, and (principally) the textile sector. In Bolivia a number of sectoral agreements have been negotiated for workers in commerce and banking, printing, and the manufacturing and construction industries. In Panama there are sectoral collective agreements for printing works and the construction industry. In Chile negotiations at the industry level have covered the textile, leather and footwear, milling, and construction industries, in which a "standard rate" (*tarifado único*) was negotiated, but the only bargaining allowed under the 1979 law is at the undertaking level.

Venezuela is probably the country in which the most progress has been made in the transition from bargaining at the undertaking level to bargaining at the industry level. In 1958 a legislative decree was passed on "collective agreements by branches of industry," and in the first few years after it came into force, between two and five agreements of this kind were concluded every year; but from 1966 on, the rate was 15 to 20 every year, and this rate has been maintained. Since the minimum duration of the collective contract is two years, about 40 contracts must now be in force. Their coverage includes the textile, ready-made clothing, printing, and construction industries, metallurgical undertakings, gasoline service stations, international press agencies, broadcasting stations, the timber industry, dyers and laundries, and the brush industry. In addition, the Federation of Oil Industry Workers (FEDEPETROL) traditionally negotiated the collective agreement covering oil workers at the sectoral level, although it was signed separately with each company. Since the oil industry was nationalized, the companies have been functioning as "operators" of the Venezuelan oil company, PETROVEN, but the previous method of negotiation has been continued. The latest development in Venezuela is the attempt to negotiate a basic industrywide model agreement between the Venezuelan Confederation of Labor and FEDECAMARAS, its counterpart organization on the employers' side.

In Argentina and Brazil bargaining is usually at the industry level. In Argentina the only company-level collective agreements appeared to be those concluded in state undertakings, particularly in public services such as the railways, the underground railway system in Buenos Aires, and the national airline; nearly all other collective agreements were sectoral ones. In the last few years, however, the practice has been to negotiate company-level agreements, probably because of the suspension of collective bargaining that followed the change of regime in 1976. Nearly all these agreements were unofficial ones, and were aimed largely at obtaining "wage flexibility," although in a few cases other points were covered as well. In Brazil it is stated in the Labor Code that collective labor agreements shall cover a sector of the economy in a given territory, such as a municipality or state. However, since the important changes that have taken place in the practice of labor relations from 1979 on, numerous company-level collective agreements have been concluded, particularly in the state of São Paulo; 606 of the 940 agreements registered with the Department of Labor between January and August 1980 were company-level agreements.

In 1982 the metalworkers' union of São Bernardo do Campo and Diadema (near São Paulo) negotiated a company-level agreement with Ford do Brasil, with a view to setting up a joint union-management committee at the company's plant. This was an important event in the development of Brazilian labor relations, since the legal framework does not provide for any form of trade union representation at the shop level and the union's demands for introducing such a representation through collective bargaining had hitherto been rejected by the employers.

Subjects Covered

Whether the content of collective agreements is meager or substantial depends on the size and kind of the undertaking, the trade union's ability to bargain, its bargaining experience, the extent to which it is interested in bargaining, and the room for maneuver that the law allows negotiators. It follows that the range of subjects covered by bargaining is very wide in some countries and much narrower in others. In Colombia, Mexico, and Venezuela the principle is widely accepted that everything is negotiable; the content of the agreements then depends on the trade union's power to push home its demands and the undertaking's ability to pay the bill. In Argentina, on the contrary, the tendency is to allow bargaining only on questions not already covered by a substantive act.

There are many intermediary positions between these two extremes: in Brazil bargaining is allowed for wage increases based on improved productivity, although more recently many collective agreements have covered a wider field. For instance, the metal trades agreement negotiated in 1982 in São Paulo included about 40 clauses, while four or five years earlier the agreements concluded in that region contained only 8 or 9 clauses. In Panama the frequent resort to bargaining that took place after the 1971 Labor Code was adopted greatly diminished after an amendment in December 1976 forbidding negotiation on job classification and the size of the work force. In Uruguay bargaining has traditionally been on two main points, wages and dismissals, and occasionally on certain social security provisions. In Peru for a number of years negotiation was allowed on only one subject, general wage increases. The main restrictions on bargaining in Chile have already been mentioned.

A table in a 1981 work[5] gives an idea of the kinds of conditions that are negotiable. Many trade unions regard collective agreements as a means, first, of improving wages and working conditions and, second, of guaranteeing greater employment security. Collective agreements are also used to obtain fringe benefits such as medical care, assistance with the cost of medicines, schools and scholarships for workers' children, holiday centers, and sports facilities. Although some authors have described these as only an extension of the paternalism traditionally attributed to Latin American employers, such benefits certainly help to fill a need only partly met by the state or local communities. Finally, signature of a collective agreement, and even more its subsequent administration, leads to the establishment of permanent bodies for talks or bargaining between the undertaking and the trade union. Grievance committees, labor relations boards, or tripartite arbitration commissions have been set up in various countries to apply and administer agreements. This development has led to quite active workers' participation in the decisions of the undertaking, admittedly hardly ever extending to top-level decisions but nearly always referring to the decisions most directly or immediately concerning the workers. Perhaps this is why the trade unions have so far shown little interest, except in a few countries, in extending participation to the running of enterprises.

Naturally, collective agreements are most complete, and the best working conditions are negotiated, in the large undertakings of the countries where there is most freedom to bargain. Many of these undertakings employ several thousand or tens of thousands of workers, and many of them are state undertakings, although this alone does not explain the generosity of some benefits granted. For example, in Venezuela the collective agreement applying to the nationalized industries in the oil sector is basically the same as the one that applied when those undertakings belonged to the multinational oil companies. In practice, what most affects the level of benefits negotiated in collective agreements is not so much whether the undertaking is public or private, or even its productivity or economic prosperity, as its role in the national economy and the ease with which it can obtain state subsidies or raise the price of its services or products to offset the cost of its concessions to the workers. Obviously, the more important the undertaking is, the more serious the consequences of work stoppages in it will be, and the greater the trade union's bargaining power and the concessions it will extract.

Collective bargaining has been criticized, sometimes harshly, on that score. It has been said that the generous benefits granted mean that costs, prices, and inflation will all be higher, and that the best-organized workers with the greatest bargaining power enjoy a preferential status that tends to constitute a privileged category of workers. These arguments have often been used in support of the restrictive measures referred to above.

It is, however, equally true that collective bargaining has been a means of improving the living and working conditions of certain important social groups and that it cannot be held responsible—at least not solely or mainly responsible—for inflation. Stabilization policies freezing collective bargaining have sometimes been more effective in reducing real wages than in containing price increases. The negotiation of improved conditions in an individual undertaking is, in any event, an inherent feature of the economic system on which collective bargaining is based. Finally, collective bargaining has an expansive force; the benefits negotiated in one undertaking today will be negotiated in another undertaking tomorrow. They will tend to become generally applied, and what is today the privilege of a few will in time be shared by nearly everybody. From this point of view collective agreements can be regarded as the vanguard of social progress.

The collective agreements on which the 1981 table mentioned above is based do not reflect the standard collective agreement in their respective countries; to some extent they are special (but not unique). It would be possible to find in each country a sizable number of public and private undertakings that apply similar agreements, while other, smaller undertakings have collective agreements that are less comprehensive, many of them doing no more than fix wages, usually fairly near the legal minimum; on other matters they either say nothing or state that such and such working conditions "shall be those laid down by law."

Duration of Agreements

In nearly all countries the regulations applicable to agreements pay special attention to various aspects of their duration. In some countries, for example, they state that the duration of agreements may be indefinite or for a fixed period. At first many agreements were concluded for an indefinite period, but the practice is now gaining ground of setting a limited period and providing for the renewal of the agreement for a similar period if agreed-upon or if advance notice to terminate it is not given. This trend follows the normal course of labor relations in other countries and reflects in the duration of the agreements the increasingly periodic character of bargaining.

It is also current practice to include provisions on the minimum and maximum duration of agreements. The shortest minimum duration (six months) is in Colombia. In Argentina, Costa Rica, the Dominican Republic, El Salvador, Haiti, Honduras, and Peru agreements may not be made for less than one year. In Chile, Panama, Paraguay, and Venezuela the minimum duration is two years. In Colombia, Chile, and Peru the national legislation does not mention a maximum duration, leaving the matter entirely to the discretion of the parties, but in Brazil and Nicaragua there is a maximum duration of two years. In Costa Rica, the Dominican Republic, El Salvador, Guatemala, and Venezuela agreements may not be made for longer than three years. In Panama the maximum period is four years; and the longest maximum period—five years—is allowed in Haiti. In two countries the durations of agreements vary according to the conditions they contain or the status of the signatories. In Mexico the prescribed duration is one year for wage clauses and two years for the other clauses of the agreement. Venezuela draws a distinction between agreements with a trade union, which must be concluded for a duration of not less than two years; and agreements with nonunion workers, the duration of which is limited to one year.

Various considerations appear to have influenced these requirements concerning the durations of agreements. Requirements for short minimum and maximum periods stem from the need to adjust bargaining dynamics to changing labor market conditions, whereas those setting longer minimum and maximum periods give priority to the need for stability and certainty in labor relations. As in other parts of the world, employers in Latin America prefer to negotiate long-term agreements, so that they can make their forecasts and organize their production with greater certainty.[6] A third consideration that has influenced the employers' preference is that long-term agreements have the desirable effect of reducing the number of potential opportunities for dispute. Employers and the authorities feel that if agreements have to be renegotiated too often, they can become a virtually permanent potential source of strife.

At times various considerations come into play in a single country. In Mexico the annual revision of wage clauses is due to the need to adjust wages to changes in the cost of living and other economic variables, while the two-year period generally observed for other clauses makes for stability and greater opportunities for undertakings to plan ahead.

In addition to the tendency to state the duration of agreements, there is a trend toward a longer duration. This greater duration is a consequence of the degree of maturity and stability reached in labor relations, and the quantitative and qualitative changes that have taken place in the content of agreements. These agreements are becoming increasingly comprehensive and complex, and their revision has accordingly become less urgent and more complicated. A comparative table prepared in 1978 by ANDI showed that in Colombia, out of 133 agreements examined, 117 (88 percent) had a duration of 2 years, and only 6 had a duration of 3 years.[7] In Mexico the great majority of agreements are concluded for two years, although occasionally one provides that its duration shall be indefinite but subject to review in accordance with the Federal Labor Act. In Venezuela the trend is toward three-year agreements; of a sample of 20 agreements recently concluded in various industries and undertakings there, 15 were of 3 years', 4 of 2 years', and 1 of 1 year's duration.[8] A similar trend appears to be emerging in Ecuador and Panama.

The trend toward longer duration of agreements may, however, be modified in the next few years because of inflation, since it is unusual in Latin America for agreements to include sliding wage scales linked to the cost of living. In some countries, such as Brazil and Chile, this adjustment takes place by means of increases decreed by the government according to a wage indexation system. A few collective agreements—for instance, in the textile industry in Peru—have provided for cost of living clauses. However, in many other countries wage adjustments can be secured only through the renegotiation of the agreement. Mexico has always recognized the right of employers' and workers' organizations to apply to conciliation and arbitration boards for amendment of the working conditions laid down by agreement "when the rise in the cost of living leads to imbalance between capital and labor."

It is unusual in Latin America for agreements to contain an explicit obligation to observe industrial peace, whether absolute or relative. Some agreements in Venezuela (as in the oil and telecommunications industries) expressly forbid claims on matters not covered by the agreement, and others state that neither the trade union nor its members may make new demands on items that have been thrown out during the negotiations, or on related matters. There is, however, reluctance to impose a specific obligation to refrain from industrial action, probably because of the importance attributed to the right to strike, its recognition in the constitution, and the fear that any such obligation might be interpreted as eroding that right. The peace obligation is, however, implicit in the legislation in force in certain countries as well as in the general tenor of the great majority of the agreements. In Ecuador, however, unions are entitled to submit a new list of demands any day after signing a collective agreement.

The dearth of provisions concerning the peace obligation is also due to the *rebus sic stantibus* clause, which allows revision of the agreement before expiry in the event of substantial change in the economic conditions on which it is based. In Colombia, the Dominican Republic, Ecuador, El Salvador, Honduras, and Mexico the labor codes allow for revision of collective agreements before their expiry should there be unforeseeable and serious deterioration in the economic situation (Colombia and Honduras), or if the economic conditions of the country or undertaking undergo substantial change (El Salvador), or when economic circumstances justify such revision (Mexico). Although this provision is not often invoked in some countries, in others it has introduced an element of uncertainty and instability into labor relations. In Honduras, for example, attempts are frequently made to revise agreements signed only a few months previously. Application for revision made toward the end of the validity of an agreement could also put its renewal upon expiry in doubt. In general it may be said that while such revision was devised as a means of preserving the real value of the wage clause, in practice it has only occasionally succeeded in doing so, and could adversely affect observance of the agreement and the guarantee of social peace that it should provide.[9]

In some countries, including Panama and Peru, the legislation provides that sale or transfer of the business shall not affect the validity of the agreement; the new employer is bound by the agreement in precisely the same way as the old employer. Under the law of several countries, dissolution of the trade union does not affect the obligations and rights laid down in the agreement. In El Salvador the law further provides that the agreement shall remain in force while a new agreement is being negotiated. Other countries provide that agreements shall be effective from the date of expiry of the previous one. Even when the law does not explicitly say so, in other countries it is assumed that the parties have power to make all or part of the agreement retroactive, as they quite often do in practice. In some countries it is also stated that expiry of the agreement does not abolish the benefits granted in previous collective agreements.

Stage of Development Reached

The foregoing analysis leads to certain inescapable conclusions, of which the most important is that collective bargaining in Latin America is spreading and that the parties are becoming more autonomous in their conduct of labor relations. Second, its development is not unattended by difficulties of all kinds. And third, it is not a universal practice and cannot reasonably be expected to take the place of the law.

At its best, collective bargaining in Latin America has reached a degree of maturity comparable with that in some industrialized countries. It is then an essential factor in stabilizing labor relations, and is considered a necessary complement to legislation as a means of improving working conditions and, more generally, the workers' quality of life. The formidable list of fringe benefits of all kinds granted in many collective labor agreements shows that the importance of such agreements in these matters is fully recognized.

The development of collective bargaining highlights a change of attitude toward it by management and labor. For employers it is no longer the "painful" experience that it may have been in the past, and is beginning to turn into an exercise forming part of routine personnel management. As for the trade unions, their growing involvement in collective bargaining means that they are becoming fully aware of their role in the system of labor relations, something quite new in Latin America, where trade unions were regarded as a cornerstone more of the political system than of the labor relations system. Conventional wisdom viewed them more as means of mobilizing the masses or transforming society than as parties in labor relations. But the political role of the trade union, however fundamental to understanding the political structures of many Latin American countries, should not obscure its industrial role. Trade unions have not abandoned their political function, nor have they any intention of doing so; they have simply come to realize that collective bargaining offers them a new and enlarged scope.

However, collective bargaining also has its limitations. In the first place, it does not cover the entire economically active population, nor even all employed persons; in some cases (such as confidential employees in Mexico) collective agreements specifically exclude certain groups of salaried employees in the modern sector. Second, it is not, nor can it ever be, a panacea for all the workers' problems. Still more important, it is regarded with some misgivings—less by the parties to it than by governments—and is therefore usually the first victim of monetarist economic policies, or of any plan for economic stabilization, or, in general, of any political system based on an authoritarian state.

The general picture is therefore one of strong contrasts, but all in all the prospects for collective bargaining appear to be good. Although merely tolerated in some countries, in others it is accepted and recognized as an essential part of the labor relations system. In a few countries it is still an exceptional procedure, but in nearly all the others it is deeply rooted and tending to spread. Many difficulties still lie in its way, but in general its successes are more numerous than its failures.

Notes

1. See John G. Simmons, "Tendencias de la contratación colectiva en Venezuela," in ILO, *La negociación colectiva en América latina* (Geneva: ILO, 1978), p. 62.

2. Ramon E. Rodríguez Perdomo, *Negociación colectiva de trabajo en Venezuela* (Lima: CIAT, 1982), p. 66.

3. B. Cavazos Flores, "El contrato colectivo de trabajo," in B. Cavazos Flores, *El derecho laboral latino-americano* (Mexico City: Editorial Trillas, 1981), p. 637.

4. See Lupo Hernández Rueda, "The Dominican Republic" (1980), in R. Blanpain, ed., *International Encyclopaedia for Labour Law and Industrial Relations* (Deventer, Netherlands: Kluwer, 1981), vol. IV, p. 156.

5. Arturo S. Bronstein, ed., *Las relaciones laborales en las empresas estatales de América latina* (Geneva: ILO, 1981), ch. 4, App. "Incidencia de la negociación colectiva sobre las condiciones de trabajo y las relaciones laborales en ciertas empresas estatales," pp. 65–85.

6. ILO, *La negociación colectiva en América latina*, p. 42.

7. Asociación Nacional de Industriales (ANDI), *Convenciones colectivas* (Bogota: ANDI, 1979), p. 304.

8. This sample was taken from the ILO collection of collective agreements.

9. ILO, "Informe al gobierno de Honduras sobre la misión multidisciplinaria del PIACT" (Geneva: ILO, 1979). (Mimeographed.)

6

Workers' Participation in Management

by
Efrén Córdova

In Latin America, as elsewhere, the term "participation" may have different meanings according to place and context. In fact, no other word in labor terminology is used in so many different ways. To start with, there are the rate of labor force participation and the references to popular participation in the development process. In both senses the term is often used in connection with the attempts to increase production and promote social change that are a characteristic feature of mobilization programs.[1] Second, there are various systems of participation in the profits and capital of undertakings, as well as, in the macroeconomic context, the participation of labor in the national income. These variants fall into a broader category that might be called participation in the benefits of production. Finally, there are experiments in workers' participation in management, and of trade unions and employers' organizations in the handling of social and labor programs that could be covered by the expression "participation in decision making." This chapter will concentrate on workers' participation in decisions within undertakings,[2] but will also contain incidental references to participation in profits and capital. (Participation by trade unions and employers' organizations in programs or bodies of national importance will be examined in Chapter 8.)

Participation in management, then, is equivalent to a recognized possibility for the workers to exert real influence on decisions within undertakings. (This means that information alone is not, in our view, a form of participation, although it is a useful form of communication and an essential requisite for bargaining.) This possibility should be recognized by the other side, be regularly exercised, and form part and parcel of the normal labor relations system. Participation in management should therefore be understood to mean a form of normal, institutionalized access of workers to the decision-making process, regardless of whether the decisions concern the overall management of the undertaking or particular labor questions, and of whether the workers participate in that decision making directly, or indirectly through their representatives. The underlying concept is therefore not as broad as that used by scholars when referring to political participation.[3] Nevertheless, participation, in the labor relations context, takes a wide variety of forms, including collective bargaining, which is so important that it is generally studied separately.

The extent to which the other forms of participation have been applied in Latin America varies a great deal. At the shop floor level, workers' participation in the organization of their own work is in general little known. There is much talk of humanization of work, but there are few actual experiments in job rotation, autonomous work groups, or self-supervised work. At the undertaking level there has been relatively little experience of works councils or joint committees, and doubts have been expressed about whether systems of workers' representation on the management of undertakings are really entrenched or can possibly become established. The question therefore arises of whether there are in Latin America socioeconomic circumstances, inseparable from the labor relations system, that prevent the introduction of participation schemes, or whether the tardy appearance or relatively meager development of participation is due to historical vicissitudes, political changes, or accidents unconnected with the system. This question should be answered before considering the history of participation in the management of undertakings or in their decision making.

Hindrances

Because Latin American labor relations have always been identified with the practice of collective bargaining, there is a tendency to believe that there were no other forms of participation there, or that they had made little progress. The most obvious reason for the latter state of affairs seemed to be that collective bargaining was carried out in nearly all the countries of the region at the undertaking level, and on the workers' side generally by an enterprise union. Collective bargaining has consequently acted as an effective form of participation directly involving the workers, and has produced tangible improvements in working conditions. Unlike bargaining at the industry level, which is done from a distance by officials of federations or industrial trade unions, bargaining at the undertaking level entails the workers' attending meetings at which their claims are formulated and the draft collective agreement approved, and direct contact is made with the negotiators. This makes for a conflictual form of participation that at first glance makes other systems of codetermination, cooperation, and cosupervision unnecessary.

This is a plausible explanation, but there is no doubt that other factors help to explain why participation was so slow in developing. While the characteristics of the labor relations system show how little importance was attached to the introduction of participation by means of legal enactments, there are other reasons why both parties showed so little interest in promoting it. Neither paternalist employers nor militant trade unions had at first the slightest inclination toward the new collaborative forms of participation in decisions within undertakings. Participation in management is of course incompatible with authoritarian or paternalist management, and collaborative types of participation are banned by some of the tenets of revolutionary syndicalism.

Later, when other forms of management gained ground, paternalism and hostility to participation were still deeply rooted and it was no easy matter to overcome these prejudices. With the exception of a very few employers belonging to the Associations of Christian Business Executives that are members of the International Christian Union of Business Executives (UNIAPAC), the great majority of employers were hostile to the proposals for participation in management made in some countries under the guise of reforming the undertaking or democratizing labor relations. This was also the usual attitude in employers' organizations, which in Latin America (as elsewhere) stoutly upheld the principles of free enterprise and management prerogatives. Many years of conditioning to decision making at the top levels only, confrontations between employers and trade unions, and vestiges of a master–servant pattern of communication made it difficult for them to accept relations based on action taken jointly or on an equal footing.

On the trade union side the picture was not dissimilar. Many leaders of revolutionary syndicalism believed that participation in management was tantamount to accepting the social system at the expense of the class struggle. Moreover, there was no lack of leaders of reformist or negotiation-minded organizations who, perhaps influenced by the trade union movement in the United States, held that such participation could compromise trade union independence and weaken collective bargaining. Even believers in other branches of trade unionism that recognized the validity of some forms of participation affirmed that these forms would be irrelevant or ineffective unless accompanied by other structural changes. In fact, it was the Christian trade union movement that was most favorable to participation, but from timidly invoking the principle contained in a number of papal encyclicals (particularly *Mater et magistra*) this movement suddenly went on to accept more or less explicitly the blueprint of a self-managing society. Generally speaking, there were few organizations willing to consider participation in management as a complement to collective bargaining instead of as a substitute for it.

These viewpoints were so firmly established that in 1974—four years after the establishment of "labor communities" in Peru—a survey of the views of Peruvian workers and their attitude toward participation showed that about one-third of the workers employed in the undertakings practicing codetermination from which the sample was taken expressed the view that they should not participate with their management in solving important day-to-day problems. Incidentally, the inquiry showed that both in undertakings under workers' management and in undertakings practicing codetermination, few workers attended meetings to take decisions; the majority went to them to put forward their grievances.[4] The conclusion drawn from the survey was that until there was a real change in the master–servant mentality, participation schemes in Peru would merely be a context in which the workers went through the motions of participation.[5]

The trouble was, therefore, not only that the parties were not interested in promoting participation, but that some of the basic prerequisites for the success of any system of participation were lacking. If the employer refused to share responsibility or mistrusted initiatives taken by the workers, and if the workers had little desire to participate or their leaders considered that it was not proper for them to do so, the conditions necessary for a good system of participation were of course not present.

Besides these subjective factors there were others that made participation extremely difficult, especially as regards workers' representation on management committees and boards of directors. The structure of commercial and industrial companies as set out in the legal codes allowed various forms of representation of capital, but hardly any country authorized the issue of shares to workers. (In Mexico the general Commercial Companies Act authorizes the issue of special shares to company employees "when provided for in the articles of association.") Before workers' representatives could take a seat on these companies' boards of directors, therefore, the commercial codes or industrial laws had to be amended; and this was not easily done. Also, serious training problems had first to be settled, lest participation should become a mere facade.

Furthermore, the social background was not propitious to the introduction of systems of participation. Any increase in workers' participation in decisions within undertakings seemed inconsistent with their passive habits and the limited political participation found in many countries. Cooperation systems were incompatible with the workers' failure to identify with the undertakings in which they worked, and within the undertaking there was much personal distrust. This sometimes meant that representatives elected to the board of directors felt uncomfortable in alien surroundings, while the workers they represented were indifferent to, or suspicious of, workers taking on the responsibilities of representation.

The Beginnings

The foregoing section will help to explain why the principle of participation made little headway for many years, but does not suggest that it was wholly unknown, or has not developed appreciably in more recent times, especially in some South American countries. In this section an attempt will be made to give a clearer idea of the development and importance of participation in Latin America.

In some countries the origins of participation in decision making go back to the 1920s. In Argentina an inquiry by the Chamber of Deputies in 1920–21 showed that in some undertakings there were councils of heads of sections and some of the older workers, formed to advise the management, but that the parties lacked sufficient maturity to go ahead with broader schemes of participation.[6]

In the following years and in various countries, projects for workers' control, or participation in decision making, were drawn up but either were ephemeral or were never taken seriously.[7] Some undertakings set up staff councils on their own initiative, as advisory and consultative bodies. In some cases, as in the Tematex firm in Argentina in 1953, these councils were instituted under an agreement with the trade union. After World War II some forms of workers' minority representation on the boards of directors of a number of big public undertakings were set up, as in the Bolivian Mining Corporation (COMIBOL) in 1952, the Volta Redonda iron and steel company in Brazil in 1961, and the Mexican oil company PEMEX in the 1940s.

Some of these experiments regarded participation as a means of workers' control rather than codetermination; workers' representatives were there to verify, advise, and check rather than to share in decision making. In Bolivia the 1952 decrees referred to workers' supervision "with right of veto." Whatever form they took in practice, these experiments were isolated or did not last long. (In some cases, as in the Argentine oil fields and national telecommunications undertakings, workers' representation on the management of undertakings was required by law but was not put into effect.) Many years passed before participation became an accepted practice more or less characteristic of labor relations in the public sector of certain countries.

In the private sector participation had made even less progress. When, for example, profit sharing was introduced into eight Latin American countries, no provisions were made for participation in decision making. In Mexico a national profit-sharing workers' commission was formed in 1963, but dealt only with fixing and revising percentages of participation in profits throughout the country. In other countries profit sharing was not accompanied by any form of participation in management. For example, the Venezuelan Labor Code states that because of profit sharing, workers shall not take any part in the management of the undertaking; it was nevertheless in Venezuela that provision was made for the right of the majority of the workers concerned to apply for examination and verification of balance sheets and inventories. In the Dominican Republic individual workers are entitled to examine the account books where there is profit sharing, but little use is made of this right in practice. In nearly all Latin American countries a share in profits has become an integral part of wages that is granted regardless of whether any profits are distributed to shareholders.

After World War II two countries introduced systems of joint work councils, but both were unsuccessful. Bolivia in 1950 and Colombia in 1955 set up joint boards to promote cooperation, improve productivity, and advise on staff policy; the Bolivian boards also dealt with vocational training and the grant of fellowships and bonuses. Neither, however, managed to establish itself, and they were even less successful as an alternative to collective bargaining. The Bolivian works councils hardly managed to operate, and the Colombian legislation was declared unconstitutional.[8] One author has even called the Bolivian joint boards nothing more than "an example of imitation."[9]

Joint committees on a smaller scale have been established in other countries. In Uruguay, for example, joint committees were formed in work places and undertakings to administer the paid holidays granted in collective agreements; they were composed of two employers' representatives, one of whom acted as chairman, and two workers' representatives. In practice they also dealt with safety at work, application of the agreements, and supervision of discipline, and had some say in the administration of the undertaking. Their operation suffered, however, from lack of trade union support as well as from the fact that not all agreements covered holidays with pay.[10] More recent attempts to encourage the formation of joint committees in Uruguay have had scant success.

Main Principles

Gradually, however, interest in participation was growing. It was even reflected in a number of principles contained in national constitutions and was intended to favor workers' participation in the management of undertakings. As early as 1946 the Brazilian Constitution introduced a provision (ratified in the 1969 Charter), dealing with integration of the workers into the operation and development of the undertaking, profit sharing, and (exceptionally) participation in management. However, the systems of participation subsequently introduced were concerned mainly with the establishment of national funds for profit sharing, savings, and loans, and did not affect decision making in undertakings. The Argentine constitutional reform of 1957 sanctioned profit sharing "with control of production and cooperation in management." Before and after this provision was promulgated, draft legislation was put forward on various occasions on profit sharing and shareholding by workers, but none was approved. A number of undertakings introduced various systems of shareholding for workers, but they had little success and most were abandoned. An Argentine scholar summed up the situation by asserting that the Argentine experience clearly showed little inclination on the part of management and labor for participation.[11]

The constitutions of Ecuador (1978) and Peru (1980) also mention participation. One section of the Ecuadorian Constitution provides for participation in net profits, and another says that the state should encourage workers' ownership and participation in management by transferring shares to them. The Peruvian Constitution recognizes the workers' right to participate in the management and profits of the undertaking, and adds that this right extends to ownership of enterprises whose legal status does not bar such extension. Both texts, therefore, include in their principles those of the three main forms of participation: in profits, in capital, and in management.

Many authors urged the need to reform the structure of undertakings, and asserted that the Latin American enterprise was evolving from the status of a capital-based company toward that of a community of labor and other factors of production.[12] Others invoked principles derived from Christian social doctrine[13] and emphasized the institutional aspects of modern industrial undertakings and their dimension as human communities. These premises led to the conclusion that all individuals in the undertaking were entitled to take an active part in its administration and government. In 1967 the Second Ibero-American Congress on Labor Law came down on the side of participation in management and capital, pointing out that both could be means of integrating workers into the undertaking. However, these theoretical statements received little support from government policy, and the undertaking's financial and organic structure remained untouched in nearly all countries.

Three Important Experiments

More significant were the experiments in participation that started in the 1970s in Argentina, Chile, and Peru. All three have as common denominator their origin in the ideology of the political regimes then in power. At first sight their similarities appear to be few; but Argentine

Peronism, the Peruvian military revolution, and the Allende government all favored a greater degree of participation and encouraged certain forms of workers' management and codetermination. Particularly in Peru participation was no longer merely theoretical or fortuitous; it became for ten years the very hub of the socioeconomic life of the country.

In Argentina, between 1973 and 1976 trade union representation was established on the management boards of all public undertakings and official banks. The most advanced form of participation was the attempt to install a workers' management system in the Greater Buenos Aires Electricity Services (SEGBA). This began in 1964 as a form of minority codetermination contained in the agreement between the undertaking and the Light and Power Trade Union, and was based on Christian social doctrine and Argentine *justicialismo*.[14] In the ensuing years the number of worker directors was increased and a consumer representative was added. In 1973 a trade union leader was made president of the undertaking and a body parallel to the undertaking's management structures, the Workers' Management Committee, was appointed. This committee shared management functions with the executive vice-president and was responsible for forming, at various levels, workers' management groups from among the various grades of the staff. Thus management boards were set up and attached to the six managers of the undertaking, together with sectional boards, each of which shared decision making with the chief of the section concerned.

The SEGBA experiment lasted barely three years, and was ended by government decision. The preamble to the act ending workers' participation in the functioning of the undertaking referred to the scheme's unsatisfactory results, but the trade union leader who was the principal promoter of this experiment maintained that on balance its results were undoubtedly favorable; according to him, there were fewer disputes, absenteeism had fallen, there had been improvements in the undertaking, and the workers had benefited. This experiment in fact combined codetermination and workers' management: workers' management was ultimately intended to bring the management of the enterprise under the control of the working community and the community of consumers, but this goal was never fully achieved. Even with regard to codetermination, the SEGBA experience appears to show that the workers' role was of tangible significance in personnel management but otherwise had little real influence.

Of much more advanced conception was the "social property" created in Peru in 1974. This was to some extent inspired by the Yugoslav experiment and harked back to the old communal affinities of the Inca *ayllú*. It was originally conceived as a workers' management scheme to end the traditional isolation of certain categories of the population from national life and to build up one of the basic sectors of Peruvian economy. Social property undertakings could be formed by any person or persons, by undertakings, or by state action with the aid of official credits and support from the National Social Mobilization Support System (SINAMOS). In its most comprehensive form the social property sector included four subsectors: cooperatives, agricultural companies operating in the general interest (sociedades agrícolas de interés social), peasant and Indian communities, and social property undertakings in the strict sense of the term. The last subsector was intended to promote full participation by its members in the administration of the undertaking, the vesting of the title deeds jointly in all the workers in the undertaking, and lifelong training of the members.

In 1979 the workers' management sector as a whole (all four subsectors) comprised more than 5,000 undertakings, whereas the social property subsector comprised only 52 undertakings with about 7,000 workers. These figures do not include about 60 undertakings administered by the workers directly after they occupied the premises when the undertakings went bankrupt.[15] At the beginning of 1983 the number of social property undertakings that were actually operating had further declined in spite of the existence of two government bodies (CONAPS and EDNAPS) in charge of promoting the development of social property projects.

Another advanced form of participation conceived by the Peruvian system was that of the labor communities. These first appeared in industry in 1970, and later spread to mining, fisheries, and telecommunications. As first organized, they comprised the three main forms of participation: in profits, in management, and in capital. Profit sharing was to be at rates varying according to the type of community (it was, for example, 10 percent in industry). Participation in the capital of the firm was to be effected by purchase of its shares to a value of up to 50 percent of its assets, with funds obtained by earmarking a certain proportion of its net income (varying from one sector to another). Participation in management began with a single representative of the community on the management board, and culminated with parity management when the community became the owner of 50 percent of the capital. No plans for participation in capital were, however, made in fishing and telecommunications communities. In industrial communities such participation was reduced to 33 percent in 1977, and subsequently the sale of its shares was allowed; these were later issued to individuals and no longer to the community.

The communities and the other forms of participation were a product of the revolutionary government's ideology; they were not a response to trade union demands, for when the legal time limit for the voluntary formation of industrial communities expired, fewer than 90 undertakings had applied for community status.[16] The immense majority of communities were established by officials of the Ministry of Industry at first, and later by SINAMOS.

The aims underlying the foundation of the communities, and the expectations they aroused, were extremely ambitious. There was talk of "conjugating" and "integrating" the undertaking's "component factors," reducing and ultimately eliminating disputes between capital and labor and interunion rivalry, transforming work into a means of self-fulfillment, and promoting workers' solidarity. These expectations were so great that no dispute settlement procedures were laid down, nor was any important role ascribed to the trade unions, which were first relegated to the background and later given unimportant functions. Trade unionists were, for example, forbidden to be members of the community council, and were indirectly prevented from being elected as workers' representatives on the management board of the undertaking. Responsibility for mobilization and publicity was transferred to SINAMOS.

The scheme as a whole made assumptions regarding training and cooperation that had no basis in fact in Peru. It raised great expectations and was somewhat utopian, but the realities of life soon circumscribed de facto or de jure the scope of the labor community, until all that was left was profit sharing, with minority participation in the management of undertakings that fulfilled the necessary requirements (having more than six employees and not less than a certain volume of operations). In 1973 the total number of recognized industrial communities was 3,352;[17] five years later it had risen to nearly 4,000, but none of them had acquired 50 percent or 33 percent of the capital and only a few had increased their original representation on the management boards. By the time the government changed in 1980, the communities had lost their initial momentum and their future was uncertain. It should be added that a limited form of profit sharing and participation in management was allowed in state undertakings, but the number of workers' representatives on the management board was limited to two.

The communities declined because of political changes and the national economic crisis. The act regulating small and medium-size undertakings was amended so that it greatly increased the number of undertakings that were not obliged to set up communities; inflation and recession caused many undertakings to shut down, and relegated the question of greater participation to the background. In 1982 a new Industries Act was adopted that gave workers a choice between a system similar to the one just described and one providing for a 17 percent profit sharing and a 20 percent representation on relevant company boards. Following a series of changes aimed at offering alternative schemes in exchange for a disbanding of the industrial communities, the Belaúnde government organized, at the end of 1982, a referendum to determine the future of workers' participation. The results indicated that 80 percent of workers voted to stay with the system introduced by the Velasco government. More than ten years after their inception, industrial communities were apparently taking hold and workers had no doubt found some advantages in their operation.

In Chile, from 1970 to 1973 participation was mainly by codetermination and was applied at various levels of decision making, but only in "socially" owned and "mixed" undertakings. The levels varied from sections, departments, or divisions of plants or production units to boards of directors, which in "social" undertakings comprised five government representatives, five representatives elected by the workers at a general meeting, and one representative appointed by the president of Chile. Participation also took place through assemblies and coordinating committees formed at various levels for advisory and administrative purposes. These basic rules were subject to subsequent definition in mixed undertakings, and were never applied to private enterprises. The scheme ceased to operate in "social" undertakings at the end of 1973.

Present Situation

Now that workers' management in Argentina and codetermination in Chile are things of the past, and the scope of the various forms of participation in Peru has been much reduced, their general effect would not appear to have been very great. None of these experiments has been taken as a model in other sectors or spread to other countries; and except for the industrial communities in Peru, they have been short-lived.

Some ideas on participation may nevertheless have survived the decline of the systems described above. In Chile, for example, in the late 1970s there were still 55 undertakings under workers' management that had begun to operate in 1969, most of them as the result of the bankruptcy of traditional undertakings. Although some of them did not exactly fit the definition of workers' management, the great majority of them did have some workers' management features.[18] Also, the Companies Law (*Estatuto de la empresa*) promulgated in 1975 granted workers minority representation on the management boards of undertakings and made works councils compulsory in establishments with 100 or more workers, although those provisions have not yet been applied, pending the approval of a new Labor Code.

New forms of participation have appeared in other countries. In Bolivia party codetermination (three workers' and three government representatives) was provided for in 1983 with regard to the management board of the state mining corporation (COMIBOL). In Panama the Labor

Code provides for the formation of works councils in all establishments and work places with more than 20 workers. Although their principal function is to deal with workers' grievances and complaints, the works councils are also supposed to promote an effective system of communication and understanding; this is thus an interesting experiment in participation that covers both conflictual and cooperative types. Nevertheless, in the view of a Panamanian author, the results obtained from works councils appeared in 1978 to be somewhat uneven; in some cases they appeared to have worked well, and in others to have failed for lack of interest on the part of employers and workers.[19]

The responsibilities of the joint vocational training committees formed in Mexico in 1978 are more precisely defined. These committees consist of equal numbers of workers' and employers' representatives, and organize and operate the contractually agreed system for improving the workers' vocational instruction and practical training.

Joint committees have been formed at the undertaking level in Brazil, Costa Rica, Honduras, and Mexico, solely to look after occupational safety and health. Preventing employment accidents and occupational diseases and mitigating their consequences have always been priority aims of Latin American social policy. By legislating for the formation of these committees, governments recognize that without the direct cooperation of employers and workers, effective prevention would be impossible. However, the parties concerned do not appear to have a clear understanding of the importance of such participation; in Brazil accident prevention committees do not operate regularly except in large undertakings, and although in Honduras more than 700 occupational safety and health committees were formed between 1974 and 1978, the Department of Labor later ascertained that they were operating—some efficiently, some less so—in only about 300 work places.[20]

It might well be argued that all the above are examples of experiments in individual countries, but two recent variants of participation tend to repeat themselves in Latin America and appear to indicate a more general trend toward participation. The first of these variants is workers' representation on the management boards of public enterprises; the second relates to joint bodies for the settlement of disputes or coordinated action established by collective bargaining.

The appointment of workers' representatives to the management of public enterprises now appears to be characteristic of labor relations in the public sector. There were two reasons for this: the desire to offer the workers some compensation for the restriction of their right to strike and the wish to stimulate productivity and promote an atmosphere of trust and cooperation. Whatever the reason, many countries have now established such participation by law or collective agreement. In Venezuela an act of 1966 introduced participation in all public enterprises and in those mixed enterprises in which the state had a majority interest. In Ecuador an act of 1976 introduced workers' representation into executive councils or committees of some ten state undertakings or institutions, including the railways, port administration, and electricity undertakings. In Peru the law requires that the workers be represented on the directorates of several public undertakings, and also provides for their participation in the educational units that plan and carry out the training of the staffs of the undertakings. In other countries workers' representation on the directorate is provided for in the particular laws concerning the establishment and structure of autonomous undertakings or institutes.

The Venezuelan system has interesting features. In the first place, the right of participation appears to be granted not to the workers of a particular undertaking, but to labor in general. This means that the representative is appointed by the Venezuelan Labor Confederation (CTV); that the appointment is determined by the relative strength of the various trends of opinion within the CTV; and that in practice the representative often disregards the views of the trade union or federation concerned.[21] Second, a workers' representative is appointed to the management board not only in undertakings owned by the state, or in which the state has a controlling interest, but also in autonomous institutes and economic development agencies. The importance of workers' representation in these circumstances is shown by its occurrence in 23.5 percent of all national economic activities.[22] Third, representation is fixed (limited to only one representative), regardless of how many members the management board has; the representative is paid the same amount as the other members and may be reelected an indefinite number of times. In general terms it can be said that in spite of the excessive control exercised by the top levels of the trade union movement over the appointment of the workers' representatives, their presence on the management boards of these public bodies has become institutionalized and forms part of national socioeconomic life.

Participation deriving from collective agreements is daily becoming more evident, and covers nearly all the countries of Latin America. It is of two basic types, the first consisting of the establishment of grievance committees that, like those in the United States, exist to settle grievances over the interpretation and application of the agreement, usually by conciliation and occasionally by arbitration. In some agreements in Colombia, such as the current one at the Cauca sugar mill, the joint labor–management committee is specifically stated to be the competent authority to decide on dismissals. In Mexico, in the rubber processing and sugar industries, there is a national or joint commission that, in addition to dealing with individual disputes not settled by the works councils, deals with strikes and economic disputes, and interprets and applies the agreement.

The second type consists of committees also provided for in a collective agreement but whose functions may extend beyond the validity of that agreement. Some of these committees are fully fledged works councils, while others deal with specific labor matters such as productivity,

grading, and welfare services (fellowships, housing, or canteen administration). In Brazil, for instance, where the labor relations system did not
foresee employee representation in undertakings, recent agreements concluded at Ford, Pirelli Ltd., and Volkswagen have provided for the establishment of works councils. In some undertakings (such as Petroperu and
the Colombian Oil Company), the collective agreement provided for more
than six different committees, but there is hardly any case in which such
committees participate in the economic management of the whole undertaking. Only very rarely is the trade union recognized as competent to
take part in decisions on investment, technological changes, the location
of the undertaking, or marketing policy. Nevertheless, it is only fair to recognize the quantitative importance of this kind of participation and its significance as a link between conflictual and cooperative participation. The
importance of these committees is also shown by the express recognition
of their purposes in legislation. Thus, the Mexican Federal Labor Act
states that collective agreements may establish joint committees "to carry
out certain social and economic functions."

In addition to the examples taken from collective agreements, recent
statements and actions by trade union organizations indicate a change in
the attitude of certain sections of the trade union movement that are becoming more favorable to participation. In Bolivia the National Labor
Center (COB) was pressing, in 1983, for greater participation in management in the traditional Bolivian sense of workers' control over the means
of production. In Ecuador the leaders of the Ecuadorian Confederation of
Class Organizations (CEDOC) stated in 1980 that it was necessary for the
workers to participate in the management boards of the state oil corporation and the Petroamazonas Company.[23] In Venezuela the CTV has, since
1977, repeatedly urged that participation be extended to the private sector
and that workers' representation in public undertakings be reinforced.
Some Latin American intergovernmental organizations are beginning to
echo these opinions; for example, the Economic and Social Advisory Committee of the Cartagena Agreement (known as the Andean Pact) has recommended that the feasibility of participation in the undertakings of the
region should be studied.

The Problems

Latin American experience of participation already seems sufficient
to highlight some of the main problems. The first is the trade union role in
participation. Experience in other countries shows that no system of rein-
forcing workers' participation could validly be conceived to take the place
of trade union action or be effectively applied without trade union cooperation.

Various systems have been followed in this respect in Latin America. In Brazil and Uruguay worker members are elected directly by the workers and the trade union is not involved in the participation scheme. Relegation of the trade union to the background is still more evident in Peru, where it was illegal for the workers' representative to be a trade union leader. In Panama and Mexico, in contrast, the trade union appoints its representatives to the works council. Bolivia and Venezuela carried this approach to an extreme by granting the trade union confederations the right to appoint the workers' representatives. Ecuador has taken a middle course; its legislation requires only that workers' representatives on the management boards of public undertakings shall be members of the corresponding trade union organization.

Some writers point to lack of trade union support as one of the reasons why the Uruguayan joint committees have failed to establish themselves and the Peruvian industrial communities had initial difficulties. As regards the communities there was a de facto attempt to change the situation by recognizing the trade union as having a complementary role in organizing and developing the "reformed undertakings." As early as 1973 the National Congress of Industrial Communities recognized the irreplaceable role of trade unions, the need to strengthen them so as to ensure that the communities functioned as they should, and the need to give each other mutual support for the benefit of the workers.[24] In the ensuing years relations among the undertaking, the community, and the trade union became closer—how close depended on the economic advantages offered the workers and the degree of politicization.

In Latin America relations between the trade union and the body in which participation takes place are particularly delicate, as is shown by the possibility of friction between them even where participation schemes were in no way intended to displace the trade union and the union had taken part in the election of workers' representatives to the board of directors. Such friction occurred, for example, in the Chilean mining company Gran Minería del Cobre de Chile in 1971–73, when parity representation was introduced into the board of directors. The trade union defended its independence to the utmost, and the workers' representatives on the board hastened to take independent positions; the result was serious confrontation.

A second problem relates to the promoters of participation having always regarded training, for the worker and his representatives, as one of their first priorities. The more advanced the system as regards the rights and duties of the representative, the greater the need to train the workers to exercise that function. The Peruvian system, for example, promoted various forms of training so that the workers could participate effectively in decision making and running the undertaking. In the "social property" undertakings a system of lifelong training was introduced that was designed to apply at all levels of decision and was carried out by committees formed in each undertaking. In the industrial communities training was at first the responsibility of the community council. When, later, the National Confederation of Industrial Communities was formed, it set up an education committee that was active in promoting self-education among the workers. It was, however, the government that took over many of the functions of participation, the Ministry of Industries looking after the technical aspect and SINAMOS mobilizing the public and encouraging it to participate.

In Venezuela training for economic codetermination was left to the trade union movement. In 1977 the CTV accordingly set up a Codetermination and Development Department whose functions included training for participation. In other countries, where participation is less ambitious or is limited in scope, the workers' representatives are trained by the trade unions directly involved, which run workers' education programs and courses in trade unionism for this purpose.

The third major problem is the effect of participation on the efficiency of the undertaking. This is hard to assess. In Venezuela the workers' minority participation in the management of public undertakings can be regarded as uneventful, and is thought to have no very significant effect on their smooth running.[25] In Peru a few authors have stated that in the first five years of the industrial communities, there was no improvement at all in the atmosphere of labor relations and that the number of strikes increased by 60 percent.[26] In general, it is believed that the communities' difficulties in Peru were due to the suddenness of the change, the employers' opposition, political divisions among the workers, and government attempts at control. In Chile a study made in 1976 of the undertakings under workers' management concluded that in spite of their shortcomings, they were perfectly viable; but the sample taken covered only 31 undertakings employing more than 10 workers.[27] A more recent investigation registered some improvements in the area of social property in respect of level of employment and productivity.[28]

Whatever its influence on the operation of the undertaking, various countries have taken steps to make participation work more expeditiously and effectively. In Panama the works councils are allowed only 48 hours to come to a decision on grievances. In Venezuela the CTV's Codetermination and Development Department aims at "supervising and coordinating the efficiency of the work of CTV representatives in public undertakings" and "encouraging affiliated trade union organizations to establish machinery and prepare human resources for economic codetermination."[29] In Mexico it is the duty of the authorities in charge of labor affairs to see that joint training committees function properly, and safety committees must give their services without charge during working hours. Experience in Mexico appears to show that the smooth running of the joint committees depends on the interest shown by the trade union and the efficiency of the labor inspectors.

The Special Place of Participation in Latin America

Worker participation in management has made more progress in Latin America than is usually admitted. After scant initial success, it has given clear evidence of its vitality, particularly during the 1970s. In a number of countries various kinds of works councils and forms of minority codetermination, introduced by law or collective agreements, have shown remarkable durability.

Nevertheless, participation has not followed a course leading to the establishment of works councils at first and systems of codetermination or workers' management later on; in some countries its development has been rushed. Attempts have been made to bring into being communitarian forms of participation seeking to promote harmony and integration in a system marked by a tradition of class struggle and the acceptance of lively antagonism as a normal state of affairs in labor relations. On other occasions workers' management was encouraged in undertakings declared bankrupt or hovering on the brink of bankruptcy. This explains the high failure rate of some of the experiments carried out in the 1970s.

Generally speaking, Latin American employers have resolutely opposed codetermination but have been more flexible about works councils and other limited forms of participation. Their attitude helps to explain why some minority forms of codetermination have developed more fully and durably in public undertakings, while works councils carrying out various functions not amounting to the economic management of undertakings flourish in the private sector.

Finally, it is easier to understand why the latter forms of participation have spread and endured if it is remembered that they spring from and complement other conflictual arrangements established at the undertaking level in Latin America. That they deal with matters of direct interest to the workers, make no claim to take the place of the trade union, and do not provoke opposition from the employers helps to explain why they are now so widespread.

Notes

1. The Sistema Nacional de Apoyo a la Movilización Social (SINAMOS), which functioned in Peru at the beginning of the 1970s, is the outstanding example of social mobilization in Latin America.

2. See especially ILO, *Workers' Participation in Decisions Within Undertakings* (Geneva: ILO, 1981).

3. See, for example, John A. Booth, "Political Participation in Latin America: Levels, Structure, Context, Concentration and Rationality," *Latin American Research Review* no. 3 (1979): 30–32.

4. A. Montalvo and M. Scurrah, *Participación laboral en la gestión empresarial: Actitudes de los trabajadores peruanos y su comportamiento participativo*, Documentos de Trabajo no. 2 (Lima: Escuela de Administración de Negocios para Graduados, 1974), pp. 11–12.

5. Ibid., p. 16.

6. See Jorge Selser, *Participación de los trabajadores en la gestión económica* (Buenos Aires: Ediciones Libera, 1970), pp. 69–70. For a discussion of the origins of participation in legislation, see Julio C. Neffa and Marta Novick, "Antecedentes de la participación de los trabajadores en Argentina," paper submitted to the Fifth World Congress of the International Industrial Relations Association, Paris, 1979.

7. See, for example, J. M. Gaitán Alvarez, *La reforma de la empresa en Guatemala* (Guatemala City: Instituto para el Desarrollo Económico Social de América Central, 1965), p. 88.

8. See ILO, *Participation of Workers in Decisions Within Undertakings*, Labour-Management Relations Series no. 33 (Geneva: ILO, 1969), p. 58.

9. Guillermo Cabanellas, *Compendio de derecho laboral* (Buenos Aires: Bibliográfica Omeba, 1968), vol. II, p. 230.

10. H. H. Barbagelata, "Uruguay," (1981) in R. Blanpain, ed., *International Encyclopaedia for Labour Law and Industrial Relations* (Deventer, Netherlands: Kluwer, 1981), vol. IX, p. 212.

11. Néstor Tomás Corte, "La participación del personal en el capital de la empresa," in *Tercer Congreso iberoamericano de derecho del trabajo* (Seville: Asociación Española de Derecho del Trabajo, 1970), vol. II, p. 200.

12. See, for instance, Jorge Enrique Marc, "La reforma de la empresa: Aspectos jurídicos, sociales y económicos," in *Tercer Congreso iberoamericano de derecho del trabajo* (Seville: Asociación Española de Derecho del Trabajo, 1970), vol. II, p. 234.

13. See, for instance, Rolando E. Pina, *Participación del trabajador en la gestión de la empresa: Los consejos de empresas* (Buenos Aires: Ediciones Depalma, 1968), pp. 63 ff.

14. See Osvaldo H. Vilas Figallo, "La participación de los trabajadores en una empresa de servicios públicos," communication submitted to the ILO Symposium on Workers' Participation in Decisions Within Undertakings, Oslo, 1974, pp. 2–4.

15. A. Meister and D. Retour, "Pérou 1968–80: Matériaux sur l'expérience autogestionnaire," *Autogestion* (Paris) no. 4 (1980): 425.

16. Jorge Santistevan, "El estado y los comuneros industriales," in G. Alberti, J. Santistevan, and L. Pásara, eds., *Estado y clase: La comunidad industrial en el Perú* (Lima: Instituto de Estudios Peruanos, 1977), p. 109.

17. See Centro de Estudios de Participación Popular, *La comunidad laboral* (Lima: SINAMOS, 1974), annex I. Note: the total number of industrial undertakings with more than six workers was 6,252 in that year.

18. See T. Jeanneret, L. Moraga, and L. Ruffing, *Las experiencias autogestionarias chilenas* (Santiago de Chile: Universidad de Chile, 1975), p. 4.

19. See Arturo Hoyos, "Panamá," in R. Blanpain, ed., *International Encyclopaedia for Labour Law and Industrial Relations* (Deventer, Netherlands: Kluwer, 1979), vol. VIII, p. 173.

20. ILO, "Informe al gobierno de Honduras sobre la misión multidisciplinaria del PIACT (Geneva: ILO, 1979), p. 66. (Mimeographed.)

21. See Osvaldo Montero, "El funcionamiento en la práctica de los sistemas de participación de los trabajadores en las empresas públicas venezolanas" (Caracas: 1980), p. 45. (Mimeographed.)

22. Ibid., p. 15.

23. *Informativo CLAT* (Central Latino Americana de Trabajadores), February 1980, p. 3.

24. See Luis Pásara: "Comunidad industrial y sindicato," in G. Alberti et al., *Estado y clase: La comunidad industrial en el Perú* (Lima: Instituto de Estudios Peruanos, 1977), p. 205.

25. See Montero, "El funcionamiento en la práctica . . . ," p. 27.

26. See, for instance, William Foote Whyte and Giorgio Alberti, "The Industrial Community in Peru," in *Annals of the American Academy of Political and Social Science*, May 1977, p. 108.

27. Jeanneret, Moraga, and Ruffing, *Las experiencias autogestionarias chilenas*, pp. 4 ff.

28. Oficina Internacional del Trabajo, PREALC, *Participación laboral: Experiencias en Perú y Chile*, Investigaciones sobre Empleo no. 21 (Santiago de Chile: PREALC, 1982), pp. 66, 67.

29. See Montero, "El funcionamiento en la práctica . . . ," p. 32.

7

Other Features of Labor Relations at the Undertaking Level

by
Efrén Córdova

Personnel Management

Collective bargaining and participation are not the only features of collective labor relations at the undertaking level. The most important of the others is personnel management, which calls for daily contact, individual and collective, between management and workers or their organizations. The general conception of personnel management also entails the drawing up of a policy or comprehensive view on how the management proposes to use its human resources and conduct its relations with the workers.

Personnel management was at first empirical and unsystematic, and reflected the paternalist and authoritarian management of the first decades of this century. Little was then expected of it; the employer exercised his powers of direction unilaterally, did all he could to discourage unionization, demanded loyalty from his workers, and tried to get them to remain in his employment by conceding certain fringe benefits.

However, it would not be appropriate to exaggerate this picture of personnel management or to claim that it lasted very long. Some authors have observed that most employers in Latin America—at least in industry—did not find it excessively difficult to accept advanced labor legislation and militant trade unionism in due course.[1]

Admittedly, there are still heads of undertakings who prefer to deal with "independent" trade unions (unions outside the big confederations) or who comply only reluctantly with the labor laws, but, generally speaking, important changes in the theory and practice of personnel management have been going on for years. As far back as the 1950s and 1960s there was some change, due to the interest then shown in human relations studies. A number of employers sincerely interested in their subordinates' welfare, and others in improving the public image of their undertakings, became enthusiastic about human relations and gave a new slant to their personnel management;[2] but these experiments were relatively unimportant except in Argentina, Chile, and Uruguay, and in fact did not last long.

Of more lasting effect, doubtless, was the demonstration effect of multinational undertakings, which almost invariably had personnel management departments and applied modern personnel policies. Seeing these multinationals' success in business, many undertakings decided to imitate the organization and policies in question. However, a more general recognition of the necessity and importance of personnel management was mainly due to the operation of the labor relations system itself and particularly to the proliferation of medium-size and large undertakings and the rise of trade unionism. Any undertaking employing a large work force had no alternative but to introduce a personnel policy and the machinery needed to apply it. If the undertaking's workers belonged to a trade union, management could not avoid the collective implications of the way it treated them.

Only one country in Latin America, Peru, has found it necessary to pass a law requiring undertakings employing more than 100 workers to set up a personnel or industrial relations office. Under that act, which dates from 1963, the industrial relations office is required to operate permanently, and its chief must have the authority and responsibility he needs to do his job and to settle personnel problems within the undertaking or with the labor authorities concerned.

In the remaining countries of Latin America the undertaking may, at its own discretion, decide whether to set up such offices, whose names vary with the importance ascribed to personnel matters or labor relations. In practice the decision whether to set up a personnel office or department often depends on the size of the undertaking, its line of business, and the composition of its work force (total number, the proportions of manual and nonmanual workers, the number of employees in positions of trust, the levels of training). An additional influence may be the kind of existing management; family undertakings in which the head of the family or a member of his family is also the manager are less inclined to establish such departments than are undertakings with professional managers. In small undertakings the boss usually acts as manager, coordinator, sales manager, personnel manager, and sole repository of powers of direction; but in big undertakings there is a natural tendency to delegate authority, and personnel management is generally included among the delegated functions. In medium-size undertakings, particularly in countries with developed labor relations, the practice is gaining ground of engaging a consultancy office to provide certain personnel management and labor relations services.

The importance assigned to the personnel office varies greatly from one country and undertaking to another. In big undertakings in Mexico, its chief usually ranks as an executive manager.[3] More frequently it is only a unit with subordinate responsibilities for making and applying staff policy. The smaller the undertaking, the less important the office and the fewer its staff, which may consist of only one or two people who look after basic personnel management questions.

Even where there is no personnel management structure, there will always be a personnel policy, however loosely defined, which will be applied by line officials following the management's directives. However, in Latin America written personnel policy is unusual; oral instructions or traditional rules are preferred. In practice this custom may cause serious problems, since it lends itself to confusion and uncertainty, and puts foremen and middle management in a difficult position, especially when there are changes in the higher levels or where communication is poor.

Personnel policy often is still somewhat a matter of routine, and the personnel office acts mainly as a placement and grievances office. Nevertheless, a more modern and pragmatic view of personnel policy, not very different from the usual one in more developed countries, is tending to gain ground in big undertakings. This is shown, for example, by the definitions contained in recent books on personnel management that include in it the functions of planning, organizing, and supervising the operative processes of obtaining, developing, and maintaining a work force capable of effective use by the undertaking.[4] Other definitions stress personnel harmonization, job satisfaction, and improved individual and collective output.[5]

It is not easy to draw the profile of the typical Latin American personnel manager. Until the late 1960s or the 1970s, chiefs of personnel were selected more or less at random and came from various occupations that included production services, the legal profession, and, occasionally, the armed forces. Even now many enterprises, particularly those regarding effective procedures for settling grievances as important and having a central office to supervise the other personnel offices, still prefer lawyers. The undertakings that employ former members of the armed forces are of course those keenest on discipline and the maintenance of order. It is, however, fast becoming more usual for personnel managers to be specialists in that subject or experts in labor–management relations; in Argentina an estimated 80 percent of the larger undertakings now employ such experts.

As regards the personnel office as a whole, the trend is, especially in large undertakings, toward a multidisciplinary approach that takes account of the need to enlist the cooperation of various experts—for example, the personnel department of PEMEX, the Mexican oil company, employs lawyers, psychologists, labor relations experts, organization and methods analysts, sociologists, and cost and labor analysts. It is also significant that the Peruvian act of 1963 should refer to the chief of the personnel office (usually called the "industrial relations officer") as a suitable person who must hold an (unspecified) certificate, diploma, or other qualification.

This professionalization of personnel management is also the result of developments in the labor relations system and the growth of direct contact between the parties. Moreover, it is only in the last few years that the shortage of executives capable of performing efficient personnel management functions has been remedied. There are now numerous training centers that satisfy the demand for personnel managers, including schools of business administration such as the Argentine Business University; higher institutes of administration such as the Ecuadorean ISEA; institutions for executive training such as the Argentine IDEA; centers for advanced administrative studies such as the Panamanian CESA; industrial relations schools such as those at Carabobo University in Venezuela and at the Ibero-American University of Mexico; and labor relations institutes that train advisers for production sectors. Some vocational training services and productivity centers also have programs for training higher and intermediate management personnel. Finally, the employers' organizations and chambers of commerce often provide courses in personnel techniques or set up specialized units to give this training, as happens in the Costa Rican Employers' Institute or the employers' centers set up by CO-PARMEX in Mexico.[6]

Parallel with these new training facilities professional organizations have sprung up, either specifically of personnel management experts, as in the countries with developed labor relations, or of managers and executives generally, as in Guatemala and Panama. At the regional level there is the Latin American Association of Personnel Management, which has already held several congresses.

The functions of personnel management depend, like its structure, largely on the size, style of management, and line of business of the undertaking. There is a tendency for such functions to expand, but few undertakings cover the entire range of activities now ascribed to personnel management: personnel planning, recruitment, selection, training, classification, job evaluation and grading; personnel movements (promotions, demotions, transfers, and dismissals); wage and salary administration; calculation and administration of social benefits; communications; processing complaints and grievances; improvement of working conditions; reduction of labor costs; safety and health; developing motivation, job satisfaction, and productivity; handling trade union relations; preventing disputes; negotiating the collective agreement; preparing counterproposals; and making and revising works rules.

In some cases the personnel management unit's activities are very limited and stress a specific aspect, such as placement or training; but there will always be other personnel functions carried out by the managers themselves, or in fragmented form by line officers. In such cases it is required in some countries (including Guatemala and Honduras) that works rules state to which management representatives requests for improved conditions, or complaints in general, are to be made, and that they shall indicate the hierarchy of management executives, heads of sections, foremen, and supervisors.

There has also been a qualitative change in the way most of these functions are carried out. The personnel manager no longer acts solely at his own discretion, as in the past, but often in accordance with established regulations or within the limits fixed by the labor laws. Consider, for example, the two basic responsibilities of personnel management, the commencement and termination of the employment relationship; both are restricted in certain countries by the requirements that recruitment must take place through the trade union, and that employment may not be terminated without just cause and observance of a stated procedure. Administration of wages and salaries is everywhere subject to regulations protecting the remuneration and stating how often, how, and where it is to be paid. The labor laws are so important that it may fairly be said that the first duty of a personnel manager in a Latin American undertaking is to make himself familiar with their content, interpretation, and scope.

Admittedly, the labor codes do not usually contain regulations for selecting, training, evaluating, and promoting personnel or for job classification and evaluation; but it is becoming the practice for these matters to be minutely regulated by collective agreements, many of which are so comprehensive and detailed that on such subjects the personnel office merely administers the agreement, in some cases sharing its responsibility with the trade union. For example, the personnel department of Ford Motors, Venezuela, has to administer some 25 fringe benefits provided for in the agreement (including medical and dental care, the provision of meals, Christmas bonuses, working clothes, and fellowships), deal with complaints as prescribed in the agreement, and deduct trade union dues from the wage and salary bill and distribute them to the organizations specified in the agreement. It has also had to take on additional duties connected with the large number of wage supplements stipulated in the agreement, which in some cases exceed the entire basic wage; some powerful trade unions in countries with developed labor relations have also managed to include in the agreement life, pension, and savings insurance schemes that supplement social security benefits and add to the work load of personnel management. In short, a personnel manager has to have an exhaustive knowledge of the collective agreement, and spend much of his time ensuring that it is properly applied.

Since personnel management is particularly important in big undertakings, and since it is in these undertakings that the labor laws are more fully applied and the collective agreements are the most comprehensive and detailed, it might be supposed that because personnel management has to live with all these factors that erode its freedom of action, it becomes a merely executive and mechanical function. Neither the law nor the agreement can, however, regulate everything, and there is always room both for an imaginative personnel policy covering other aspects of labor force development and for a personnel management applying the appropriate regulation or clause of the agreement.

Personnel management may well have lost some of its powers of discretion on individual aspects of its terms of reference (recruitment, classification, promotions, dismissals, wage and salary administration), but it has gained in importance and in freedom to exercise its imagination in collective matters. It is constantly faced with the challenge of gaining the cooperation of the whole staff, promoting a measure of harmony with the trade union or, at worst, maintaining peaceful coexistence with it, and helping to settle the difficulties arising from relations among individuals and groups.

Experience in Latin America shows that besides his part in preparing, negotiating, and administering the collective agreement, the modern personnel manager is beginning to interest himself in improving vertical, lateral, and diagonal communication, standardizing the principles applied in dispute settlement, and encouraging workers' participation in the organization of their work. Ultimately, the traditional pattern of behavior laid down by rules tends to be enlarged in an effort to turn personnel management into a dynamic endeavor to prevent rather than cure. In taking this approach, many heads of undertakings recognize that this is the kind of personnel management that may most influence the state of human relations in Latin American undertakings.

Works Rules

Works rules constitute another feature of collective relations at the undertaking level. They consist of the body of rules governing the carrying out of the work and the day-to-day operation of the undertaking, which must be observed by employer and workers alike. They are sometimes drawn up jointly by the employer and the trade union, though the former usually plays the leading part.

The role of works rules in practice depends on whether there is a collective agreement. It might even be said that their value as rules binding on all, and as a means of channeling collective relations, is in inverse proportion to the extent of development reached by collective bargaining in the undertaking. If collective bargaining is well established and leads to comprehensive and detailed agreements, it may be assumed that the works rules are unimportant, or even that in practice there are none. The parties and the government will, however, regard works rules as important if there is no agreement, or if bargaining is still in its first stages. The notion of works rules as a complement to collective bargaining rather than as a substitute for it has not yet taken root in Latin America, except in big undertakings in Mexico.

This explains why the countries of Central America and of the greater part of the Andean group pay special attention to regulating works rules, whereas such rules are of little importance in Argentina, Chile, and Uruguay, where there is sometimes a complete lack of awareness of any need to adopt regulations concerning them. Some Central American countries, such as Costa Rica and El Salvador, have set up a works rules section in their ministry of labor to examine and approve draft works rules submitted to it. Others have deliberately promoted the formulation of works rules as a means of filling in the gaps left by collective bargaining and providing the workers with an ad hoc system of protection, especially in occupational safety and health. In Costa Rica in 1979 more than 60 standing committees of workers were formed to draw up and approve works rules.[7] In El Salvador the Ministry of Labor registered 272 works rules in 1979–1981.[8]

It could also be argued that the pattern of work intrinsic in the functioning of a big undertaking makes for internal organization of labor of a kind not always found in a collective agreement, and still less in individual employment contracts, which are almost invariably verbal. Even if the agreement contains many regulatory clauses, it may have to be supplemented by a long list of prescriptions or practical instructions on how services are to be performed and properly coordinated, and how orderly and regular performance of work is to be maintained. This is why attention is still being paid to preparation of works rules in Mexico although collective bargaining is very advanced there. In Venezuela many undertakings have works rules, although there is no regulation expressly requiring them to be made. In Argentina, where there is no legal requirement for works rules, many employers are reluctant to put into writing rules to be observed in doing work, for fear that in a dispute the workers may use them as a pretext for the form of protest known as "working to rule."

Not only are there many countries in which there is no regulation of works rules at all, but even in countries where such regulation does exist, it is not clearly stated to be compulsory. The minimum number of workers whose permanent employment in an undertaking makes preparation of works rules compulsory varies; generally it is 10, but in Colombia and Honduras only 5 for commercial undertakings and 20 in agricultural, stock-raising, and forestry undertakings. In Bolivia the number is everywhere 20, and in Peru 100.

Works rules continue to be associated in principle with the employer's prerogative of managing his undertaking, but there is a trend toward their approval by agreement. In Ecuador, for example, a few years ago works rules were regarded merely as an example of "what the boss says goes"; the labor codes placed hardly any restrictions on them beyond requiring them to be approved by the labor authorities, who in practice raised very few difficulties.[9] In other countries the rules are neither bilateral nor produced unilaterally by the employer; their draft text is given to the undertakings by the department of labor. Few countries allow the employer simply to produce works rules out of his own pocket, some expressly stating that the trade union must take part in formulating them or must first be consulted, others that they must be made known to the workers; almost everywhere they must be registered and approved by the department of labor.

Only in the Dominican Republic is the employer expressly allowed to formulate and amend works rules on his own, provided he then deposits two copies of them with the Department of Labor. In Costa Rica, Honduras, Mexico, and Paraguay works rules are formulated by a joint committee of workers' and employers' representatives. In Peru draft rules may not be approved until the labor authorities have made a visit of inspection. If the works rules do not comply with the law, the authorities must return them to the employer for correction, but since the law does not always fix a time limit for making the corrections, the process of adopting the works rules often comes to a standstill.

As regards their value as a source of law, the rules generally come after legislative enactments, general regulations, and the collective agreement. In some countries they come still lower, after usage and custom; this might be challenged on the grounds that usage and custom should be taken into account when the rules are drafted but that thereafter, and once they have been approved, a new written order of things is introduced that should take precedence over the unwritten order. The problem arises when the value of works rules is examined in relation to individual contracts; in this event the employer's power of administration, which might entail certain quasi-legislative powers within the undertaking, conflicts with the contractual character of the employment relationship, which prevents that relationship from being changed unilaterally by one of the parties.

Some countries consider that works rules may not infringe the rights granted in the individual contracts already in force when they are adopted, but could be regarded as supplementing such contracts should the rules introduce conditions not contractually agreed to by the parties. In the latter connection, it is assumed that the workers show their tacit acceptance of the works rules by accepting employment in the undertaking. The Uruguayan courts, however, have maintained that works rules form part of the individual contract and are therefore subject to legal supervision. This means that the propriety of dismissals under the works rules, for example, must be judged by the courts in accordance with the general principles of labor law, and not only according to the works rules.[10]

Many labor codes require works rules to contain certain basic provisions and sometimes spell out in more detailed fashion the subjects that must be included in them. In practice, however, most works rules do no more than reproduce certain statutory provisions (generally on safety and health) and add to them a few rules on working hours and rest periods. The parties appear to feel certain inhibitions against making full use of the works rules; the workers look on them as an example of the employer's power, and the employer fears that they may be used against him in unexpected ways. Neither party has been willing to realize that works rules offer the opportunity to supplement the collective agreement, improve working conditions and the quality of life, and streamline production. Trade unions especially have preferred to ignore works rules or regard them as a poor substitute for collective bargaining, without realizing that when the law requires that the unions shall be consulted before works rules are adopted or revised, it opens the door to a new form of participation, however minor; and the employers often cannot see that works rules and their revision are an effective way of exercising the *jus variandi* (the employer's prerogative of amending certain working conditions not laid down by contract).

Examination of the provisions that the codes require to be included in works rules shows notable similarities in regard to working hours, kinds of wages and forms of payment, discipline, and safety and health. Works rules occasionally include substantive requirements, as in Honduras (where they contain a list of permissible disciplinary measures, such as reprimand or suspension for a limited number of days) and Ecuador (on the classification of the permanent work force). At other times they lay down rules of procedure for dealing with grievances within the undertaking (such as the appointment of works council members or of the officials to whom complaints must be submitted). Practice differs as to whether works rules shall also include technical or administrative rules made directly by the employers for the smooth running of the undertaking (including the production process). Honduras, Mexico, and Paraguay expressly exclude them; Costa Rica, the Dominican Republic, and Guatemala regard them as suitable for inclusion.

Finally, for works rules to serve their purpose, they have to be known by all members of the undertaking, which means that they must be given adequate publicity. This is usually done by displaying them at various places in the establishment where the workers will see them, especially on the bulletin board. In some countries the law requires that works rules shall be printed in pamphlet form and that the pamphlet shall be distributed to the workers free of charge.

Trade Union Action

In spite of its political leanings and avowed aim of changing society as a whole, the Latin American trade union movement has always been extremely active at the undertaking level, mainly because of its basic structure, almost everywhere relying on enterprise unions, and the law, which from the first decided to concentrate the labor relations system at that level. Government intervention has been decisive here; it was legislation that gave enterprise unions advantages over industrial unions and even hindered the operation of some industrial unions. In some countries the law has required the trade unions to appoint a member of their managing committee to maintain contact with the undertaking and the employers' organizations.

Even where there are no provisions for workers' representation in the undertaking and even if bargaining is at the level of a branch of the economy, there is nearly always such representation in practice. In Argentina, where the current system does not recognize enterprise trade unions, it is nevertheless usual to establish internal committees at the undertaking level, their members being appointed in accordance with the collective agreement, and to have shop stewards who, although elected by the workers, must be trade union members and are in fact yet another trade union body. In Mexico the national industrial trade unions are in the habit of forming sections or local branches at the undertaking level that, although not empowered to conclude collective agreements, play an important part in labor relations in undertakings. The only country to which this preliminary observation is perhaps inapplicable is Brazil, where the trade unions are organized on a geographical basis and play only a secondary part in undertakings except in the industrial areas of greater São Paulo.

Admittedly there are also, in various countries, other bodies at the undertaking level that at first sight appear to have been conceived to take the place of the trade union—for example, the works councils in Ecuador and Panama. However, the Ecuadorian works council was formed as a trade union cell at the undertaking level to conclude collective agreements, to take part in collective disputes, to defend workers' rights, and to further its members' economic and social advancement. As an Ecuadorean author explains, they were a product of the weak and slow trade union development, which made it necessary for the law to establish a body enjoying certain prerogatives to represent and protect the workers.[11] For all practical purposes, therefore, it is an enterprise union under another name, established by law and not necessarily linked to the rest of the trade union movement. The Panamanian works council's parity composition (two of its four members are appointed by the trade union) makes it a form of workers' participation exercised through the trade union.

Generally speaking, the scale of trade union action in practice depends largely on the protection and facilities allowed the trade union by law, the relevant clauses in collective agreements, and the powers given by the trade union's constitution to the official(s) representing the workers within the undertaking.

Reference was made in Chapter 2 to the first of these factors. It covers the whole system of protection for the leaders and founders of the trade union, and is known in nearly all the countries of Latin America as the charter of trade union rights (fuero sindical). Although in many countries trade unions have now reached a degree of institutionalization that goes beyond the protection provided by such a charter, the latter still serves to facilitate the establishment of a trade union, particularly in countries where labor relations are still in the formative stage. The charter is not generally extended to cover unorganized groups, and this helps to explain why the collective relations established by such groups are so precarious.

The collective agreement clauses at times attempt to extend the scope of the charter of trade union rights recognized by law so that it covers, for example, the trade union's sectional committee, trade union delegates, and members of certain committees. It is, however, more usual for such clauses to seek to confer functional and economic facilities not granted by law. A 1981 ILO study on labor relations in public undertakings found that the following facilities were generally included in the agreements made in this sector in nine countries of Latin America: provision of premises for meetings or funds to build or rent them, means of transport or funds for their purchase and maintenance, a trade union bulletin board, paid leave of absence (for the general secretary, members of the executive committee, and other officials), fares and travel allowances for certain trade union functions, facilities for trade union training, and facilities for access to the undertaking as well as for the collection of trade union dues.[12]

Some of these facilities appear typical of the atmosphere of cooperation that prevails in many public undertakings, but many of them also appear in collective agreements made in the private sector. In Venezuela, for example, collective agreements concluded in the manufacturing industry provide that time spent by trade union delegates in attending to the workers' demands shall be considered as part of the working day and paid at basic wage rates. When the matter is very important, some agreements add that the company will consider granting paid leave of absence to the entire executive committee of the trade union.[13] It is, however, more usual to fix limits on the number of trade union officials entitled to leave of absence or to stipulate the total number of hours or days of paid leave of absence granted to the trade union; this rule also leads some collective agreements to limit the number of trade union delegates, which is generally proportionate to the number of workers in the undertaking.

Equipped with such protection and facilities, many trade unions in Latin America are extremely active in representing and protecting their members' interests, and this activity directly or indirectly affects the most important of the employer's functions, from recruitment of personnel to termination of employment. These activities may be carried out in a spirit of cooperation or confrontation, and they may be provided for in the agreement or form part of the trade union's routine functions. It used to be thought that the trade union's activity in undertakings lay in its traditional function of challenge and protest, but in many cases there is without doubt also an element of supervision, and even of cooperation and codetermination, that is often underestimated and has not yet been sufficiently appreciated.

It might be supposed that recruitment and selection are basic functions of personnel management, but there is certainly a de facto or de jure situation in various countries of Latin America that greatly restricts that function. The de facto situation occurs in nearly all the ports of the region and in some trades, such as the construction sector, for which the trade union normally supplies labor. The de jure situation applies above all to Honduras, Mexico, and Venezuela, where the union security clauses are accepted and where, in many undertakings, recruitment is done through the trade union. In Mexico the union keeps side by side its lists of members and lists of applicants for job vacancies and for membership in the trade union. When a vacancy occurs, the trade union submits a number of candidates within a prescribed period and the undertaking chooses one of them. In Honduras a number of undertakings in Tegucigalpa and San Pedro Sula are in the habit of informing the trade union of vacant posts so that it can submit the names of candidates. This trade union function is still more prevalent in Venezuela, where about three-quarters of the workers in undertakings that have a collective agreement are appointed from a list submitted by the trade union.

Less obvious in the law, but very general in practice, is trade union action to defend workers whose employment is terminated by the employer. This is explicitly provided for by law in only a few countries, such as Peru, and then only with regard to redundancy for economic or technical reasons or force majeure. Practice under the collective agreements is, however, extremely rich in this respect; it may even be said that in several countries dismissals cannot be made without first informing or consulting the trade union. In Venezuela a number of agreements merely state that "the company undertakes to inform the works council or trade union in advance of intended dismissals, except where cause is shown for doing otherwise." Other agreements are even stricter and require the undertaking not only to notify the union of dismissals but also to submit its recommendations to the trade union for consideration. It is more usual in Venezuela for the agreement to state that in the event of collective dismissals, a meeting of the leaders of the undertaking and the trade union shall be held to "review and consider" the final decision, and that individual dismissals shall be submitted to the works council or grievance committee before the employer takes a decision.[14]

Perhaps the extreme examples of trade union intervention in dismissals are in the Mexican oil industry, where the collective agreement in force requires the employer to consult the trade union from the time the facts are investigated up to the final decision, and to discuss the effects of commutation with it. Moreover, in Mexico the employer is obliged to dismiss workers who resign or are expelled from the trade union, in compliance with a union security arrangement called the "exclusion for separation" clause—a clause that would be null and void in nearly all other countries of the region.

Besides recruiting the worker and protecting him in a dismissal situation, the trade union performs a wide variety of functions, of which probably the most important are putting forward its members' grievances, looking after their interests, and seeing that the collective agreements are complied with. Sometimes (as in Chile, El Salvador, and Venezuela) the unions may not present the workers' claims unless expressly requested to do so in writing by their members; on other occasions the representation functions are determined by the terms of the constitution of the union, and in various other countries (Bolivia, Colombia, and Panama) they are established by law. In Argentina a distinction is made between representation within the undertaking, for which the trade union enjoys an implicit legal mandate, and representation in dealing with judicial and administrative bodies, for which prior application by the person concerned is necessary.

Monitoring the proper application of a collective agreement may mean either seeing that the employer duly applies its normative and "relational" clauses, or guaranteeing that members of the trade union will observe it. In some countries (Colombia, Honduras, and to a certain extent Panama) the labor code provides that the trade union shall promote closer relations and cooperation between itself and the employer. In Colombia, for example, one of its main functions is stated to be the promotion of closer relations between employers and workers, founded on justice, mutual respect, and observance of the law. Similarly, the Labor Code of the Dominican Republic includes among trade union aims that of seeking a just and peaceful settlement of disputes over the implementation of labor contracts entered into by union members. In other countries (such as Venezuela and Chile) the legislation expressly states that one of the trade union's functions is to report irregularities in the application of the law to the labor authorities.

Another important activity of trade unions in the undertaking relates to the establishment and operation of the various committees and bodies to be formed in accordance with the collective agreement. There are, first of all, the grievances committees, which are steadily becoming more usual, the disciplinary committees, job classification or grading committees, training committees, safety and health committees, and welfare committees, which are also steadily becoming more common in the region. In some undertakings in countries with developed labor relations, in which cooperation is well advanced, trade unions are especially consulted about working hours, staggered holidays, and staff changes.

Union Security Clauses

For the trade union to do its job efficiently, it needs maximum support from the workers and adequate funds. These conditions are not easily fulfilled where unionization rates are still low, the status of members fluctuates, and trade union dues are meager or not paid regularly. Only when all these conditions are present can the trade union discuss with authority, be equipped to negotiate, obtain the services of advisers, represent its members effectively, and carry out social welfare on a large scale.

Some countries have tried to meet these needs by including union security clauses in the collective agreement—for instance, the closed shop clause stipulating that workers may not be employed in the undertaking unless they first join the trade union. In this Mexico was the pioneer country: the Veracruz and Tamaulipas trade unions were the first to win this concession under the 1917 Constitution, and the validity of closed shop clauses was first sanctioned by legislation in 1931. Honduras and Paraguay followed the Mexican example and expressly recognized the legitimacy of the clause in question; but in Honduras it may not have retroactive effect, and in Paraguay it is in practice little used. In Venezuela recognition is given to trade union preference clauses whereby, other things being equal, employers are bound to give preference in hiring to a certain proportion (in practice between 66 and 75 percent) of workers put forward by the trade union. Venezuela is one of the few countries in the world to have incorporated the validity of union security clauses into its Constitution.[15]

Nevertheless, union security clauses have everywhere provoked heated debate, as their application raises problems concerning the freedom to join or not join a trade union, their possible effect on the right to work, and the erosion of certain of the employers' prerogatives. It is therefore not surprising that many Latin American countries (Argentina, Brazil, Costa Rica, Chile, the Dominican Republic, Guatemala, Haiti, Nicaragua, Panama, Peru, and Uruguay) expressly prohibit such clauses.

To remove some of the objections to union security clauses, some countries have developed the "trade union solidarity levy" (equivalent in practice to the agency shop). Trade union membership is not compulsory, but all workers, whether trade union members or not, have to pay a contribution as compensation to the trade union for the benefits it obtains for all workers. In this Colombia was the pioneer country, introducing this contribution as far back as 1950; the present position there is that nonunionized workers benefiting from the agreement pay half the normal contribution or the full contribution, depending on whether fewer or more than one-third of all workers in the undertaking belong to the union. In Ecuador, Honduras, and Panama no such distinction is made, all nonunionized workers being obliged to pay the full amount. While in Colombia and Honduras this form of checkoff is contingent on the existence of a collective agreement applicable to all the work force, no such condition is required in the other two countries. In Argentina an agency shop system was in force for more than 20 years, the trade union contribution being fixed by the union and applying to all workers in the activity. This system was discontinued in 1979 by the Trade Union Act, limiting periodic contributions to trade union members and allowing only a single annual contribution to be levied on nonunionized labor benefiting from an approved agreement.

Solidarity levies, although apparently favored by most recent thinking, still provoke spirited discussion. One side argues that a levy on nonunionized labor gives the trade union powers that are almost those of a taxation office, and coerces a nonunion worker into paying trade union dues, with the aggravating factor that their amount is fixed by the body receiving them.[16] The other side says the agency shop is a natural consequence of the principle that the agreements should be generally applied (*erga omnes*) and is a means of ensuring that the presence of workers who receive the benefits of the agreement without contributing to the maintenance of the bargaining agent (free riders) does not lead to an overall weakening of the trade union.

A third way of meeting the trade union's need for funds is to levy contributions on trade union members by deducting them from pay.[17] Where this "checkoff" is provided for in the agreement, the employer undertakes to act as an agent for collection and payment of union dues and the trade union is spared the difficulties of collecting contributions directly from members. The checkoff may be compulsory or voluntary, depending on whether it applies automatically to all members or only to those who have stated in writing that they agree to it. The latter variant obliges personnel management to ascertain in advance to which trade union (if there is more than one) dues are payable, to verify that the worker is a member of that union, and to see that his authorization to deduct the dues is in order and renewed as necessary. Both variants often oblige management to split the contribution among the trade union, the federation, and occasionally the confederation, paying each the percentage fixed in the collective agreement or stipulated by the trade union. The checkoff system is voluntary in the Dominican Republic, Guatemala, and Peru, and compulsory in Bolivia and El Salvador.

The Brazilian *contribuição sindical* deserves special mention. It is required by the Brazilian Consolidation of Labor Laws and applies to all workers, whether unionized or not. The amount of the contribution is one day's wage in March of each year, and is paid by checkoff; 5 percent of the total amount collected by the employer goes to the trade union confederation, 15 percent to the trade union federation, 54 percent to the trade union, 20 percent to the Department of Labor's unemployment fund, and the rest to the Bank of Brazil. This contribution and a special checkoff fixed in the collective agreement, or by the labor courts when wage increases are agreed upon, are the trade union's main sources of income; in 1974 Mericle estimated that both represented 59 percent of trade union income in Metropolitan São Paulo.[18] For Brazil the total of the *contribuição sindical* at the start of the 1980s amounted to between 70 and 90 percent of the income of the small and medium-scale trade unions. In 1980 the total checkoff deducted for the *contribuição sindical* was estimated at 6 billion cruzeiros. The use of these funds is strictly regulated by law so as to prevent the formation of strike funds and to control trade union affairs.[19]

Brazilian experts justify this contribution on the grounds that the activities of the trade union are in the general interest, since it cooperates with the state as a technical and advisory body, provides welfare services, and is responsible for furthering the interests of the occupational category or labor sector concerned. They accordingly feel that the state should grant the union the subsidies or financial aid it needs to do this work.[20] The strongest trade unions could, however, do without the contribution, and a few have refused to levy it, on the grounds that it would compromise their independence.

Extent of Joint Action

The main conclusion to be drawn from this chapter is that at the plant level there is much more bilateral and joint action than might be supposed at first sight. As an Argentine writer points out, in this sector of labor relations (at the undertaking level) the forces at work make not only for opposition (those generally get most attention); they also make for cooperation, bringing the parties to understand that they are each part of a whole and share some interests.[21] As will be seen in Chapter 8, this aspect of cooperation is also evident at higher levels.

Notes

1. See, for instance, Frank Brandenburg, "The Development of Latin American Private Enterprise," in Stanley M. David and Louis Wolf Goodman, eds., *Workers and Managers in Latin America* (Lexington, Mass.: D. C. Heath, 1972), p. 183.

2. See Eduardo Groba et al., *Lecturas sobre administración de personal* (Buenos Aires: Ediciones Macchi, 1974), pp. 7–8.

3. See "Contrato colectivo de trabajo celebrado entre Petróleos Mexicanos y el Sindicato de Trabajadores Petroleros de la República Mexicana" (Mexico City: PEMEX, 1979), p. 28.

4. See, for instance, Claudio Fuchs, José A. Muga, and Luis Orlandini, *Tres enfoques al desarrollo de la empresa a través de sus recursos humanos* (Santiago de Chile: DERTO, Universidad de Chile, 1976), p. 8.

5. See, for instance, Raymundo Amaro G., *Administración de personal* (Santo Domingo: Impresora UNPHU, 1974), p. 22.

6. See ILO, "Las organizaciones de empleadores y su papel en la formación de ejecutivos, especialmente para pequeñas y medianas empresas y en materia de relaciones laborales," document submitted to a regional technical seminar for Latin American employers' organizations (Lima: ILO, 1978), p. 3. (Mimeographed.)

7. Ministerio de Trabajo y Seguridad Social de Costa Rica, *Memoria anual 1979* (San José: the Ministry, 1980), p. 29.

8. Gobierno de El Salvador, *Informe de labores, octubre 1979–marzo 1981* (San Salvador: the Government, 1981), p. 4.

9. Hugo Valencia Haro, *Legislación ecuatoriana del trabajo* (Quito: Editorial Universitaria, 1979), p. 359. In Colombia the Ministry of Labor in 1980 approved 518 works rules and rejected 242. See Ministerio de Trabajo, *Memoria* (Bogota: Sección de Biblioteca y Publicaciones, 1981), p. 53.

10. See H. H. Barbagelata, "Uruguay" (1981), in R. Blanpain, ed., *International Encyclopaedia for Labour Law and Industrial Relations*, vol. X (Deventer, Netherlands: Kluwer, 1981), p. 92.

11. Valencia, Haro, *Legislación ecuatoriana del trabajo*, loc. cit.

12. Arturo S. Bronstein, ed., *Las relaciones laborales en las empresas estatales de América latina* (Geneva: ILO, 1981), pp. 59–61.

13. See Federación de Trabajadores Petroleros, Químicos y sus Similares de Venezuela (FEDEPETROL), *Resumen de los contratos colectivos de trabajo celebrados en la industria del petróleo de Venezuela* (Caracas: FEDEPETROL, 1972), p. 84.

14. A summary of relevant collective bargaining clauses in Venezuela is in Antonio Espinoza Prieto, *Estabilidad en el trabajo* (Caracas: Imprenta Nueva, 1969), pp. 255 ff.

15. For more detailed discussion of these clauses, see E. Córdova and M. Ozaki, "Union Security Arrangements: An International Overview," in *International Labour Review,* Jan.–Feb. 1980, pp. 19–38.

16. References to the extent of this debate in Argentina are in A. Ruprecht, *Asociaciones gremiales de trabajadores* (Buenos Aires: Victor P. de Zavalía, 1980), pp. 100–06.

17. See E. Córdova, "The Check-off System: A Comparative Study," in *International Labour Review,* May 1969, pp. 463–91.

18. Kenneth S. Mericle, "Conflict Regulation in the Brazilian Industrial Relations System" (Ann Arbor, Mich.: University Microfilms International, 1976), p. 114.

19. Amaury de Souza, "A CLT procura novos caminhos nas vésperas de seus 40 anos," in *Jornal do Brasil,* Spec. Supp. Apr. 12, 1981.

20. Arnaldo Sussekind, Delio Maranhão, and Segadas Vianna, *Instituições de direito do trabalho* (Rio de Janeiro; Livraria Freitas Bastos, 1974), vol. II, pp. 809–11; and Arnaldo Sussekind, "A contribuição sindical compulsoria e o desconto de salário em favor do sindicato," in *Tendências do direito do trabalho contemporâneo* (São Paulo: Editoria LTr, 1980), vol. II, pp. 74 ff.

21. A. Vázquez Vialard, *Derecho del trabajo y seguridad social* (Buenos Aires: Editorial Astrea, 1978), p. 487.

8

Tripartite Cooperation

by
Efrén Córdova

Rationale and Development

The origins of present-day cooperation go back to the first decades of this century. In Argentina, for example, the tripartite councils responsible for mediation in labor disputes date from 1912. In Chile employers and workers have been represented in the administration of social insurance since 1924. In Mexico the Federal Conciliation and Arbitration Board was set up in 1917.

Although tripartite cooperation has been through many ups and downs, and although it is sometimes more nominal than real, it has nevertheless reached sizable dimensions in most Latin American countries. This development has been due largely to the requirements and special features of labor relations in the region. The need was felt to raise labor relations to the highest plane of national life, to the power centers where social policy is made or applied; it was also thought appropriate to palliate, through tripartite cooperation, the confrontation and conflict that had for many years been typical of labor relations in Latin America.

Tripartite cooperation has also served to fill the vacuum created by the relative lack of direct contact, basic agreements, and high-level joint committees that in other countries contribute to channeling and promoting collective labor relations. The ILO, too, has encouraged tripartite cooperation by embodying the principle in a number of international conventions and recommending its wider adoption in resolutions adopted at regional conferences.[1]

The department of labor has always been the hub of tripartite cooperation. Its functions include responsibility for drawing up and directing the government's labor policy and promoting a balance between conflicting social forces. In Latin America departments of labor have been an obvious meeting place for employers and workers and representatives of their organizations, all of whom looked to the departments to solve their problems. Labor administrators have also been interested in encouraging employers and workers to take part in developing and applying labor policies. Many years of frustration in applying labor legislation had made them realize that without the support of the organizations directly concerned, it would not be possible to implement government policy. Tripartism, moreover, served a double purpose: first, tripartite cooperation provided departments of labor with the opportunity to join forces with organizations of employers and of workers so as to strengthen their own position in relation to other government agencies and to the community as a whole, and thereby accentuate their role in the process of economic and social development; second, discussions between the parties and the labor authorities made it possible to reach at least the degree of social consensus required for the normal conduct of production activities. To some extent tripartite cooperation represented a government effort to induce labor to accept the existing social structure by giving it representation in a number of sociopolitical organs.

Management and labor also displayed interest in gradually strengthening their direct contacts and their links with the labor authorities. They had learned from experience that when neither side had the opportunity to know the point of view of the other, or when no use was made of the intermediary function of departments of labor, the activities of both employers and trade unions were inevitably restricted and precarious. The development of tripartite cooperation was resisted only by the most obdurate employers, who sometimes refused to recognize the existence of the other party, and by the most uncompromising trade unionists. Otherwise, the tendency both in the more moderate and pragmatic trade unions and on the part of professional management as it evolved in the region was to accept and promote tripartism.

With the converging of these two different interests—that of the parties concerned and that of the labor authorities—tripartism flourished in Latin America. The initial somewhat sporadic contacts, dating back to the establishment of departments of labor, gradually gave way to more institutionalized forms of rapprochement and even to systems of collaboration.

More recently the trend toward tripartite cooperation has been reflected in the texts of the constitutions of a number of Latin American countries. In Argentina, Brazil, Ecuador, Guatemala, Honduras, and Mexico, for example, the constitution provides for tripartite bodies to determine minimum wages, settle labor disputes, or administer social security. In others, such as Panama and Uruguay, the constitution provides for the setting up of economic and social councils, including representatives of management and labor.

Where tripartite cooperation is not provided for in the national constitution, it usually operates under special legislation or, in some cases, under decrees or regulations. In several Latin American countries (including Mexico and Panama), the labor code contains a special chapter on different forms of tripartite cooperation in relation to industrial relations problems.

There have been few cases in the region where tripartite cooperation has been instituted by basic agreements or joint statements of management and labor. A few isolated examples of agreements of this kind at the national level are the *Pacto obrero-industrial* signed in Mexico in 1945 between the Confederation of Chambers of Industry (CONCAMIN) and the Confederation of Workers of Mexico (CTM), the *Triángulo de Esquintla* in Guatemala in 1947, the tripartite conference in Colombia in 1967, the National Compromise Agreement (*Acta de compromiso nacional*) of 1973 in Argentina, and the Alliance for Production (*Allianza para la producción*) of 1977 in Mexico; but the practical significance of these agreements has not been great. In 1981 the major trade union confederations in Colombia and the principal national organizations of employers signed an agreement on labor relations that begins with a clear reference to the adoption of a policy of concerted action and goes on to announce what measures should be adopted, along the lines of those typical of the Scandinavian basic agreements, to improve the conduct of labor relations. The agreement states, for example, that collective agreements must establish procedures for the settlement of complaints, grievances, and disputes over interpretation.

In addition to the basic agreements there are a few cases of informal arrangements for facilitating contact and the study and consideration of labor problems. The outstanding example is that of the Venezuelan high-level commission that met monthly and was composed of the president of the republic, the minister of labor, and the chairmen and vice-chairmen of the Federation of Chambers of Commerce and Production (FEDECAMARAS) and of the Confederation of Labor of Venezuela (CTV). However, arrangements of this kind are exceptional, and cooperation usually occurs on government initiative and is provided for in the law. Contrary to the practice in other countries, such as Spain, which has sought consensus through agreements that have led in some cases to the formation of tripartite bodies, in Latin America the priority has been the formation of tripartite bodies that sometimes lead to agreements, but only rarely on basic problems.

The statutory nature of tripartite cooperation should provide a firm basis for its development in Latin America, but in some cases the recognition of tripartism has not gone beyond the words of the constitution or the relevant statute. In some countries there has been a tendency to recognize the desirability of tripartite cooperation as a principle but to postpone action to make it a reality, or to restrict it to narrow fields. Alternatively, tripartite cooperation is resorted to sporadically when difficulties are encountered in the application of some aspect of social policy or when a crisis threatens, without any clear intention of making it permanent.

The highly politicized context in which tripartite cooperation has evolved in many countries and the practice of direct appointment of labor and industry representatives by the government go far to explain the weaknesses in the application of the tripartite principle. This does not mean that there have not been countries (or industries in a country) where tripartism has been practiced successfully. The results of years of effort to develop the concept and to make it a reality show that tripartism can be applied to many different types of subject and with widely varying powers. In Latin America tripartite bodies have been set up with various types of functions: consultative, administrative, supervisory, standard-setting, and judicial. The last two types are mainly found in labor relations, where it has been government policy to enable the concerned parties to participate in setting labor or industrial relations standards and arriving at decisions on disputed matters in these fields. Administrative bodies have mainly been used in areas bordering the labor field, such as social security and the administration of certain social services. Bodies with powers limited to making recommendations or advising the government are found in many areas of activity, especially in economic and social development planning.

As for its structure, tripartite cooperation has been carried out by permanent boards or by short-lived ad hoc committees with limited terms of reference, and frequently by purely informal and circumstantial contacts. Generally these do not last long, but there are examples of contacts or meetings that tend to become institutionalized, as occurred in Venezuela with the high-level commission.

Scope

No survey of the magnitude and scope of tripartite cooperation in Latin America would be complete without some mention of the matters to which this cooperation relates. These are either specific labor questions or matters of a general character.

Three Main Specialized Areas

The three areas in which tripartite consultation has been most widespread are the determination of minimum wages and other terms of employment, the settlement of labor disputes, and the administration of social security. The activity of tripartite bodies in these areas has been so extensive that, according to some specialists, it already forms a permanent part of Latin American labor law.[2]

In the case of minimum wages, it has long been regarded as appropriate and useful to include representatives of employers and workers on the wage-fixing bodies so as to associate the holders or beneficiaries of a right in the determination of its extent.[3] Nearly all countries in the region have established tripartite bodies that participate in the fixing of minimum wage scales. Commissions have been set up in some countries on a territorial basis (states and municipalities), and in others on an industry basis. In addition to the local bodies there is usually a national commission that includes members appointed by the most representative employers' and workers' confederations: such commissions exist in Argentina, Brazil, Colombia, Costa Rica, the Dominican Republic, Ecuador, El Salvador, Guatemala, Haiti, Mexico, Nicaragua, Panama, and Paraguay.

The functions assigned to the wage commissions vary to a marked extent, depending on the legal system. In some countries their role is confined to recommending scales as a basis for a subsequent decision by the government; in others they not only actually lay down minimum wage rates but also supervise their application. The commissions also have power to require the production of past records and to carry out investigations or studies as necessary.

Participation in the determination of minimum wages can be an instructive experience in promoting labor relations for employers' and workers' representatives alike—and for those they represent, if the representatives explain and obtain their support for decisions—since it involves them in an exercise resembling negotiation. To cite only one example, it has been argued in Uruguay that one of the greatest benefits of the wage councils system set up in the 1940s was its contribution to the development of the trade union movement.

From minimum wage determination, tripartism moved on to cover other forms of remuneration. In Mexico, for example, the proportion of profits to be allocated to profit sharing is determined by a national commission on workers' participation in the profits of enterprises, consisting of a chairman, a tripartite council of representatives, and a technical director. The establishment of this commission in 1963 was a notable development, since until then nowhere in Latin America did workers have any voice in decisions on profit sharing.

Other conditions of employment, such as paid leave, productivity bonuses, and the introduction of special pay systems, usually involve some form of tripartite cooperation if they are to be set in a way that is fair and satisfactory to the parties. In some cases, such as holiday schedules or bonus rates, sound labor–management cooperation at the enterprise level may be enough. In other cases the social repercussions of certain conditions of employment or of proposals to extend them to all workers may make it preferable for the matter to be studied and decided in a tripartite framework. Thus, to improve holiday facilities and provide and promote establishments for this purpose, a national commission on recreation has been set up in Guatemala and a commission to promote popular tourism has been established in Uruguay.

The advantages of tripartite cooperation in the settlement of labor disputes were also widely recognized. In many countries the basic design of conciliation and arbitration machinery provides for representation of the two sides of industry so that the background of the dispute can be fully ascertained and a solution reached through compromise to which the parties have contributed. In the same way the purpose of including workers' and employers' assessors in labor courts was to supplement the academic legal knowledge of the judge with their experience of labor problems.

In some countries there are examples of tripartite bodies with wide terms of reference extending across conventional boundaries to cover matters that would normally be regarded as falling within the competence of other authorities. In Mexico, for example, the conciliation and arbitration boards have standard-setting and judicial functions that include both the issuance of rulings with force of law in relation to collective economic disputes and the application of the law in legal disputes. (There is a somewhat similar situation in Brazil, whose system of judicial bodies with a tripartite structure will be studied in Chapter 12.)

As regards the bodies responsible for applying or interpreting the law, acceptance of the principle of tripartite cooperation is not unanimous. Some authors consider that the administration of justice should be entrusted only to impartial persons with special legal training, since employers' and workers' representatives are bound to reflect the particular interests of those they represent.[4] The opponents of tripartism in this context also refer to practical difficulties, particularly the inadequate training of lay judges, especially on the workers' side. Some Latin American authors argue that the collaboration of employers' and workers' representatives with the state in the exercise of the latter's judicial functions should not be underrated, for it is bound to strengthen the concepts of legality and equity on which the labor courts rely when they invite the parties to reach an understanding and themselves work out the rules that should govern their relations.[5]

In the field of social security, participation machinery is concerned primarily with management but may also cover some aspects of supervision and control. In countries where social security is operated by independent funds for each industry, representation of employers and unions on the boards of the funds is required by law. In countries where there is a single nationwide social security scheme or where a central coordinating body has been created, it is usual for the employers—who contribute to the scheme—and the workers—who are the main beneficiaries—to be represented. Two examples will illustrate the scope of the management functions assigned to tripartite bodies in a unified social security system. In

Ecuador the Social Security Institute is headed by a board responsible for directing, planning, operating, and supervising social security; it is made up of the representatives of government, of employers, and of workers. In Mexico an amendment to the Social Security Act (1971) retained the principle of tripartite membership of the three organs of the Social Security Institute: the general meeting, the technical council, and the supervisory commission.

To a great extent the adoption of the tripartite cooperation principle for the managing bodies of social security is attributable to historical circumstances. In some countries the first systems developed from existing mutual benefit schemes and inherited some features of their administration. In a number of cases the enactment of social security legislation followed union pressure, and this was reflected in the arrangements made for directing and managing the new agencies. Thus, an element of private initiative and self-government was evident from the start. Even today the main social security system is frequently supplemented by insurance schemes established by the parties through collective agreements or arrangements giving the unions joint responsibility, so that autonomous, jointly administered institutions are established.

In addition to the considerations already mentioned, there are administrative advantages in associating employers and workers in the management of social security. As the preamble to the Mexican Social Security Act points out, a tripartite system enables the social groups sharing in the creation of the basic assets of the system to see that a service in which all have a direct interest is run properly. Nor should one overlook the influence of the ILO Conventions, which from the start laid down the principle that protected persons, employers, and public authorities should participate in the administration of insurance schemes.

It is hardly necessary to add that participation in social security bodies can be significant in two ways: first, by contributing to better administration of insurance in the direct interest of contributors and beneficiaries, and, second, through the assistance to community development schemes given by investment of social security funds.

Expansion of Tripartism

The tripartite principle has been extended to other sectors of social policy. In employment, for example, there has been a move from sporadic and sometimes rather halfhearted participation by unions and employers' organizations toward systematic cooperation arrangements. While the general tendency today is to reemphasize the employment service's public function, it is also recognized that the workers and employers primarily affected by the success or failure of employment policies can, and should, make a continuing contribution to the formulation and implementation of those policies. On the employers' side there is no doubt that the representative organizations can provide advice on desirable policies in matters of selection and vocational guidance, recommendations on the use of suitable technologies and practical ways of making intensive use of manpower, information on labor market fluctuations, and encouragement to their members to use the employment service. The trade unions can provide particularly useful advice on the organization and operation of the service, voluntary registration of the unemployed, occupational and geographical mobility planning, and development of socioeconomic programs to influence the employment situation.

When these activities are combined and institutionalized in a tripartite consultative body, the usefulness of the employment service and its effectiveness in human resources utilization can be enhanced. It then becomes easier to guide and organize the employment market, to distribute human resources rationally, and to coordinate absorption of manpower in the private sector. A number of countries, including Brazil, Colombia, Chile, Mexico, Peru, and Venezuela, have therefore begun to experiment with this type of tripartite cooperation. In Brazil the Federal Manpower Council was formed in 1976. It includes representatives of both sides of industry and acts as a high-level advisory agency recommending means of making more intensive use of labor and improving the working of the labor market. In Mexico there has been, since 1978, a federal tripartite advisory committee composed of five representatives of each sector, in addition to a state advisory council. In the Dominican Republic a national committee on employment was set up in 1983. Needless to say, where the system of labor exchanges is still in use, representatives of employers and workers are usually included in the bodies managing them.

Closely related to the consultative commissions on employment are the vocational training bodies set up at the national level, which have been particularly ready to accept tripartism. A 1980 publication reports that in almost all countries of Latin America, there is some form of participation by employers and workers in the promotion and management of vocational training (a subject whose nature leads them to approach it in a spirit of harmony and cooperation) and that vocational training is one of the areas in which participation arouses least resistance.[6] The national apprenticeship councils in Brazil, Colombia, and Guatemala, and the management boards of the vocational training institutes or services in Chile, Ecuador, Honduras, Panama, Peru, and Venezuela, are striking examples of tripartite cooperation. In Venezuela tripartism has helped to provide a firm base for the institutional structure of the National Institute for Educational Cooperation (INCE) and to give backing to its extensive program of activities and publications.

Provisions for participation in occupational safety and health deserve a special mention. The legislation of a number of countries (including

Mexico and Honduras) requires safety and health committees, composed of employers' and workers' representatives, to be appointed in every establishment or plant. National councils are a more recent development, but there are already a number—for instance, in Costa Rica (the National Council for Occupational Safety and Health), Guatemala (the Permanent Commission for Accident Prevention), and Mexico (National Advisory Commission on Safety and Health). These developments tend to confirm the assumption that efforts to promote safety in industry are more effective if there is regular cooperation between the labor administration authorities and the organizations concerned.

Apart from these official safety and health bodies, there are nongovernmental ones that are subsidized by the state or maintained by private contributions. Brazil, for example, has the National Center of Safety, Health, and Industrial Medicine and the Technical Commission on Industrial Health and Safety. Both have links with the industrial social service run by the employers and include a representative of the National Confederation of Industrial Workers. The Colombian Industrial Safety Council, financed by private industry but having the status of a semipublic autonomous body, is similar in character.

The Brazilian Commission for Trade Union Affairs (Comisión de Encuadramiento Sindical) determines the sphere of trade union competence and trade union mergers, divisions, and dissolutions. In collective bargaining Argentina set up, in 1958, the National Council for Labor Relations, having representatives of employers and workers, to eliminate unfair labor practices and promote voluntary negotiation between workers and enterprises. It was dissolved in 1979.

There are many other tripartite bodies dealing with labor questions in particular sectors of the economy. In the shipping industry, for example, there are bodies of this kind with consultative functions (as in Brazil and Panama) or with regulatory, executive, and control functions (for instance, the tripartite commissions on stevedoring in Uruguay). In the building, transport, clothing, and other industries, tripartite commissions have been set up to study problems in the industry and to make recommendations to the government authorities concerned. In Uruguay the commercial salesmen's tripartite commission has proved exceptionally long-lasting.

Tripartite Bodies with General Responsibilities

A study of the functions of tripartite bodies with general responsibilities gives an even better idea of the potential role of such cooperation in the labor field.

In several countries, since early in this century, tripartite commissions have been appointed for codifying labor law or consultating with the two sides of industry in connection with the drafting or revision of labor legislation. More recently, attempts have been made to place such cooperation on a permanent footing through the creation of national labor councils. The basic idea underlying their establishment is the achievement of a consensus between the key groups and sectors in the economy before making substantial changes in labor law. Bodies of this kind have been set up—for example, in Brazil, Colombia, Ecuador, Guatemala, and Peru—to assist in preparing laws and regulations on labor questions and to give opinions on matters of general concern referred to them by the government. They thus serve as a forum for discussion on the major problems of the labor sector and are in a position to exert considerable influence on the process by which the main lines of labor policy are formulated.

In some countries the councils are supposed to study the results of labor policy and propose changes in the light of experience and to provide a high-level means of communication between the department of labor and the employers' and workers' organizations. This function could, in fact, be regarded as one that is preparatory and complementary to legislative action, since the existence of the councils makes it possible to test the initial degree of social acceptability for an intended measure and to improve it subsequently with the support of specialists and practitioners. The councils also provide opportunities for developing at the highest level the willingness to compromise and the spirit of tolerance that are essential for the success of tripartite cooperation. In practice, however, they have not always operated as intended; in some cases they have practically ceased to function, or meet only sporadically.

The economic and social councils set up on the French model after World War II resemble labor councils in a number of respects. While they do have functions in connection with the drafting of labor legislation, their scope is wider and includes questions of domestic and foreign trade, production, monetary and credit policy, health, and housing; they were conceived as a means of stimulating and coordinating the social aspects of the country's life and to suggest broad lines of policy. This wide scope explains why these councils include representatives of other sectors, such as consumers and members of the professions.

Perhaps the best-known example of this type of body in Latin America is the Argentine Economic and Social Council (CONES), established in 1973. Much was expected of this council when it took shape, since it was designed to provide a setting in which the different sectors of society would be able to participate in preparing the decisions of the central government;[7] however, the General Confederation of Labor was reluctant to appoint delegates because the council was only a consultative body, and the government soon lost interest in its functioning. The council was dissolved in 1976.

Among the tripartite cooperation bodies forming part of the political structure of the countries concerned are the councils of state required under the constitutions of Guatemala and Paraguay. These stand at the summit of the politico-administrative hierarchy and are responsible for commenting on draft laws, on financial, economic, and international policy questions, and on appointments to certain civil service posts. In Paraguay the council at present includes two members for agriculture, one for manufacturing, one for commerce, and one for labor. In Guatemala there is provision for separate representation of urban workers and rural workers, in addition to that for employers. In Ecuador, 12 out of 45 members of the Senate were at one time elected by private organizations representing industrial, agricultural, commercial, and labor interests.

The participation of employers' and workers' organizations in the work of planning bodies is more recent. It relates to a variety of questions in the development process, but mainly to economic matters. Most of the bodies of this kind are consultative in character and have duties in relation to the formulation of economic plans. However, some of them provide advice for both policy-making bodies and technical services, and their responsibilities cover plan implementation and evaluation as well. The National Development Councils of the Dominican Republic and of Ecuador and the Venezuelan Council for the National Economy are examples of this type of tripartite cooperation.

Other variants of tripartite bodies with general responsibilities are the national tripartite commissions set up in Mexico in 1971 and in Peru in 1981. In Mexico the commission had wide responsibilities, including the search for solutions to problems of unemployment, investment, industrial decentralization, the cost of living, housing, and environmental pollution. These problems were then studied by specialized bodies, also tripartite, such as the National Institute for Promoting Workers' Housing (IN-FONAVIT). In government thinking the tripartite commissions were in no way substitutes for the political bodies established by the constitution, but were considered as "complementary to them and an extension of the decisions, compromises and exchanges of views of employers and workers for the greatest social progress and also for the best economic growth."[8] In Peru the National Tripartite Commission first concentrated on the study of wage adjustment, the cost of living, and alternative employment for dismissed workers. In 1982 it was replaced by the National Council of Labor and Social Cooperation, the purpose of which was to promote consultation and collaboration between employers and workers in labor policy making and tripartite cooperation in applying that policy. Although structurally the council is a typical Latin American tripartite cooperation institution, it shows noteworthy interest in adopting agreements by a consensus of the government and employers' and workers' representatives composing it, and in promoting harmonious labor relations and social cooperation.

The above examples show the wide acceptance gained by the principle of tripartite cooperation in social policy and labor administration. Some impressive examples can be quoted of the quantitative growth of tripartite cooperation in labor relations: there are 80 tripartite bodies in Brazil, a few years ago 25 bodies were recorded in Peru, and in Mexico a government report of 1974 listed 14 separate fields in which there were tripartite commissions, boards, councils, or committees.[9] The tripartite principle has gained so much ground that it could easily be regarded as containing the embryo of a new conception of labor administration that would substitute for an exclusively government body one that included representatives of the main social groups or classes.

Government policy on tripartite operation has not, however, been one of uninterrupted progress. Political events have frequently put a stop to some forms of representation of employers' and workers' organizations in labor or social security institutions, and sometimes even a change of administration can affect the continuity and extent of cooperation. This explains why in many countries it appears fragile and sporadic. Such lack of continuity has also had an unfortunate effect on some of the most successful experiments that have taken place in the region.

This fact will perhaps explain why the formation of tripartite bodies, especially those with general responsibilities, has not lessened conflict and the pursuit of claims and counterclaims that in Latin America seem to be immune to the attempts at cooperation made at the national level.[10]

Problems

Basic Principles of Cooperation

From the previous sections it is apparent that tripartite cooperation has made appreciable progress, as shown by the diversity of the fields in which such cooperation exists and by the importance attached in some Latin American countries to the organic forms of participation. However, in many instances the action taken and the results obtained have fallen considerably short of the objectives that these bodies had been set up to achieve. It is almost universally recognized that tripartism is a good thing, and often the requisite machinery is created; but the principle involved is all too frequently misapplied, or difficulty is encountered in putting it into practice.

These difficulties arise above all from the basic principles underlying the system. No proper tripartite cooperation can exist unless certain conditions and requirements providing a framework and a foundation for the machinery of cooperation are met. Thus, it is essential that both trade unionists and employers should be reasonably well organized. Second, it is essential that employers' associations and workers' organizations should be able to operate in full freedom, with due recognition for the responsibilities they have to shoulder. Third, the trade union movement must be suitably structured, with bodies able to operate at the national level. Although such organizations exist in the region, the ideological clashes and trade union multiplicity mentioned in Chapter 2 hinder progress in tripartite cooperation. And, last, the proper representation of employers and workers presupposes capable leaders in sufficient numbers. All these things are essential, and little purpose would be served by flinging the doors wide open to "participation" if the organizations involved represented an insignificant portion of employers and workers, or if they were unable to express their views freely, or if the employers or the trade union movement were divided or inarticulate, or if the leaders were untrained or not qualified for other reasons.

Since the problems concerning the participating institutions were dealt with in Part I of this study, attention will now be concentrated on the other difficulties, starting with the qualifications and training of the persons taking part in tripartite cooperation, and attitudes of the relevant organizations. Participation is effected through representatives, and the efficiency of such cooperation depends on what grasp the individuals concerned have of problems affecting their organizations and society at large, and on their ability to study those problems and discuss them with the authorities.

Some countries have tried to tackle this difficulty by demanding, among other things, that the employers' and workers' representatives on certain bodies have at least an elementary education. Other systems, such as those in Brazil and Chile that govern the election of representatives to the boards of social security or provident funds, demand that candidates be experienced; for instance, they must have several years' seniority in the undertaking and some knowledge of the subject. Nevertheless, it is usually agreed that some forms of tripartite cooperation, including the granting to workers of a right to share in planning decisions, require special training or supplementary technical instruction.

Apart from the question of ability, there is the problem of the attitudes of organizations and their leaders. Cooperation presupposes a serious and continuing endeavor, on the part of governments, employers, and workers alike, to work together to promote mutual understanding, good relations, and the general interests of the country as a whole. It may not be easy for people in whom many years of tough labor–management bargaining have developed an ingrained militancy and combativeness to adopt the necessary attitudes overnight. It is not infrequent, on the other hand, that different trade union confederations in a single country may not see eye to eye on tripartite cooperation. In Peru, for example, the CGTP's unwillingness to cooperate with the National Council of Labor and Social Cooperation contrasts with the CTP's recent declaration that it was ready to contribute to the national effort against inflation and underdevelopment, and recognized that "cooperation entails negotiation and in practice means that sacrifices must be shared."[11] At the same time the efforts made by the government to win the support of high-level officials of both CTP and CGTP generated, according to some authors, a process of internal confrontation between the rank and file and their leadership that diminished the effectiveness of the council.[12]

Representativity and Methods of Representation

Even if all the above conditions are fulfilled, tripartite cooperation will rest on unsure ground unless there is some means of ensuring that each of the sectors concerned is properly represented on the bodies set up for the purposes of cooperation. Not only must attempts be made to ensure that each organization really represents its sector; it is of equal importance to ensure that the people holding seats on tripartite cooperation bodies really represent their organizations. Organized participation can be effective only insofar as the occupational organizations really represent their members and act through suitable and genuine representatives.

Certain experiments in cooperation failed because representatives were appointed for political reasons, without prior proposal by the organizations concerned. In such circumstances the persons appointed acted in a personal capacity, and at best as nonofficial spokesmen for their organizations; they did not enjoy the legitimacy that would have given a real value to their contributions.

Such anomalies seem to be deplorably frequent in Latin Amrica, and affect both employers' and workers' organizations. The problem arises above all in places where there are several organizations, in which event considerations of equity would seem to demand that the choice should fall on the most representative ones simultaneously, in turn, or on the basis of some system of proportional representation.

In most instances the most representative organization is authorized to appoint or put forward the name of a representative. In practice this has meant the choice of the organization that, on the basis of objectively discernible factors (including membership), carries most weight. The use of membership as a criterion seems especially necessary in dealing with trade union organizations and other voluntary associations whose influence clearly derives from the number of their members. For employers' associations other systems have sometimes been used, such as the amounts paid out in wages and salaries, or to the state in the form of taxes, by the membership.

Just as important is the question of the methods used to appoint the persons who are to sit on participatory bodies as employers' and workers' representatives. Appointment may, for instance, be by a majority of the votes cast at a convention, assembly, or referendum in which unorganized as well as organized employers and workers take part. In Honduras and Mexico employers' and workers' representatives on minimum wage boards and conciliation and arbitration tribunals are elected at employers' or workers' conventions, periodically convened by the Department of Labor, for the various branches of industry. In Uruguay the Trade Union Act of 1973 authorizes the government to carry out a referendum within a trade union federation, although in practice elections are usually organized in accordance with proposals made by the registered trade unions.

In other cases the appointment may be made directly by the employers' associations or trade unions concerned. This system is used mainly in countries where there is a single confederation or national organization for a particular branch of industry, or when there can be no doubt that one is the most representative. Argentina and Venezuela have on occasion had resort to this method of appointment.

In some instances appointment is made by the government itself, without taking into account any proposal or recommendation that the organizations or individuals concerned may have put forward. Only a few years ago this system of direct government appointment was still practiced in four Latin American countries; it of course tends to perpetuate the risks of favoritism and political partiality. As one Latin American author points out, it is essential for members of participatory bodies to be truly representative, since otherwise there will be no genuine contribution of opinion or social commitment.[13]

The most widespread system is that under which the government appoints representatives on the basis of lists supplied, or proposals made, by the organization concerned. Various views have been expressed on the advantages and shortcomings of this procedure. The workers have argued that the trade union movement tends to feel that the representatives so designated may not really represent it, the more so where the persons selected are frequently chosen on political grounds and do not necessarily enjoy the full confidence of the workers. They also argue that the system lends itself to maneuvers designed to foment squabbling and rivalry within the trade union movement.[14]

Governments argue that they should be free to decide who would be best able to help put through an official program, and to reject candidates lacking the requisite abilities and attitudes. It is also maintained that the system allows a distribution of seats among the various organizations that submit proposals, and avoids a state of affairs in which the same organizations tend always to nominate the same people.

Once representatives have been appointed, new problems arise, this time in connection with the part they should play on tripartite bodies. There is, for example, disagreement as to whether a representative's hands are tied by the will of his electorate and whether he should follow its instructions. Because of the system used for the appointment of representatives, and because mandates can be revoked, it is often felt that the individual representative can act only as the spokesman (or perhaps adviser) for those who have elected him, with no margin to act independently, "to the best of his knowledge and understanding." The result may be embarrassing, especially in bodies invested with powers of judicial decision or standard setting, when spokesmen are tempted to act, not as judges, but as parties to the dispute, and systematically dissent, abstain from voting, or take extreme positions.

Such problems as these are even more bothersome when we turn to revocation of the mandate conferred on representatives. If it can never be revoked, a representative ceases to be a representative, and sits on the participatory body in a purely personal capacity. Even so, not every Latin American country gives explicit statutory recognition to the principle of revocation. Some systems state that a duly elected representative becomes a member of the body in question for a fixed period of time; others provide for replacement of official representatives, but not of non-governmental representatives. However, the view is gaining ground that in both cases the representatives should continue in office as long as they enjoy the confidence of their constituents and that it should be possible, in certain circumstances, for the latter to replace them. Some systems of tripartite cooperation, such as the Mexican one, give some solemnity to the act of revocation and require that it be approved by two-thirds of the employers or workers concerned, the majority in question being verified by the competent authorities.

Organization and Structure of Tripartite Bodies

One major organizational problem of tripartite cooperation is that of finding the most suitable location for it within the government machinery. In some countries cooperation bodies are regarded as decentralized semi-public agencies having considerable independence; in others they are attached to a department (most likely the department of labor) and are hierarchically and functionally under the authority of the responsible minister. Advisory tripartite bodies with general terms of reference usually fall in the first category, and those with more specialized terms of reference in the second. But there are many exceptions to the rule, and there is a need to define just how independent a cooperation body should be.

Another problem of organization especially important to tripartite bodies is that of securing proper internal balance. It sometimes happens that there is no proper balance among government, employers, and workers, or that the employers' representation and that of the workers are unequal. In the Dominican Republic, for instance, in 1983 a national workers' federation (CUT) refused to participate in the National Employment Commission, on the grounds that the representation accorded to the workers was not sufficiently important vis-à-vis government and employers. In fact, there are not many participatory bodies with general terms of reference in which the nongovernmental sector enjoys numerically equal representation with government, and many are the instances of participation, even in the three basic areas, in which the official sector clearly predominates or employers have more representation than the unions or vice versa. It is usually the trade union representatives who are at a disadvantage, but in some Latin American social security organs the reverse has occurred, there being but one member to represent the employers and several to represent the workers (their number being fixed on the basis of the number of workers contributing to the scheme).

The determination of qualifications for members of a tripartite body gives rise to problems for governments as well as for employers and workers. On the government side there is some doubt whether governments should be represented exclusively by civil servants or whether more flexible procedures that would lead to changes in the membership of tripartite cooperation agencies (such as representation of the nongovernmental public interest) could be envisaged.

On the employers' and workers' sides, difficulties sometimes arise in connection with the internal balance of their respective delegations or the question of whether certain social groups that are neither employers nor workers should be represented as well. The problem of balance arises above all in national bodies with broad terms of reference, in connection with which a decision has to be taken on whether the employers and workers should be represented as a single group or with separate representatives for each sector. In some countries national minimum wage boards are made up of persons representing trade unions and employers in manufacturing industry, mining, trade, banking, transport, stock breeding and agriculture, arrangements sometimes being made for certain specific interests in the last-mentioned sector (those connected with coffee, sugar, or tobacco growing, for instance) to be represented. For this purpose a classification of sectors and subsectors has to be attempted, and a choice made of those that by reason of their importance ought to be represented.

Apart from these problems, the question sometimes arises of whether interest groups (consumers' associations, mutual benefits societies, cooperatives, women's or youth organizations) not usually forming part of the trade union movement or represented in employers' associations should be given representation on tripartite bodies. On the one hand, it is frequently held that tripartism should not be interpreted so rigorously as to exclude other valid systems of representation. The nature of some organs is such as to demand, at times, a multipartite membership, including governments, employers, workers, and other interested parties. Thus it is natural that bodies called upon to give advice on, say, the encouragement and protection of female labor should include representatives of women's organizations side by side with representatives of employers and unions. Again, it is understandable that in some social security schemes the managing bodies should include representatives of contributing members and pensioners in addition to representatives of contributing employers and government.

On the other hand, some experts feel that representation of other groups or social activities should not be carried too far; otherwise the most important representatives (the employers and workers) could become minorities in a heterogeneous array of delegates with relatively little to contribute to the discussion of general problems of economic and social development.

Certain standards are generally observed in the internal organization of tripartite cooperation bodies. Some of the general bodies, by reason of their size and the scope of their terms of reference, need administrative support to enable them to dispatch their business promptly and efficiently. It was not considered desirable, for example, to leave it to the plenary meetings of national labor councils to undertake the detailed discussion of all the business referred to them. Provision is often made for standing or ad hoc subcommittees or sections that discuss problems in their respective fields and report back to the plenary meeting. In Latin America this is the course followed by a number of bodies with general terms of reference. In Colombia the National Labor Council has four technical committees (for manpower, productivity, social security, and cooperatives).

Working of Cooperation Machinery

Apart from these structural and organizational questions, problems arise in connection with the procedure to be followed by tripartite bodies. The relevant national legislation does not always deal with this point in detail. Sometimes there is a very long wait before the requisite regulations are adopted. In other cases tripartite cooperation has come to a standstill because the rules of procedure are so complicated and legalistic that the participants have become discouraged and the working of the machinery has suffered.

It is generally accepted that the regulations governing tripartite cooperation should facilitate the working of the individual collegiate bodies. They should include rules concerning the quorum, frequency of meetings and publicity to be given them, voting procedures, members' rights and duties—including access by employers' and workers' representatives to the information they need to do their work—and rules for the taking of decisions. It might be thought that some of these matters are of relatively little importance, but in some countries they have been an essential element in the smooth working of the machinery.

The rules on the minimum frequency of meetings are of particular importance. Where certain councils and committees have been dormant for lengthy periods, rules have been enacted requiring them to meet at prescribed intervals. But some difficulties have arisen because members of these bodies have other duties as civil servants, trade union officials, or officials of employers' organizations. They must, accordingly, be released from other functions, or paid fees, or their expenses must be refunded, on a scale suitable to their duties. These duties must not be allowed to become either a burden or a sinecure.

Apart from these general problems there are others specifically linked to the various kinds of tripartite cooperation. In participation in planning it has been noticed, for instance, that the aspirations of cooperation bodies tend to be out of proportion to their achievements, and that the planning bodies tend to pay little attention to the views expressed by consultative bodies. In regard to cooperation with employment services, experience shows that the main difficulties are encountered in coordinating the activities of the new organs, the departments of government concerned, and the national planning bodies. With regard to the activities of minimum wage boards, some countries report that the work done is sometimes superficial or technically unsound, the decisions taken frequently being no more than compromises between employers' and workers' views. Conciliation or arbitration boards are criticized on rather different grounds; they are alleged to be slow and rigid in their handling of collective labor disputes. In some countries dissatisfaction has been expressed with tripartite bodies dealing with social security matters; their members are said to be inexperienced in the management of insurance schemes or in the investment of capital.

Most of these criticisms relate to the practical working of tripartite cooperation but do not detract from the validity of the principle itself. In some countries attempts have been made to overcome the difficulties mentioned above—which goes to show that tripartism can develop and adapt itself to changing conditions. In Ecuador and Mexico the legislation promulgated in 1970 and 1974, respectively, provided for the creation of a technical unit of the national minimum wage board to undertake research and inquiries. Elsewhere, action has been taken to stimulate and improve the efficiency of tripartite conciliation boards, human resources development committees, and vocational training bodies.

Nevertheless, it is clear that the problem is more than one of taking measures in isolation to improve the functioning of a particular tripartite body. What is needed is a determined effort to reinforce the basis and all the different manifestations of tripartite cooperation as a system.

Notes

1. See especially the resolution concerning social policy and economic development (Buenos Aires, 1961), the resolution concerning social participation in the development process (Caracas, 1970), and the resolution concerning the strengthening and furthering of tripartite cooperation (Mexico City, 1974). A detailed account of the resolutions adopted up to 1974 appears in ILO, *Strengthening and Furthering of Tripartite Cooperation*, Report III, Tenth Conference of American States Members of the ILO, Mexico City, 1974 (Geneva: ILO, 1974), pp. 3–4.

2. See, for example, Guillermo Cabanellas, *Compendio de derecho laboral* (Buenos Aires: Bibliografia Omeba, 1968), vol. II, p. 418.

3. Mario de la Cueva, *El nuevo derecho mexicano del trabajo* (Mexico City: Editorial Porrúa, 1972), p. 332.

4. See, for example, I. E. Banchs, "Nueva organización y procedimientos uniformes de los tribunales bancario y de seguro," *Derecho laboral* (Buenos Aires), May 1973, pp. 263 ff.

5. Ernesto Krotoschin, *Instituciones de derecho del trabajo*, 2nd ed. (Buenos Aires: Ediciones Depalma, 1968), p. 612.

6. Héctor Hugo Barbagelata, *El tripartismo y la formación profesional en América latina*, Estudios y Monografías no. 53 (Montevideo: CINTERFOR/ILO, 1980), p. 26.

7. See Mauricio Birgin, "El Consejo Económico Social y nuestra realidad nacional," *Derecho laboral* (Buenos Aires), June 1972, p. 323.

8. *Reseña laboral* (Mexico City), Aug. 1973, p. 5.

9. Secretaría del Trabajo y Previsión Social de México, "Fortalecimiento y ampliación de la cooperación tripartita en México," working paper submitted to the Tenth Conference of American States Members of the ILO, Mexico City, 1974.

10. Efrén Córdova, "Conflicto y concertación: Algunas comparaciones entre España y América Latina," in Instituto de Estudios Laborales y de Seguridad Social, *2° Encuentro iberoamericano sobre relaciones de trabajo* (Madrid: the Institute, 1983), pp. 135–146.

11. Confederación de Trabajadores del Perú, *Lineamientos económicos en el marco de la concertación social* (Lima: CTP, 1982), p. 7.

12. See Denis Sulmont, "Coyuntura laboral. Trabajadores: ¿Retomando la iniciativa?" *Cuadernos laborales* (Lima) no. 12 (May 1982): 3.

13. Ildefonso Recalde, *Desarrollo nacional y participación: Consejos económicos y sociales* (Buenos Aires: Talleres Gráficos Stylos, 1970), p. 38.

14. Organization of American States, Third Interamerican Conference of Ministers of Labor on the Alliance for Progress, "La representación de los trabajadores en los organismos de desarrollo y gubernamentales," report submitted by the Inter-American Regional Organization of Workers of the ICFTU (Washington, D.C.: OAS, 1969), p. 9. (Mimeographed.)

Part III: Disputes

9
Labor Disputes: Their Nature and Settlement

by
Efrén Córdova

Collective Disputes in the Latin American Context

Disputes have always been part and parcel of Latin American labor relations. The parties have tended to take an aggressive stance very early on, and disputes and strikes have played a prominent part in the development of collective labor relations. A number of authors explain the dynamics and characteristics of some systems of labor relations by relating them to the parties' propensity to disputes or governments' efforts to arrange their peaceful settlement.[1]

The first strikes—those, for example, in the Argentine printing industry, the Cuban tobacco industry, and the Mexican textile industry—took place more than a century ago. In some countries the great strikes of the first stages of labor relations—the "tragic week" in Argentina (1919), the period of the great strikes in Colombia (1924–34), the events at Iquique in Chile (1907), and the Cananea and Rio Blanco strikes in Mexico (1906–07)—left their mark on the parties' subsequent attitudes; in other countries, such as Bolivia and Honduras, they were the starting point of the trade union movement. Everywhere the history of labor-management relations has been marked by periods of acute agitation. Writings on Latin American labor matters include many works devoted exclusively to important disputes and strike movements.[2]

It is, accordingly, not surprising that procedures for the peaceful settlement of strikes appeared at an early date. As far back as 1912 the Argentine Department of Labor included in its duties the setting up of boards to settle labor disputes between employers and workers. In Mexico a fairly complete system of conciliation and arbitration boards was operating by 1927. The first strike control measures introduced in Peru date from the beginning of the century and are virtually the earliest of all labor relations procedures.

The fear of disputes and a desire for their peaceful settlement became part of the foundations of labor policy, so much so that settlement procedures accounted for much of collective relations. Until a few years ago most collective bargaining took place as part of peaceful settlement procedure, with which, as time went on, a complex system of bodies and authorities were involved. Bolivia, Colombia, and Paraguay each have a special code of procedure in labor matters (código procesal del trabajo), regulating procedures for the settlement of individual and collective disputes. In Mexico the Federal Labor Act, as amended in 1980, devotes more than one-third of its provisions to regulating the procedure to be followed in labor disputes. In Brazil the system for settlement of disputes is still basically designed to take the place of collective bargaining, eliminate open conflict, and give the courts standard-setting powers. Elsewhere, with the trend toward voluntarism the parties have managed to get rid of a number of controls imposed on the dispute settlement system, and disputes are beginning to be accepted as part of the dynamics of collective bargaining; but there is still a tendency to follow outdated practices and resort frequently to bodies whose job it is to settle disputes, formally or informally.

In some countries the authorities responsible for dealing with labor matters are present at the very beginning of the presumed dispute, and settlement procedures revolve around them. In Bolivia, the Dominican Republic, Ecuador, Paraguay, and Venezuela the workers must submit their demands to the labor inspector, who notifies the employer of them and gives him a certain time to reply. In Paraguay the employer's reply must be sent through the labor authorities. In Peru demands may be submitted direct to the employer, but a copy must be sent at the same time to the administrative authorities, who must be kept informed of all meetings held for direct negotiations; in addition it lies within the competence of the administrative authorities to approve collective agreements concluded by direct negotiation.

Perhaps in reaction to their excessive channeling through complicated official procedure, disputes in Latin America have been notable for their tendency to take unofficial and anomic forms. As will be seen in Chapter 13, there have always been many more illegal strikes than legal ones. Strikes accompanied by backup measures and demonstrations have found more favor than those limited to stoppage of work. This may be a historic vestige of the revolutionary spirit and defiance of the social order that inspired the first strikes. It may also be because direct action, especially strike action, is difficult and has been ineffectual as a means of bringing economic pressure to bear on employers. In any event, control of disputes in all their forms was quite strict from the beginning.

Whatever the cause of this trend toward illegal and anomic disputes, signs of it are found in the behavior of some trade unionists and in the approach to and style of collective labor relations. Professor Francisco de Ferraris observed some years ago that disputes broke out in Uruguay without respect for precedent or order, as acts of war or breaches of the peace, and that open conflicts went on in the street, leading to mass meetings that often retained the romanticism of the workers' movements of the last century, largely because of the ideological kind of trade unionism still prevailing in Latin America. The influence of ideological trade unionism is also seen in the terminology almost universally employed in collective relations, and especially in the use of the Spanish equivalents of "demands" (*reivindicaciones*) and "conquests" (for the benefits provided for in collective agreements), "social antagonists" (for the signatories), and "the trade union struggle."

The state's cautious attitude following the great strikes of the first years of labor relations is exemplified in the legislation of various countries, such as that of Bolivia forbidding persons unconnected with the undertaking, factory, or piece of work affected by the dispute to act as workers' representatives. This ban on participation by the national leaders was made to prevent factors unconnected with the original reasons for the dispute from being added to it, and its possible spread to other sectors, even at the price of foregoing the help that those leaders could give.

The above reasons may help to explain why in recent years there have been new forms of trade union militancy, and new kinds of unruly demonstrations, such as the occupation of public buildings, cathedrals, and embassies, as well as work places in the course of a dispute.

In Mexico, even in legal strikes, when strikers stop work, they continue to take symbolic action, such as the display of red and black flags. In the Dominican Republic it was probably the memory of the great strikes of the past that prompted a provision of 1964, still in force, that for reasons of discretion and the conciliator's personal safety, all conciliation meetings should take place at the State Secretariat of Labor, and only exceptionally in or near the work place.

Many of the above-mentioned regulations and attitudes have undergone important changes since the 1960s. The workers' protest is no longer the sole determining factor of labor relations, nor even the principal one; cooperation, institutionalization of contact, and bargaining have been gaining ground in the general context of the system. But the scars left by the initial stage are still visible, both in the symbols used and in the way of conducting bargaining and settling disputes.

Frequency and Causes

As will be clear from the previous section, in Latin America there are many labor disputes and many forms of anomic protest,[3] but relatively few legal strikes. The disputes are many because in most countries the parties have not yet reached the stage of mutual understanding and trust, and a variety of procedures is available for filing claims and for dealing with them. At the same time there are not sufficient means of calling strikes of any considerable duration in economic disputes, or it is difficult to do so because of restrictive legislation, particularly in countries where labor relations are undergoing change and in Brazil.

The frequency of disputes is, moreover, proportionate to the extent of collective bargaining. In Paraguay, for example, where bargaining was still at its very beginning, only four cases of conciliation and one of arbitration were recorded in 1971.[4] Significantly, in Mexico the total of individual and collective disputes being handled by the Federal Conciliation and Arbitration Board in December 1977 was 50,534, including 6,386 strike calls, a high proportion of the total number of cases of collective bargaining. In Brazil there are nearly half a million disputes (*dissidios*) every year, a high figure even if compared with the total economically active population (about 40 million).[5] In Venezuela, if the number of cases handled in 1977 by the tripartite labor commissions (21,054) is added to the number of individual and collective complaints handled in that year by labor inspection officials (54,712), and to the number of cases passed to the labor courts, the total is considerable.

The socioeconomic factors explaining these high figures are very complex, and the occurrence of the dispute is affected by a large number of variables. The aggressive attitude of the trade union movement and its tradition of class struggle (stronger in some cases than in others) of course influence the number of disputes, but are themselves conditioned by the ideological position and the affiliations of the various wings of the trade union movement in Latin America. There seems to be no doubt, however, that especially in countries where labor relations are still in the formative stage, many trade union leaders are predisposed to labor disputes. In Ecuador, for example, surveys carried out in 1975 showed that about 85 percent of the general secretaries of trade unions interviewed thought that disputes were a good thing for a militant labor movement.[6] In a study of the genesis of the industrial relations system of Chile, James O. Morris gave credence to this view by asserting that labor leaders and organizations meant what they said when they preached revolution (while engaging in collective bargaining), and that in industrial relations conflict sprang fundamentally from totally different systems of thought.[7]

The results of the politicization of the trade union movement may or may not be positive, depending on the links with the government party. If trade unions are an ally of the party in power, they often refrain from economic strikes in the hope of a favorable settlement through arbitration or "favored" conciliation; they will nevertheless be disposed to provoke disputes and to refuse any direct agreements that do not particularly benefit them. If, on the contrary, trade unions are in opposition to the government, they will try to avoid disputes and make direct agreements, but may occasionally become involved in political strikes or demonstrations.

Other factors related to trade union dynamics also act as variables of limited influence. If the union is weak and has no strike fund, the form and timing of disputes will be affected rather than their frequency. A trade union without the human and financial resources needed to exhaust all stages of administrative conciliation, appeals to conciliation boards, and arbitration feels more inclined to rush into an illegal strike, as an immediate way of expressing its protest that puts the stamp of urgency on subsequent action; but the strike will probably be short, for lack of means and because of the purpose for which it was called.

While trade unions generally lack the power of economic resistance, they have had what some authors have called a "capacity for violent destabilization."[8] This is typical of sociopolitical movements rather than of occupational organizations, and its normal form of expression is nearly always an open conflict. It has been used particularly in the formative stages of the labor movement and where collective or political bargaining and procedures are inoperative; this explains the use of unofficial or illegal methods.

In countries or sectors in which trade unionism has greater economic and organizing power and in which bargaining procedures have been established, frustration is caused by the contrast between expectations and methods of action, which resemble those observed in industrialized countries, and the economic background, which is still that of a developing region. In Latin America the spirit of confrontation and protest by the workers does not suffer from idiosyncratic inhibitions, and the cultural background is not especially conducive to harmony. The process of articulating interests and demands thus goes ahead vigorously, but in an atmosphere remarkable for the structural deficiencies of the Latin American economies. Latin American undertakings have been exposed almost continuously to fluctuations in the prices of raw materials, cyclical contractions in demand, the limitations of the domestic market and difficulties encountered by economic integration schemes, the high cost of imports of machinery and energy sources, the lack of inputs due to failure of foreign exchange policy, and the substantial welfare costs that are payable by the employers and increase their total costs (because they are made responsible for providing benefits that are elsewhere a government responsibility).

All this gives rise to an atmosphere of insecurity and financial straits that makes frequent adjustment necessary and leads to defensive conflictual action. Some authors assert that the great strikes were not due to ideological causes but to the need to defend economic interests.[9] In Mexico it has been said that the intensified disputes of the last few years are due to the fall in the workers' real income.[10] Many other disputes originate in the frustration generated by the contrast between the energetic terms in which demands are formulated and the meager results of bargaining; but this should not obscure the importance in some countries of ideological factors. In Ecuador, for instance, solidarity feelings were rated in 1975 as the third main cause of collective disputes (job security and wage increases being the first and second).[11]

It could be argued that the high levels of structural unemployment characteristic of Latin America could tend to reduce the propensity to open conflict; but there is no direct relation between higher unemployment and less frequent disputes. There are other institutional factors that to some extent arrest the possible effects of high unemployment, such as the prohibition in nearly all countries of the use of strikebreakers in economic disputes and the effective legal protection given in many countries to workers lodging complaints against the employer. Furthermore, in any one country the labor market is fairly well segmented and there is a marked difference between the levels of vocational training of employed and unemployed workers. All these factors usually prevent unemployed workers from being considered as suitable replacements for workers taking part in the dispute.

The employer's attitude must similarly be classified as a variable; it generally depends on the prevailing type of management, the sector involved, and even on the kind of undertaking (whether a multinational corporation, a small or medium-scale national undertaking). However, in some periods of Latin American labor history the employers' attitude was responsible for serious tension and strong resistance to recognition of trade unions. Some authors assert that Latin American management has not been favorable to the establishment of a pluralistic approach to standard setting, nor to real cooperation with trade unions.[12] Nor did it make much effort to develop adequate communication with the staff or to promote the formation of works councils as a means of fostering cooperation or channeling workers' protests; had it done so, disputes might have been less likely.

Besides this variety of influences, three general factors may be identified that could be called constants. The first relates to the system adopted for the conduct of collective relations and in particular of bargaining. In Latin America, except in Argentina and Brazil, a decentralized system has been adopted that promotes bargaining at the level of the undertaking and therefore makes conflicts much more likely. Not only is the number of potential disagreements much greater than in industry-level bargaining, but the negotiators may lack the experience and expertise of leaders of federations or national industrial trade unions and employers' organizations. Personal friction and resentment are also more likely because of the parties' direct interest in the discussion. At the same time, however, there is no doubt that the decentralized system does reduce the scale and effect of individual disputes, although their total cumulative effect is probably similar. It is also possible that where the decentralized system is accompanied by a free functioning price system, a market operating normally, and access to foreign trade, it is easier to recognize the legitimacy of open conflict and accept the outcome of strikes.

The second factor is the function of disputes in the general context of labor relations. The government's dominant position as regulator, dispenser of benefits, and composer and arbitrator of labor relations makes a dispute not so much a break in negotiations with the employer as a signal to the government to intervene. In the last resort, satisfaction of the workers' aspirations and demands traditionally depended more on the government than on the employer; the government thus became the intermediary in bargaining, and its intervention the immediate object of the dispute. Where negotiations offer little prospect of a prompt settlement, either party, but especially the trade union, will tend to provoke a dispute without exhausting bargaining possibilities. The government is then subjected to pressure by the workers' organization or the employer. This pressure will take the form of conflict or of a public demonstration that may attract government attention, and perhaps put it in an embarassing position. The dispute thus becomes a useful bargaining weapon to get a settlement from the third, omnipresent party to the system. Labor disputes in Latin America are therefore so frequent because of the initial distortion of collective labor relations during the stage of strong government interventionism.

The third factor, an institutional one, has taken diverse and sometimes contrasting forms, but in general has made disputes more frequent. On the one hand, in many countries workers involved in a dispute enjoy guarantees and protection that in practice encourage disputes. These include the general prohibition of reprisals ("even the least reprisal," as in Costa Rica), the prohibition of dismissals or transfers of trade union officials and workers, or the retroactivity of any agreement or award made as a result of a dispute. On the other hand, in nearly all countries there are strict institutional restrictions that, for example, in the past prevented unionization of agricultural workers and now deprive public servants of the right to collective action. The agitation of the 1950s, 1960s, and 1970s on the farms and plantations in Central America and some South American countries, and the present effervescence in the civil service in all the countries of the region, are doubtless features of the campaign for trade union recognition and the consequent right to bargain and to strike.

Classification

The accepted meaning of "dispute" is not entirely uniform in Latin America, being wider in some countries than in others. In some countries it is equated to the bargaining process, whereas in others it is more correctly regarded as the breaking off of bargaining. In many countries the legislation appears to restrict the notion of dispute to strikes and lockouts, without specifically making clear that the latter are merely manifestations of open conflict.

The distinctions drawn by many experts between disputes and controversies are, of course, much more refined. According to some Argentine and Brazilian authors, a dispute means a mere clash of interests or a discrepancy in interpreting and applying a rule,[13] and becomes a controversy or *dissidio* when the claimant submits his complaint to the state—that is, when either party applies through the normal channels for adjudication or settlement of the dispute. These criteria are not universal, so Mexican authors prefer to regard the two terms as identical, whereas a Brazilian author distinguishes between dispute, collective action, and controversy, controversy appearing, according to him, only when collective action is denied or rejected.[14]

The markedly legal character of discussions in Latin America regarding classification of disputes is immediately noticeable. National legislation makes relatively few classifications, but the courts and commentators have become involved in complicated discussions on the meaning of the various possible classifications. Several criteria have been followed in this connection. The main ones relate to the nature of the parties concerned (there are disputes between trade unions, between workers, between employers, between a trade union and its members, and between labor and management), the interests at stake (individual or collective), the nature of the dispute (over rights or over interests), and the prohibition of unfair practices.

Disputes Between Trade Unions, Between Workers, and Between a Trade Union and Its Members

Many Latin American experts maintain that it is necessary to make a preliminary classification of disputes according to what parties are involved, distinguishing between labor–management disputes, disputes between trade unions, disputes between employers, disputes between workers, and disputes between a trade union and its members. In general labor codes deal only with labor–management disputes, and leave the settlement of other kinds to the parties concerned (in some countries to the administrative authorities supervising the register of occupational organizations). Mexico and Nicaragua are exceptions to this rule, since the Mexican Federal Conciliation and Arbitration Board and Nicaraguan labor judges are empowered to deal with and settle labor disputes not only between workers and employers but also between workers only or between employers only, provided they are occasioned by labor relations or closely related matters.

Some authors are of the opinion that Latin American law pays scant attention to disputes between trade unions or between employers because the interested parties do not want the government or any other party to intervene in their internal disagreements. This line of argument is less acceptable in regard to disputes between a trade union and its members, since the latter may be the victims of discrimination or arbitrary action, and trade union rejection of their complaints could leave them unprotected. In fact, except for administrative complaints or their possible classification in some countries as an unfair labor practice, there is no special procedure in Latin America for the settlement of such disputes. However, in the countries that recognize the validity of the closed shop clause, certain means of protection against expulsion are prescribed.

In practice, disputes between workers are usually about promotion and seniority rights under an agreement, and this would justify classifying them as disputes over rights between labor and management. There is hardly any record of disputes between employers, although the growing importance of employers' organizations could lead to disputes with their members or other organizations in regard to the extent of their competence and authority. For the time being, some codes state only that the employers' organization represents only the occupational interests of the employers who are members of the association.[15]

Labor–Management Disputes

Labor–management disputes are generally divided into individual and collective disputes, or disputes over rights and disputes over interests, these being the classifications disseminated in the region by the ILO in 1949.[16] At present nearly all countries know and apply both distinctions, in legislation and in the courts. Even the countries that normally have only one body to settle all disputes, such as Brazil's labor courts and Mexico's conciliation and arbitration boards, lay down different procedures for different kinds of disputes. All countries recognize that there are individual and collective disputes, as well as disputes over rights and over interests; some countries emphasize the first classification, others the second, and the great majority prefer to combine both. In Bolivia, Ecuador, and Uruguay, for example, the legislation particularly emphasizes the difference between individual and collective disputes. The Dominican Republic, El Salvador, and Panama expressly distinguish legal disputes (or disputes over rights) from economic disputes (or disputes over interests), but the other terms of the classification are not unknown in those countries; in all other countries both classifications are used in conjunction with each other.

These comments are based on examination of the global treatment of the subject by legislation, jurisprudence, and practice, since the codes or laws of some countries either do not expressly refer to the classification or refer to it unsystematically or under other names. In Venezuela, for example, the original distinction in the Labor Code refers to collective disputes and contentious matters (*asuntos contenciosos*), the latter being defined as those to which conciliation or arbitration is inapplicable or that arise in regard to the application of legal or contractual provisions. In some countries the legislation describes disputes over interests as "economic and social" or "socioeconomic" disputes. The present legislation in Chile and Peru does not expressly refer to the various classes of disputes, but implicitly distinguishes between individual and collective disputes.

Individual and Collective Disputes

Countries making a primordial distinction between individual and collective disputes take it for granted that these terms are clear and need no definition. It is hard to find in legislation any precise indication of what is meant by individual or collective disputes. It is possible that the law is not explicit on this point because in practice individual disputes may sometimes turn into collective ones if a group of workers considers itself affected by an individual dispute and decides to act in defense of the common interest to arrive at a generally applicable settlement.

Even though statutory definitions may be lacking, legal experts and case law have clarified some aspects of this classification. In principle the classification is based on the number of workers involved in the dispute, but this merely quantitative basis may be inadequate, since the case law of various countries has established that an accumulation of individual grievances, or discussion of the subjective rights of a number of workers, does not necessarily constitute a collective dispute. The Mexican Supreme Court of Justice, for example, has ruled that what constitutes a collective dispute is not the number of complainants or the fact that the grievance concerns the interpretation or application of a collective agreement, but the nature of the interests at stake: a collective dispute exists when what is at stake are the interests of a group of workers, or occupational category, whereas an individual dispute is one affecting only individual interests and occurring between the parties to an individual employment relationship.

The number of workers concerned is not, then, the decisive factor; but certain provisions relating to collective disputes may require a minimum number of workers for the complaint to be entertained. In Chile that number is eight, and relates to the capacity to initiate a collective bargaining process. In Peru precedent and certain regulations require that there shall be at least five workers involved before a dispute becomes collective, and that if the number falls below five in the course of the action because of waiver, abandonment, or any other reason, the collective action may not proceed. In Brazil no definite number of workers as plaintiffs is required.

The criteria for the identity of the parties to a collective dispute also lack uniformity. In most countries of the region only organizations may act on the trade union side in a collective dispute, but in six countries that allow unauthorized groups to negotiate, these groups may also be parties to a dispute (see Chapter 5). In Mexico economic collective disputes may be started by trade unions of workers covered by collective agreements, or by the majority of workers in an undertaking or establishment, provided that occupational interests are affected. In Haiti the workers in general are mentioned "as parties empowered to appoint delegates and take action in the dispute."

Disputes over Rights and over Interests

Although few countries accept the distinction between disputes over rights and disputes over interests as the sole basis of classification, there is no doubt that this classification is exceptionally important in practice. It attempts to differentiate disputes according to their nature, and this is no doubt highly relevant to determining which body and procedure are appropriate. If a dispute over rights refers to the interpretation or application of an already existing provision, the bodies competent to settle it will obviously be those appointed to "lay down the law"—that is, the labor courts. A dispute over interests concerning the introduction of a new norm or the amendment or abolition of an existing one must, however, be passed for settlement to bodies empowered to compose or settle conflicting interests, the conciliation and arbitration boards. This is clearly stated, for example, in the Dominican Republic's Labor Code, which regards disputes over new working conditions or the amendment of existing ones as economic.

In practice there is a growing tendency to treat legal disputes on the same footing as grievances over the interpretation or application of a clause of an existing collective agreement, and to treat disputes over interests in the same way as those that arise when collective bargaining breaks down. The Panama Labor Code expresses this distinction in similar terms when it states that collective legal disputes are those arising from the interpretation or application of a law, decree, works rule, custom, contract, or collective agreement and involving a group or collectivity of workers; and that collective economic disputes or collective disputes over interests are those whose purpose is the conclusion of a collective agreement, and those that in any other way express collective interests that are socioeconomic or contained in workers' demands.

This classification is also important because of its effect on the right to strike; it assumes that the right to strike should be exercised only in connection with disputes over interests and not in disputes over rights, since there are bodies and procedures empowered to settle disputes of the latter kind by interpreting and applying the law. This is expressly stated in Argentina, Chile, and Uruguay, but in Mexico the law also entertains the possibility of a strike called to enforce an agreement.

Combination of Classifications

The prevailing tendency in Latin America is doubtless to combine the two classifications. In fact 13 countries nowadays distinguish three kinds of disputes: individual disputes; collective disputes over rights; and collective disputes over interests. While some authors entertain the possibility of an individual dispute over interests,[17] this is usually regarded as unimportant because such a dispute would have no practical repercussions. The tendency everywhere is therefore to treat all individual disputes as legal disputes.

Nevertheless, the only explicit reference to all three types of disputes appears in the 1980 Mexican legislation reforming labor procedure. Although all disputes in Mexico are handled by conciliation and arbitration boards, individual and collective disputes over rights follow a procedure different from that for collective economic disputes or disputes over interests. The latter are defined as those whose object is to amend working conditions or introduce new working conditions, or to suspend or terminate collective labor relations.

The distinction between collective disputes over rights and collective disputes over interests is clearly established in the labor codes of El Salvador and Haiti. The Salvadoran code neatly defines collective disputes over rights as those caused by failure to interpret or observe an agreement, or those seeking enforcement of the law or of works rules, provided that a group of workers is affected. The code states that collective disputes over interests spring from the imbalance of collective economic interests between employers and workers, or from the defense of the workers' common occupational interests. The Haitian code distinguishes disputes arising from differences of opinion on legal matters or regulations from disputes occurring as the result of deadlocks in the negotiation or revision of an agreement.

In most of the other countries the above distinction is only partially or indirectly made by legislation, or is made to a rather greater extent by court decisions and circulars of the department of labor.

The formula is therefore not the same from one country to another, but it can be said that there is a basic consensus as to the distinction between individual and collective disputes, and between disputes over rights and disputes over interests. There is also fairly general agreement as to which body should be competent to deal with individual disputes, and which should deal with collective disputes over interests. The exceptions are Brazil and Mexico, which have opted for a single body; in the other countries the labor courts are competent to settle individual disputes, and the conciliation and arbitration boards to settle collective disputes over interests. There is at times overlapping or confusion, as in the Labor Code of Ecuador, which states that justice shall be administered by labor courts and conciliation and arbitration boards, or in Costa Rica, Guatemala, and Honduras, which make labor courts responsible for the determination of the legality of strikes. However, except for these particular cases there appear to be clear statutory provisions distinguishing bodies competent to settle individual disputes from those competent to settle collective disputes over interests.

Some doubts arise regarding settlement of collective disputes over rights: according to one school of thought, the legal aspects should take precedence over the collective ones, and such disputes should therefore be settled by the labor courts; according to another school, their social repercussions require separate treatment. Bolivia, Colombia, Chile, El Salvador, and Haiti subscribe to the former opinion; they believe that all legal disputes, whether individual or collective, should be submitted to labor courts. The Dominican Republic and Peru hold the latter opinion; they have established bodies and procedures similar to those acting in collective economic disputes. Argentina makes a threefold distinction: it assigns individual disputes to labor courts, collective legal disputes on the interpretation of collective agreements to the joint committees, and collective disputes over interests to Department of Labor conciliators. However, the joint committees' decisions are subject to legal review.

While some authors have suggested that collective disputes over rights are not strictly a separate category of dispute, the prevailing opinion is that expressed by Ernesto Krotoschin: that collective legal disputes are fundamentally what might be called an extension of disputes over interests that were inadequately settled by an agreement.[18] This opinion to some extent gives such disputes a special character that places them halfway between disputes over rights and disputes over interests, and this explains why in some countries they are first subject to conciliation, and sometimes to arbitration, before going on to the labor courts, and why in others settlement procedures partake of both methods, since they entertain the possibility of a strike within a virtually judicial procedure. In Panama the 1972 Labor Code prescribes that before submitting a collective dispute over rights to the labor courts, either of the parties may call for mediation by a conciliation officer from the Department of Labor and Social Welfare.

In practice collective disputes over rights or disputes over interests, and also individual disputes, may all be handled by administrative conciliation, and in fact many of them are submitted first to departments of labor, so that this method of settlement is tending to become a general prior procedure applicable in principle to nearly all disputes. This means that the above classifications are really important only when conciliation has failed and it has to be decided whether final settlement of the dispute shall be by the labor courts or by arbitration.

On what basis is it decided whether a dispute shall or shall not first be submitted to administrative conciliation? In most cases it is essentially a practical matter, depending above all on the immediate or potential importance or magnitude of the dispute. If a grievance is put forward by a single worker but may lead in practice to a strike or protest action, or be converted on solidarity grounds into a major dispute, or if the aggrieved worker is firmly backed by his union, the dispute will probably go first to the department of labor for conciliation. This tendency to give uniform initial treatment to all disputes is rarely reflected in the specifically relevant legislation; except in Panama it tends to be a practice sanctioned by the general powers conferred by the legislation under which the department of labor was set up.

Unfair Labor Practices

There is another special category of disputes recognized by certain Latin American countries, those connected with unfair labor practices, which are specifically regulated by law in Argentina (in 1958 and 1979), Colombia (1962), Chile (1979), the Dominican Republic (1958), and Panama (1972). Although the concept of unfair practices was imported from the United States, each country has formulated and applied it differently. In the Dominican Republic and Panama only the employer is considered to commit unfair practices; in the other countries either party may do so. In Argentina they are defined in terms of acts or failures to act that are contrary to the ethics of labor relations; in Panama they are regarded as practices contrary to trade unionism and the workers' rights; and in Chile as practices detrimental to freedom of association and to collective bargaining and the procedure laid down for it.

Complaints of unfair practices lodged against employers are generally of four main kinds: dismissals, maltreatment or reprisals ordered by employers against trade unions or individual complainants; interference by employers to promote or subsidize one organization to the detriment of another; obstruction of the right to join a trade union; or rejection of collective bargaining. The last two kinds usually also appear among the unfair practices of which trade unions can be accused; Argentina includes trade union interference in the operation of employers' organizations, but this is unimportant in practice. Where the practice of refusing to take part in collective bargaining is prohibited, there is no mention of the question of recognition, or of bargaining in bad faith, or of withholding of information necessary to negotiation.

In fact, what some countries describe as unfair practices are also directly or indirectly forbidden in others, although the same expression is not used. Similarly, most of the situations covered could in any event provoke individual or collective legal action. It is therefore not surprising that complaints of unfair practices almost everywhere go to the labor courts. Only Argentina has set up a special body to deal with unfair practices, the National Labor Relations Court (formerly Council), but this was dissolved in 1979, and competence to deal with complaints against unfair practices was transferred to the labor courts.

In practice it does not appear that the system has really flourished in the region. Not many complaints have been made under it; in Panama, for example, there are normally not more than a dozen complaints of unfair practices every year. Possibly many lawsuits brought for unfair practices are couched in other terms and invoke other legal provisions, but it does not appear that the content and usefulness of unfair practices legislation has been made sufficiently known. This may be because in Latin America unfair labor practices were conceived as additions to an already established system, and never attained the central importance accorded them in the United States.

Settlement Procedures

Reference has already been made to the labor courts and the conciliation and arbitration systems. We must now identify more exactly the means used in Latin America for the settlement of labor disputes. Latin American analysts tend to classify them in three major categories: direct settlement by the parties; settlement by a third party; and self defense (which will be discussed in Chapter 13). Other ways of ending disputes that are frequently used and consist of suppressing or controlling their external manifestations are compulsory resumption of work and military call-up of strikers. However, such actions do not really settle the dispute, which can remain latent for long periods; it merely prevents it from being expressed in certain ways, particularly by direct action.

To consider only those means of peaceful settlement that deal with the substance of the dispute and seek to remove its causes, the two major categories, direct settlement and settlement by a third party, can be divided into seven means of settlement: negotiation or direct arrangement between the parties (the only real form of settlement by the parties themselves), mediation, conciliation, arbitration, judicial intervention, fact-finding or inquiry, and legislative action.

The two last means are hardly known in Latin America. Fact-finding or inquiry has absolutely no traditional background because it was never tried in the first decades of the twentieth century, when it was in fashion in Anglo-Saxon countries. Since it is based on objective investigation of the facts in dispute and publication of the findings and recommendations of the committee appointed for the purpose, it would be advisable to give it a trial now that schooling is more widespread, publicity media are more advanced (in many countries special sections of the daily press are devoted to labor news), and public opinion carries more weight. However, no country has yet enacted the appropriate legislation.

Some countries in the region prescribe that if conciliation fails, the conciliator must in his final report state the causes of the conflict. In Argentina and Venezuela, if conciliation fails and the parties reject voluntary arbitration, it is assumed that the conciliator or conciliation board will end its work by publishing a report containing a statement of the causes of the conflict, a summary of the negotiations, and the settlement plan proposed, and indicating which party accepted or refused it. Only exceptionally have reports of this kind been prepared, and they have not always been given due publicity. It is also usual for many departments of labor to make statements to the press or put out press releases giving progress reports on disputes, particularly those with important implications.

The practice of enacting legislation to establish new conditions of employment, or to set out the terms governing labor relations as a means of settling labor disputes, has not often been followed in Latin America, perhaps because recourse to parliamentary action has not always been available.

In recent years settlement of disputes directly between the parties themselves (also called direct arrangement, direct negotiation, collective negotiation, or collective renegotiation) is tending to become more important, in keeping with the trend toward voluntarism. There was previously little regard for these forms of settlement, since it was thought that once the parties had disagreed, they were incapable of reconsidering their attitude, and the idea of dispute thus became associated with that of intervention by a third party. In 1962 the ILO noted the virtual monopoly of settlement procedures thus exercised by the state, and reported that there was hardly a country whose government allowed the interested parties to settle economic disputes on their own.[19]

In practice direct negotiations between the parties failed at that time for two reasons: first, for causes similar to those met with in the collective bargaining of the time (both parties' tendency to take up extreme positions), and, second, the certain knowledge that sooner or later the dispute would inevitably be settled by the authorities responsible for dealing with labor matters; this raised both parties' hopes that they would gain more or lose less than by compromising. However, as collective bargaining gradually became more rational, and as the parties gained confidence in their own abilities and realized the advantages of settling the dispute by themselves, the prospects of direct negotiation began to improve.

Nowadays direct settlement is specifically mentioned as a means of settling conflicts of interests in Costa Rica (where, however, the phrase "direct arrangement" also covers understandings between employers and unorganized groups of workers), the Dominican Republic, Ecuador, Haiti, Paraguay, and Peru. In Costa Rica it is stipulated that a direct arrangement may be concluded only between the parties themselves or with the help of amicable referees (which of course brings it nearer to conciliation). Other countries distinguish between direct negotiation and conciliation: in conciliation the parties may be accompanied by advisers (who may be lawyers or trade union or employers' leaders), whereas at the direct negotiation stage only the parties may take part, and persons unconnected with the process are excluded. This distinction, which is prescribed in Bolivia and Peru, seems to be a reaction against the excessive use of advisers (particularly legal advisers) who occasionally hinder frank and direct discussion between employers and workers.

As for procedure, in Peru the basic regulations for direct negotiation limit its duration to 20 days, and make attendance at meetings for direct negotiations compulsory (although this applies only to the employer). Peruvian labor policy shows its interventionist spirit by regulating even direct negotiation by law and requiring accords or agreements concluded by direct negotiation to be approved by the administrative authorities. In Haiti rules are also laid down for direct negotiation, limiting its duration to ten days and the number of persons composing each delegation to three. Other countries prefer not to regulate direct negotiation, perhaps regarding it as a matter for the parties concerned to settle by themselves.

The Sixth Ibero-American Congress of Labor Law and Social Security (Caracas, 1977) stated in one of its conclusions that settlement by direct negotiation by the parties themselves is the ideal way of settling labor disputes. It also recognized that negotiation is a way of overcoming difficulties arising between the parties, as well as of fixing working conditions.

There are no exact statistics on the relative importance of direct arrangement as a means of settling disputes. In some countries it is not possible to distinguish between agreements reached at the bargaining stage and those obtained by renegotiation after the dispute has been submitted to the labor authorities, and in others the figures for voluntary agreements do not distinguish agreements arrived at directly from those obtained by conciliation. The major importance of direct settlement nevertheless appears to be beyond doubt. Even in Peru, where arbitration was initially regarded as the principal means of settling disputes, the number of arrangements by direct negotiation rose from 80 in 1966 to 998 in 1975 and 965 in 1976.[20] In 1980–81, 18 of the 26 cases of wage bargaining in the Peruvian mining industry were concluded by direct agreement, 3 by conciliation, and 5 by decision.[21] In 1982–83, out of 24 negotiations carried out in the same industry, 20 were settled by direct negotiations, 2 by conciliation, and 2 by decision.[22]

Notes

1. See, for instance, Kenneth S. Mericle, "Conflict Regulation in the Brazilian Industrial Relations System" (Ann Arbor, Mich.: University Microfilms International, 1976), p. 300.

2. See, for instance, José Alvaro Moisés, *Greve de massa e crise política (Estudo da greve dos 300 mil em São Paulo—1953/54)* (São Paulo, Livraria Editora Polis, 1978); L. Díaz Cárdenas, *Cananea: Primer brote de sindicalismo en México* (Mexico City: Secretaría de Educación, 1936); Mario Gill, ed., *La huelga de Nueva Rosita* (Mexico City: Imprenta Mapri, 1959); H. Landsberger and F. Camtrot, *La huelga de Molina de 1953* (Santiago de Chile: Editorial del Pacífico, 1967).

3. See, for example, the heading "huelga" in *Recopilación de la prensa diaria: Indice mensual* (Mexico City: Secretaría del Trabajo y Previsión Social de México, Instituto Nacional de Estudios del Trabajo, Servicio de Información sobre Asuntos Laborales, various issues).

4. Data provided by the Department of Labor.

5. Coqueijo Costa, "Arbitration and the Role of Courts: The Administration of Justice in Labour Law," *Reports and Proceedings, International Society for Labour Law and Social Security, Ninth International Congress, Munich, 1978* (Heidelberg: Verlagsgesellschaft Recht und Wirtschaft, 1978), vol. II/1, p. 37.

6. Abdón Calderón, "Los conflictos colectivos en el Ecuador en el año 1973," *Revista del Instituto de derecho del trabajo e investigaciones sociales* (Quito), July–Dec. 1975, p. 133.

7. J. Morris, *Elites, Intellectuals and Consensus* (Ithaca, N.Y.: New York State School of Industrial and Labor Relations, Cornell University, 1966), passim.

8. Juan Carlos Blasco, "Relaciones laborales en América latina," in R. Katzman and J.L. Reyna, eds., *Fuerza de trabajo y movimientos laborales en América latina* (Mexico City: Colegio de México, 1979), p. 151–93.

9. See Henry Landsberger, "The Labor Elite: Is It Revolutionary?" in Seymour M. Lipset and Aldo Solari, eds., *Elites in Latin America* (New York: Oxford University Press, 1967), pp. 256–300.

10. Francisco Zapata, "Investigación sobre las relaciones entre la legislación del trabajo, las relaciones laborales y el desarrollo económico y social en México" (Mexico City: El Colegio de México, 1979) p. 39. (Mimeographed.)

11. Euclides Ramón, "Los conflictos colectivos en el Ecuador durante los últimos seis años," *Revista del Instituto de derecho del trabajo e investigaciones sociales,* July–Dec. 1975, pp. 196–97.

12. See the summary of relevant material in Juan Carlos Blasco, "Relaciones laborales en América latina," pp. 174–77.

13. See Octavio Bueno Magano, "Solução dos conflitos coletivos de trabalho," *Revista LTr* (São Paulo), June 1978, p. 690; M. Tissembaum, *Las controversias del trabajo: La huelga y el lockout ante el derecho* (Buenos Aires: Victor P. de Zavalía, 1952); and Guillermo Cabanellas, *Derecho de los conflictos laborales* (Buenos Aires: Bibliográfica Omeba, 1966), p. 45.

14. Coqueijo Costa, *Direito judiciário do trabalho* (Rio de Janeiro: Forense, 1978), p. 89.

15. See, for instance, the Code of the Dominican Republic, art. 87.

16. ILO, *Labour Courts in Latin America,* report submitted by the International Labour Office to the Fourth Conference of American States Members of the International Labour Organisation (Montevideo, April 1949) (Geneva: ILO, 1949).

17. See Guillermo Cabanellas and Mozart Victor Russomano, *Los conflictos colectivos de trabajo y su solución* (Buenos Aires: Heliasta, 1979), p. 18.

18. Ernesto Krotoschin, *Tratado práctico de derecho del trabajo* (Buenos Aires: Ediciones Depalma, 1977).

19. ILO, *Some Aspects of Labour–Management Relations in the American Region,* Labor–Management Relations Series, no. 11A (Geneva: ILO, 1962), p. 20.

20. Information from Peruvian Department of Labor.

21. *Análisis laboral* (Lima), Mar. 1981, pp. 10–11.

22. Ibid., May 1983, p. 12.

10

Conciliation

by
Efrén Córdova

The original system of collective labor relations in Latin America did not regard conciliation as vitally important; but in practice conciliation has become the most significant and effective means of settling labor disputes. It stands halfway between settlement by direct negotiation (which in the long run is what makes conciliation successful) and intervention by a third party, being limited to helping the parties to seek an agreement. Conciliation also serves to maintain continuity between the new trends toward voluntarism and the old interventionist traditions. Many countries, including Argentina, Mexico, and Panama, have made it the hub of a dynamic policy for settling disputes.

The preamble to the draft labor code submitted in 1979 to the Chamber of Deputies of the Dominican Republic considers conciliation as the best possible way of settling labor disputes.[1] Similarly, the preamble to the text of the procedural amendments made in 1980 to the Mexican Federal Labor Law describes conciliation as the most suitable means of settling disputes with the least possible waste of time and money; it seeks to promote contact between workers and employers in the presence of the authorities, whose amicable intervention helps to clear up misunderstandings and settle conflicts.[2]

This explains why in recent years various countries have decided to run training programs for their conciliators, hold seminars to study their problems, and compile statistics on the kinds of disputes submitted for conciliation and the results obtained. Other countries, which still follow the traditional approach that considers conciliatory meetings as improvised or emergency actions and conciliators as part-time members of a department that also does other work, are nevertheless coming to realize, little by little, the enormous value of conciliation in promoting collective labor relations. Even in Brazil, where the labor courts play a predominant role, conciliation is not regarded as a preliminary to the collective award but as an immediate objective of the proceedings.[3] The conviction has thus been gaining ground everywhere that industrial peace, or at least reduction of the number of disputes to a reasonable level, depends primarily on strengthening the conciliation system.

Conciliation and Mediation

Although in practice hardly any country distinguishes between conciliation and mediation, a distinction is attempted in some codes, and still more by the legal experts. In Chile and the Dominican Republic, for example, the deliberate distinction between the two terms is noticeable in the legislation, although it is made for different purposes: the Labor Code of the Dominican Republic speaks of conciliation for legal disputes and mediation for economic disputes, while in Chile it is believed that the legislature used the term "mediation" to refer to the use of a conciliator empowered to suggest the terms of a settlement.

Latin American authors have used various criteria to differentiate between conciliation and mediation. The most common one is the degree of initiative supposedly taken by the third party. According to some authors, a conciliator tries only to narrow the gap between the parties and to facilitate a compromise, but makes no proposals, whereas a mediator does not confine himself to promoting frank discussions and understanding, but also puts forward proposals and seeks a compromise. Other authors have used the same criteria of differentiation in an opposite sense; but the intention behind these distinctions is clearly to place conciliation, mediation, and arbitration in an order of different degrees of intervention. Deveali, for example, writes that "mediation is an especially intense form of conciliation."[4] Russomano adds that it is also "a gentle form" of arbitration.[5]

Other authors distinguish conciliation from mediation by the purpose of each. The conciliator concentrates on obtaining an equitable settlement of the dispute; the mediator tries to reach an agreement as best he can and to avoid open conflict—that is, to reach agreement for its own sake, irrespective of the degree of justice or equity it will bring. This distinction has perhaps influenced the system of the Dominican Republic.

Finally, there is no lack of authors who believe that the real distinction lies in the status of the conciliator or mediator. They believe that conciliation is always a matter for civil servants, whereas mediation may be by prominent personalities unconnected with the government; in Latin America high dignitaries of the Roman Catholic Church have sometimes acted as mediators in important disputes. In 1981, for instance, mediation by the Catholic Church was successful in resolving a lengthy dispute between the Bolivian government and the tin miners. In Costa Rica leading figures of a political party are called upon to participate at the critical stages of negotiations on the banana plantations.

Characteristics of Conciliation in Latin America

Like other aspects of labor relations, conciliation has special characteristics in Latin America. Its function is basically the same as elsewhere, but it is applied and exercised in special circumstances that should be identified from the start.

The first concerns the type of dispute for which conciliation is to be used. In other parts of the world, conciliation is regarded as an appropriate means of settling disputes over interests, since it is in such cases that a third person, the conciliator, can suggest compromises, seek an understanding, and obtain agreements. Any attempt to use conciliation to settle a dispute over rights in which the point at issue is simply interpretation of an already established standard and ascertaining its scope could jeopardize inalienable rights and be looked on almost as an incongruity (*contradictio in adjecto*).[6] There is, however, no doubt that in Latin American labor relations conciliation is used as much for disputes over rights as for disputes over interests—not only to save legal costs,[7] but also because it is recognized that many disputes over rights are basically due to faulty interpretation, lack of knowledge, or difficulties of communication. Where many workers are not aware of their rights and some employers are reluctant to recognize their obligations, conciliation may obviously be useful to remedy this state of affairs and clear up misunderstandings.

Figures taken at random from the annual reports of government departments may illustrate the frequent use of conciliation in disputes over rights. In Costa Rica in 1979, the Department of Labor and Social Security intervened in 8,990 grievances, in relation to which conciliatory meetings were convened in 4,962 cases; in the same year it dealt with only 26 disputes over interests.[8] In Ecuador in 1975, under 20 percent of the industrial disputes dealt with by the labor authorities concerned improvement of labor conditions.[9] In El Salvador in 1972–73, the Collective Relations Department intervened in fewer than 100 disputes over interests but acted as conciliator in 2,590 legal disputes.[10] In Panama in 1974–75, the Ministry of Labor's Complaints and Grievances Section recorded 6,507 cases of conciliation in individual disputes and 1,503 cases of collective mediation.[11] In Peru every year the number of complaints filed by trade unions with regard to nonobservance of rights greatly exceeds the number of economic demands handled by the department of labor. In other countries, particularly in Central America and the Caribbean, the annual number of meetings called to conciliate legal disputes is often ten times higher than that of meetings for disputes over interests.

It may be that these figures reflect a lack of maturity in negotiating collective agreements, which do not always cover all negotiable aspects or fail to clearly regulate working conditions and relations between the parties. Since the conclusion of the agreement does not clear up all outstanding claims, there is often a residue of discontent that shows itself in subsequent individual or trade union complaints dealt with by conciliation. However, available data also seem to suggest that administrative conciliation is in fact taking the place of other institutions, not only negotiation itself but also labor courts.

The delays, expenses, and vexations of court proceedings are such that in nearly all countries (except Brazil) the parties prefer to apply first to the department of labor, where more energetic and receptive officials can promptly clear up the controversy. It is therefore understandable that the 1975 annual report of the Costa Rican Department of Labor and Social Security announced with satisfaction that of 8,990 complaints on matters of law, 5,358 were settled out of court, with or without the help of the Labor Relations Division, so that "the workers did not have to go to the labor courts to settle their differences."[12]

An important characteristic of Latin American practice in disputes over interests is that in many countries, the parties frequently resort to conciliation even though they have virtually reached agreement by direct negotiation. The reason for this is the fear of criticism or the distrust that a direct agreement might provoke within the rank and file. Many years of confrontation have ingrained the habit of representing directly negotiated agreement as the result of a dispute that could not have been settled without the intervention of the labor authorities. By resorting to conciliation, generally by an administrative official, the parties can convince the people they represent that the concessions made were necessary. This saves face and prevents protests from possible opponents of the line taken by the trade union.

Another characteristic, admittedly not confined to Latin America, is the dual procedure in force in many countries. There is administrative conciliation, possible at any time but generally preceding resort to conciliation and arbitration boards or labor courts. Whereas administrative conciliation is informal, flexible, and adaptable, conciliation by the boards or courts is legalistic, somewhat rigid, and formalistic. These contrasting approaches have been partly responsible for the boom in administrative conciliation and the growing tendency to shun the boards and labor courts; the boards' quasi-legal procedure is probably due to the use of conciliation both for disputes over rights and for disputes over interests.

When the first boards were set up, bargaining was still in its early stages, and in some countries, such as Mexico, they also acted as labor courts; the procedure laid down in the labor codes was therefore particularly suitable for the numerous disputes over rights that constituted the main business of the boards. Only slowly did the idea of conciliation as a means of peaceful settlement by bringing the parties together, clearing up misunderstandings, and creating areas of joint interest emerged. When at last it became established, the previous system was nevertheless kept in existence, so that there was a dual conciliatory procedure; but the boards are now used to determine the validity of strikes and give them legal status rather than to settle disputes.

Composition of the Conciliation Body

Everywhere the composition and status of the conciliation body have given rise to long discussions. The debate on the advantages and disadvantages of the individual conciliator versus conciliation bodies is a long-standing one in many countries. Whether the conciliation body should be independent or attached to the department of labor is also the subject of much thought and discussion.

In Latin America the two questions have, so to speak, merged into one. As will be seen from Table 10.1, there are three main kinds of conciliation systems and a fourth, less important, approach. Eight countries of the region prefer an individual conciliator, while seven others prefer tripartite boards. In three countries conciliation is by tripartite boards chaired by a judge, and in only two countries (Costa Rica, as regards direct arrangements, and Colombia), is conciliation carried out by a single conciliator or by a conciliator for each party (each appointing its own) known as an "amicable conciliator" (although in practice there are also department of labor conciliators).

One difference among these bodies lies in whether the chairman of the board is an official appointed by the executive power or a member of the judiciary. This difference obviously affects the degree of independence of the conciliation body; some boards chaired by administrative officials are independent, but most are dependent in some way on the department of labor, whereas boards chaired by a judge are independent by definition. The contrast is of course greater if boards chaired by a judge are compared with the individual conciliator, who is nearly always an administrative official attached to a unit of the department of labor. There are also, of course, hybrid forms of composition, as formerly existed in

Table 10.1.   Composition of the Conciliation Body, by Country

Individual Concili-ator (department of labor official)	Tripartite Board (chaired by govern-ment official)	Tripartite Board (chaired by a judge)	One or two concili-ators appointed by each party
Argentina	Bolivia (labor in-spector)	Brazil	Colombia
Chile	Ecuador (labor in-spector)	Costa Rica	Costa Rica*
Dominican Republic	Honduras (official of the labor depart-ment)	Guatemala	
El Salvador	Mexico (govern-ment representa-tive appointed by the labor depart-ment)		
Haiti	Nicaragua (strikes judge appointed by the labor department)		
Panama	Paraguay (official)		
Peru	Venezuela (inspector)		
Uruguay			

*For direct arrangements only.
Source: Data available in the ILO documentation service.

Nicaragua, where the chairman of the standing board was a specialized judge (*juez de huelgas*) freely appointed by the parties.

Table 10.1 calls for two more remarks. The first is that some countries could be included in more than one group. Uruguay could, strictly speaking, be placed in any of the three main groups, since its constitution provides for the establishment of conciliation and arbitration courts, which have not yet been set up; a 1977 decree mentions conciliation bodies composed of one or more persons; and a later regulation authorizes the Directorate of Wages and Labor Relations to intervene in disputes over interests.

The second remark is that inclusion in one or another of the three main groups has been governed by the body's real nature and not merely its name. This explains why Haiti has not been included in the group of countries using the system of amicable conciliators although its labor code uses that expression, for in that country the expression refers not to private individuals but to intervention by the director-general of labor. In certain other countries the conciliation boards are composed of a government representative and the representatives of the parties to the dispute (and not of national employers' and workers' organizations); but such representatives can hardly mediate in a dispute between themselves, and it therefore seems obvious that, in spite of its name, the system is really that of the individual conciliator. If we now recall that in Brazil, where a true collegiate body does exist, conciliation is initiated by the chairman of the board, who is a judge, it may be concluded that the system of the individual conciliator is the one that is gaining most ground.

The Colombian system of amicable conciliators has been criticized by Colombian writers on the grounds that the conciliators are not necessarily suitable or impartial. One writer states that "they feel themselves to be representatives of the parties rather than conciliators, and conciliation turns into a veiled opening of the direct arrangement system."[13]

Individual Conciliators versus Conciliation Boards

At the beginning tripartite boards appeared to be favored by the government labor policy, which at that time sought to democratize justice by bringing the principal parties to the system into dispute settlement, and securing the benefit of their practical knowledge of labor problems. Another factor that may have helped the growth of the system is that the ILO emphasized the advantages of a tripartite approach. In 1946, for example, the resolution on voluntary conciliation and arbitration adopted by the Third Conference of American States Members of the ILO (held in Mexico City) recommended that "in those countries which have formal conciliation machinery and in which the agencies operate on a group basis they should be tripartite in character."[14] Many years before, however, Chile and Mexico, whose legislation was to influence Latin American systems of settling disputes, had introduced tripartite conciliation and arbitration boards. Boards were also previously known in Cuba, Ecuador, and Venezuela.

It had not, however, been foreseen that in a society of legalistic leanings, this tripartite composition would lead to an adversarial, formalistic, and inflexible approach to conciliation proceedings. The presence of a judge of course encouraged this approach, but even where the chairman was an administrative official, the pressure on the board of representatives of the parties directly concerned prompted the government to adopt rules intended to ensure that its proceedings should be impartial. This semilegal slant was accentuated by the boards' having to decide in some countries whether to declare a strike legal or illegal.

Gradually, therefore, the boards became courts of a sort and their operation became slow, cumbersome, and difficult. Little by little their failure became evident in some countries. In Chile, for example, various authors have pointed out that some of the reasons for this failure were that the boards were excessively formalistic and legalistic, and lacked financial and technical support.[15] Many countries having conciliation boards were, accordingly, obliged to resort to the system of individual conciliators, which appeared more effective in practice; but in some of them the chapter on conciliation boards was not deleted from the labor code and they continued to exist as a stage in conciliation parallel or subsequent to administrative conciliation.

The upshot was, first, a duality of conciliation procedures (still found in Bolivia, Ecuador, and Mexico) and, second, an expansion of administrative conciliation at the expense of resort to the conciliation boards. In Ecuador, for example, an expert observed that the parties expected so little from the operation of the Conciliation and Arbitration Board that trade union leaders prepared a strike declaration, obtained the necessary signature to it in advance, and took it with them to the hearing by the board.[16] Similarly, a Mexican author writes that conciliation by the Conciliation and Arbitration Board "is merely a precautionary formality without useful result," and that settlement by conciliation is not normally achieved by the board but by the parties' meeting in the presence of the administrative authorities.[17] Some countries, including Chile and Panama, have recently decided to do away with the boards altogether.

Bipartite Arrangements for Conciliation

Table 10.1 reflects the various legislative formulas for the composition of the conciliatory body but does not deal with bilateral arrangements. These are not much used in disputes over interests, but are beginning to take shape in some countries in disputes over rights. This development is mainly noticeable in the big undertakings' collective agreements, which generally contain one or more clauses on the settlement of disputes arising during the life of the agreement. Agreed arrangements might even be classified into those providing merely for conciliation procedure and those setting up a conciliation body (sometimes with powers of arbitration). In the first case the intention is merely, in the words of the Orinoco (Venezuela) Iron and Steel Company's collective agreement, to "exhaust amicable and conciliation procedures to settle disputes over the interpretation and observance" of the contract or the law.[18]

For this purpose the various stages of a conciliatory procedure are specified; they actually amount to an attempt at a direct arrangement, and often include a three-tier discussion: (1) between the trade union representatives and the worker's immediate supervisor, (2) between a member of the trade union leadership and the labor relations department, and (3) between the general secretary of the union and the management. In the case of conciliation bodies, collective agreements require a committee to be formed and to meet regularly while the agreement is in force.

Latin American experience shows that conciliatory bodies of the type required by collective agreements are joint bodies, nearly always established at the plant level. In Panama, for example, the works councils that may be formed by agreement in establishments with at least 20 workers normally comprise two representatives of the undertaking and two from the trade union. In the same country, however, there are examples of industrywide conciliation bodies that also deal with disputes over interests, such as the voluntary conciliation machinery set up by the Chamber for the Construction Industry and the corresponding trade union.

In other countries the bodies formed in accordance with collective agreements and covering an entire branch of the economy are generally tripartite, as in the case of the misnamed joint committees in Argentina chaired by a government official (known as the secretary for labor relations) and the joint committees in the Mexican sugar and rubber industries. In Mexico the *contrato-ley* covering the rubber manufacturing industry indicates that the joint committee shall comprise four representatives of the employers, four of the workers, and an official of the Department of Labor and Social Welfare appointed with the agreement of the two other parties or, failing them, by the secretary of labor. Even where these joint committees act as arbitrators rather than conciliators, their decisions are mandatory only if adopted unanimously.

Trend Toward Specialized Conciliation

The preference for individual conciliators has brought greater specialization in conciliation. The first conciliators were, possibly for budgetary reasons, labor inspectors who attempted to settle disputes in their first stages. This practice still obtains in Bolivia, the Dominican Republic, Honduras, and Venezuela. It is argued in its favor that the inspector's proximity to the parties and firsthand knowledge of the labor problems from which the dispute arises can help him to bring about effective conciliation between the parties.

In other countries it was considered that a labor inspector's duties, including enforcement of existing provisions, were essentially different from conciliation and even incompatible with it, and that inspection and conciliation were both full-time jobs. In those countries it was therefore preferred to appoint officials who were specifically conciliators, or to have conciliation sections attached to the department of labor. Specialized units covering the whole area of labor relations began to appear later, and were at times concerned in settling labor disputes. A third and more recent stage is that of divisions specifically responsible for carrying out conciliation, and occasionally arbitration as well.

On the fringe of formal systems are other forms of conciliation used in special circumstances and involving officials who were not originally conciliators. Nationwide disputes, or disputes likely to lead to an emergency, may involve conciliatory action by senior officials of the department and even by the minister of labor himself. In some exceptionally serious disputes—in Colombia, Mexico, and Venezuela, for example—the president of the republic has seen fit to mediate.

In fact, although conciliation is tending to become a specialized function, experience shows that on certain occasions it is not the sole preserve of the individual or collegiate conciliators specially appointed for the purpose; in practice it may also be carried out by administrative or legal bodies appointed for other purposes or, in the last resort, by any person whose main qualification for intervening in the dispute is his high reputation or position, or the confidence he inspires in the parties. Examples of mediation by the president of the republic or high dignitaries of the Catholic Church have already been mentioned; there has also been mediation by state governors in Venezuela, members of parliament in Costa Rica, and military commanders in Honduras.

Voluntary or Compulsory Conciliation

Although the Mexican resolution of 1946 and the conclusions of the Ibero-American Congresses came out in favor of voluntary recourse to conciliation, there appears to be a definite trend toward making it compulsory. In all countries the parties are of course free to accept or reject the proposals of the conciliator or conciliatory body, but without prejudice to this freedom the prevailing opinion is that when a dispute arises, employers and workers should give the government the right to intervene in an attempt to reach a peaceful settlement, and accordingly should recognize the obligation for both sides to attend conciliatory meetings. Another reason for making conciliation compulsory is that in some countries prior resort to conciliation is essential for a strike to be declared legal. Compulsory resort to conciliation may, however, be subject to limitations: in Haiti, for example, it applies only at the second summons to a meeting; and in Honduras, while mediation by conciliation boards is compulsory (although very rare in practice), mediation by the Department of Labor is not.

In most countries of the region the parties are obliged to attend all meetings to which they are summoned by the conciliation official, but this obligation may take various forms. In Costa Rica the conciliation body has the power to send the police to fetch representatives who have failed to appear at any of its meetings, and also to fine them. In the Dominican Republic failure by any of the parties to attend conciliation meetings is an offense, and in Panama it may be regarded as contempt of court. In Peru a law of 1936 that is still in force requires trade union constitutions to contain a clause making conciliation compulsory in the settlement of collective disputes; and a 1971 act states that when a dispute goes to conciliation, if the trade union fails to send a representative to the conciliation proceedings, it shall be regarded as abandoning its claim, and if the employer's representatives fail to attend, they shall be regarded as accepting the workers' demands.

In some countries the attitude is still that resort to conciliation should be completely voluntary, and that the parties should be free to attend or stay away from conciliatory meetings. In Mexico it is considered that workers and employers alike are free to use the services of the Federal Conciliation and Arbitration Board if they wish. In Venezuela, if either of the parties repeatedly fails to appear at conciliation meetings, the only inference drawn is that the party in question assumes that further conciliation would be useless. In Chile resort to conciliation was formerly compulsory but now depends on the parties' agreement, apparently because it is believed that where the parties voluntarily submit to conciliation, they are more likely to come to an agreement than where it is forced on them. This regards the parties' wishes and the conciliators' prospects of success as more important than the public nature of conciliation services or concern for the harm that might be done to the general interest if either party refused to attend conciliation meetings.

Procedure

The key to successful conciliation lies not only in the conciliator's ability to bring the parties closer together and their willingness, however minimal, to reach an agreement, but also in the conciliation procedure. In principle proceedings should be initiated in good time, and be quick, informal, and free of charge, and any agreement to which they lead should be valid and binding.

Not all Latin American countries have laid down fixed rules concerning the most favorable moment for conciliation. In some countries (such as Brazil and Chile) the law states in general terms that conciliation may be set in motion or ordered at any time. In others its timing is related to the strike or lockout; in Venezuela, for example, the law states that work may not be stopped by either the employers or the workers until the conciliation procedure has been exhausted. In other countries a sequence of direct negotiation, conciliation, and arbitration is laid down by law.

However, there is no express requirement (except in Brazil) that any procedure laid down by a collective agreement for settling grievances or disputes over interests shall be exhausted first, although, if this is not done, resort to conciliation could be premature and the parties could become conditioned to intervention by a third party. Delay in resort to conciliation is in practice less fequent, and occurs mainly in countries maintaining a twofold conciliation system; it could, of course, affect the successful outcome of conciliation, since after some time the parties tend to become intractable, and agreements more difficult.

There are two approaches to the conciliation process that correspond to different stages in the development of conciliation. In the beginning, when conciliation boards were the more usual system, observance of legal formalities was much in favor, despite the fact that such formalities, however suitable for other purposes, were not appropriate for conciliation. There was much talk of hearings, evidence, challenges, remedy of appeal and nullity, and even of writs of execution of agreements and judgments.

At a later stage, that of the individual conciliator and the influence of individual conciliation on the previous system, conciliation was, wherever possible, stripped of its previous formalism and made more flexible. In Costa Rica, for example, the law states that the conciliation board shall meet without delay, if possible on the premises at which the dispute has arisen, and shall not accept challenges concerning the qualification of the board's members, or dilatory exceptions or motions of any kind. The Labor Code of Panama states that procedure must be simple, flexible, and informal. It expressly adds that formal presentation of a case and the taking of oral evidence must be eliminated, and that other evidence shall be admitted only where the conciliator deems it necessary to the proper conduct of conciliation. Often there is a mixture of formality and informality. In Paraguay, for example, conciliatory procedure consists of a hearing at which the board acts as an amicable conciliator; if it does not at once effect conciliation, it may call for reports to be submitted or require the parties to complete such questionnaires as it deems fit.

Whatever the approach, there is a general desire for conciliation proceedings to be summary. It is, for example, current practice to fix a maximum duration for conciliation: 8 days in Haiti, 10 in Chile, 12 in Panama (working days here, and two extensions are allowed), 15 in Colombia (from the date on which the conciliators agree to act), 15 in Uruguay (with extension), 20 in Peru, and 30 in Venezuela. In Venezuela, however, the Labor Act states that the conciliation board shall continue to meet until an agreement has been reached or it has been decided that conciliation is impossible.

Another way of expediting conciliation procedure is to give collective disputes preference over individual disputes. While this practice has been followed in Brazil, it has been estimated there that if the case goes through the first and second steps in a proceeding, it takes more than seven or eight months to deal with a collective dispute.[19]

It is fairly widely accepted that conciliation procedure should be free of charge, first because it is thought that settlement of a collective dispute is also in the interest of society and that the government therefore should not charge for the conciliator's services; and second because it is recognized that if conciliation were charged for, it would be a heavy expense for the workers and might deter them from using means of peaceful settlement. There are exceptions, however: in Chile the cost of mediation is equally shared between the two parties, and in Brazil, where conciliation forms part of the settlement process for collective disputes, the cost is borne by the losing party. The final cost is, in any event, considered to be extremely low.

Latin American legislation is more specific on the principles to be followed by the conciliator or the boards than might at first be supposed from the flexible nature of conciliation. Admittedly there are countries, such as Bolivia or Honduras, in which the law requires the inspector to confine himself to acting as chairman of the board, without expressing an opinion or voting on the substance of the matter. But there are others that lay down guidelines, however general, for the exercise of conciliation. In Colombia the law merely establishes that the function of the conciliators is to bring about an equitable arrangement "taking account of the parties' mutual interest." In the Dominican Republic the code mentions prudence, good judgment, and equity as the conciliator's basic guiding principles. Costa Rica also uses the word "prudence" with regard to the proposals or general basis of agreement that the judge may suggest. The law of Panama prescribes that the conciliation officer must do no more than act as an intermediary, chair the discussions, and take an active part only in clarifying the facts. In Venezuela the Labor Act prescribes that the inspector may be guided by reasons of expediency but that he may not express an opinion or vote on the substance of the dispute.

Two more points must be made about conciliation procedure. First, nearly all countries use the system of separate meetings, especially in administrative conciliation, since they enable the parties' respective positions to be ascertained precisely and possible concessions to be discussed frankly. Only in Haiti, however, does the code mention the existence of this conciliation technique. Second, it is everywhere customary to prepare minutes of all conciliation sessions. Venezuelan law specifies that the document shall contain an extract of the discussions. In other countries the provisional minutes record only the agreements, and it is left to the final report to explain the points on which no compromise was reached and to sum up each party's position and arguments. Some countries require the conciliator to make a special report containing an analysis of the dispute and of the attempts at conciliation, and why they succeeded or failed. In Chile, for example, the mediator must submit a report on his handling of the case that records the last proposal made by each of the parties. This requirement is for the purpose of subsequent arbitration.

Results

Its favorable results in recent years appear to confim that conciliation can become the keystone of dispute settlement policy. It would not be an easy matter to compare one country with another or establish trends in developments within a single country because standards of classification vary and data are not always available. The following indications may nevertheless show how far conciliation can contribute to peaceful settlement of disputes.

It is curious that at first sight the results are at times more impressive in individual disputes than in collective disputes. In Costa Rica, for example, in 1979, 77 percent of disputes over individual employment contracts were settled by a conciliatory agreement.[20] In Uruguay, over 50 percent of the 20,391 individual grievances submitted in 1978 were settled at the conciliation stage.[21] These percentages contrast with the data for the settlement of collective disputes in Ecuador where only 46 percent of collective disputes in 1975 were settled by compromise.[22] Favorable results regarding collective or interest disputes are however higher in most other countries for which some data are available. Table 6 shows some recent figures concerning eight countries of the region. It may be noted that the percentage of favorable results passes the 90 mark in Mexico and Venezuela and reaches satisfactory levels in countries where administrative conciliation is widely practiced.

Whatever the results it is everywhere customary to end the conciliation process by certain formalities. The previous chapter mentioned that in case of disagreement the minutes or final report were required in some countries to state the causes of the dispute and each party's position, and in other countries merely to give an extract of the discussion. If a compromise is reached it is customary for the minutes to be specially detailed and to state the points contained in the initial application for conciliation and

Table 10.2. Number of Conciliation Meetings (CM) and Conciliation Agreements (CA) in Eight Countries (1979–1982)

Country		1979	1980	1981	1982
				Year	
Argentina	CM			8,420[1]	416
	CA			4,707[1]	247
Costa Rica	CM	42	107	5,040[1]	5,023[1]
	CA	26	92	3,727[1]	3,960[1]
Dominican	CM		8,288[1]	7,477[1]	3,770[1]
Republic	CA		2,264[1]	3,314[1]	1,330[1]
El Salvador	CM		783		
	CA		525		
Mexico	CM	4,396		6,245[2]	
	CA	3,226		6,087[2]	
Panamá	CM		122	135	144
	CA		95	48	60
Perú	CM	471	401	510	471
	CA	132	144	211	173
Venezuela	CM		192	199	
	CA		188	181	

[1]Include both individual and collective disputes.
[2]Calculated on the basis of strike notices.
Source: Annual reports of Departments of Labor or data obtained directly from labor authorities.

those on which an agreement terminating the dispute was reached. Not infrequently a distinction is drawn between agreements made directly by the parties and agreements based on the recommendations of the conciliation body. As regards the points on which no agreement was reached, a distinction is sometimes drawn at the request of the trade union side between points waived and points on which the parties did not reach an understanding but that were not considered to stand in the way of final agreement (probably because they were postponed to a more favorable occasion).

In some countries the final document containing a compromise has the force of a collective agreement, but in others, more inclined to legal terminology, they are considered as equivalent to writs of execution. In

Argentina the law provides that agreements arrived at by the interested parties with the help of conciliation by the joint committees have the force of law. These differences again show the contrast between the use of conciliation merely as a means of settling disputes over interests and its use as virtually a judicial process for settling disputes over rights. In any case it is current practice to fix a duration for the validity of an agreement reached by conciliation—a minimum varying from six months (in Bolivia) to two years (in Chile), and a maximum that in the Dominican Republic is as much as five years. Any revision of such an agreement is generally regulated in the same way as a collective agreement.

Some Current Problems

The foregoing discussion identifies some of the present problems of conciliation. The first is of course the need to give administrative conciliation the institutional and legal support that its practical importance requires. This problem is especially acute in countries maintaining the twofold procedure of conciliation boards (to which the labor codes pay special attention) and conciliation officers (whom the labor codes practically ignore); but it also arises in countries using only individual conciliators and in which the labor relations system inadequately recognizes the work of these officers. The conciliator's authority and prestige are so important to the success of conciliation that it is essential to put an end to the discrimination that exists against administrative conciliation in some cases and in others to strengthen its institutional foundations so that it can make its maximum contribution to the peaceful settlement of disputes.

Second, the purposes of conciliation must be clearly stated and associated with modern approaches to labor relations. These purposes are generally stated as being to "settle the dispute," to "prevent the outbreak of strikes and lockouts," or to "facilitate agreement by the parties." Conciliation in collective labor disputes is sometimes stated "to have as its fundamental purpose the establishment of a balance between production factors."[23] The view is slowly gaining ground that the main purpose of conciliation is not merely to settle a dispute but also to help the parties to establish better relations for future coexistence,[24] although this view is not yet reflected in legislation. For example, hardly any practical use is made of the preventive side of conciliation; the tendency is to associate it with the outbreak of a dispute, and above all with a strike. Similarly, not enough attention is paid to the possible effect of conciliatory action on collective bargaining; prematurely convened conciliatory meetings prevent the parties from using their own machinery for peaceful settlement or accustom them to leaning too heavily on state intervention.

There is also a need to state clearly the qualifications required to work as conciliator, and to make recruitment and promotion of civil service conciliation officers depend essentially on merit. A number of countries continue to attach prime importance to legal knowledge without giving due weight to what is in fact more important: a flair for diplomacy, human relations, and industrial psychology. Moreover, all too often the recruitment conditions duly laid down by law are in practice disregarded for political reasons. Similarly, little attention is paid to the conciliation officer's problems in regards to career prospects, salary, and rank.

One specially relevant point in some countries is that a single person combines the function of conciliator and arbitrator. As well as confusing separate functions requiring a different set of abilities, this affects the efficacy of conciliation. It often happens, for example, that the conciliator refrains from proposing an arrangement for fear of being accused later of prejudging the case; the parties may also be inhibited from making concessions before a conciliator who would subsequently settle the dispute as an arbitrator. Perhaps one of the reasons why conciliation has not developed as far as it could in Peru is that the conciliation officer or his immediate superior sometimes has powers of decision, and these encourage him to relegate the conciliatory meeting to the background or to devote insufficient effort to it, because he is sure that he or his superior will settle the dispute in any case. The result is that far too many cases of conciliation fail and that the parties become more conditioned to government intervention.

Although for many years some departments of labor neglected to provide the premises and material facilities necessary for conciliation to be fully effective, more attention is beginning to be paid to this. The ILO pointed out this need as far back as 1968, when its report to the government of Peru stressed that interviews and hearings should be held behind closed doors in meeting rooms that were large enough and adequately equipped for negotiation between the parties and with the conciliator, thus helping psychologically to bring the parties closer together instead of driving them further apart.[25] Some governments now recognize in their annual reports that the conciliator must work in a serene atmosphere and in suitable premises, where employers and workers alike will be predisposed to accept his recommendations or suggestions.

The problem also arises of ridding proceedings of the hindrances, complications, and formalities that still typify them in many countries. Conciliation should be divorced from the process of declaring a strike legal or illegal, and the conciliator should be relieved of the legal formalities he now has to carry out. It is none of his business to judge or arbitrate, and he therefore does not need to call for evidence or take decisions on the substance of the case unless these would facilitate conciliation. It would also seem advisable to centralize conciliation by making a single body or system responsible for it, thereby preventing the proliferation of conciliation and mediation bodies, with all the resulting confusion (although this reform should not prevent geographical decentralization).

Finally, there should be more diversification of studies on conciliation, which now generally deal with legal matters and not enough with conciliation techniques, measurement of their results, and socioeconomic aspects. At an international congress on labor law held in Mexico City in 1980, and at the Seventh Ibero-American Congress of Labor Law and Social Security, held in the same year, nearly all the papers on conciliation dealt almost exclusively with legal problems.

Notes

1. See Henry Molina, *El nuevo Código de trabajo* (Santo Domingo); p. 22.

2. See *Gaceta* (Academia Mexicana de Derecho Procesal del Trabajo), spec. iss., Feb. 1980, p. 54.

3. Coqueijo Costa, "Arbitration and the Role of Courts. . . ," in *Reports and Proceedings, International Society for Labour Law and Social Security, Ninth International Congress* (Heidelberg: Verlagsgesellschaft Recht und Wirtschaft, 1978), vol. II/1, p. 35.

4. Mario L. Deveali, *Curso de derecho sindical y de la previsión social* (Buenos Aires: Victor P. de Zavalia, 1957), p. 254.

5. Guillermo Cabanellas and Mozart Victor Russomano, *Los conflictos colectivos de trabajo y su solución* (Buenos Aires: Heliasta, 1979), p. 120.

6. Johannes Schregle, "La conciliación en América latina: Algunas reflexiones," paper submitted to the International Congress of Labour Law, Mexico City, 1980, p. 7.

7. Ibid., p. 9.

8. Ministerio de Trabajo y Seguridad Social de Costa Rica, *Memoria anual 1979* (San José: the Ministry, 1980), pp. 27–28.

9. Hugo Valencia Haro, *Legislación ecuatoriana del trabajo* (Quito: Editorial Universitaria, 1979), table 11, p. 501.

10. Gobierno de El Salvador, *Informe de las labores desarrolladas por el poder ejecutivo en el ramo de trabajo y previsión social (1972–1973)* (San Salvador: the Government, 1973), p. 92.

11. Ministerio de Trabajo y Previsión Social de Panamá, *Memoria 1974–1975* (Panama City: the Ministry), p. 30.

12. Ministerio de Trabajo y Seguridad Social de Costa Rica, *Memoria anual 1979*, p. 27.

13. Guillermo Camacho, *Derecho del trabajo*, vol II, *Relaciones colectivas* (Bogotá: Editorial ABC, 1973), p. 229.

14. ILO, *International Standards and Guiding Principles, 1944–1973*, Labour–Management Relations Series, no. 44 (Geneva: ILO, 1975), p. 97.

15. Ramón Rivas Guzmán et al., *Código del trabajo: Organización sindical y negociación colectiva* (Santiago de Chile: Revista Técnica del Trabajo y Previsión Social, 1980), p. 328d.

16. Hugo Valencia Haro, *Legislación ecuatoriana del trabajo* (Quito: Editorial Universitaria, 1979), pp. 475–76.

17. Miguel Cantón Moller, "La conciliación y los conflictos colectivos de trabajo," in Academia Mexicana de Derecho del Trabajo y de la Previsión Social, *Ponencias, Congreso internacional de derecho del trabajo del 21 al 24 de julio de 1980* (Mexico City: the Academy, 1980), p. 8.

18. C. V. G. Siderúrgica del Orinoco, C.A., "Contrato colectivo de trabajo," 1974–1977, clause 93.

19. Coqueijo Costa, "Arbitration and the Role of Courts. . . ," p. 37.

20. Ministerio de Trabajo y Seguridad Social de Costa Rica, *Memoria anual 1979*, p. 27.

21. Information from Uruguay: Department of Labor.

22. Hugo Valencia Haro, *Legislación ecuatoriana del trabajo*, table 15, p. 504.

23. Secretaría del Trabajo y Previsión Social de México, *Memoria de labores, septiembre de 1974/agosto de 1975*, op. cit., (Mexico City: the Secretariat, 1975), p.71.

24. See Rivas Guzmán et al., *Código del trabajo*, p. 328.

25. ILO, "Informe al gobierno de la república del Perú sobre la mediación y conciliación de los conflictos colectivos de trabajo," Labour–Management Relations Series, no. 30 (Geneva: ILO, 1968), pp. 15–17, 33. (Mimeographed.)

11

Arbitration

by
Efrén Córdova

Under the traditional conception of the settlement of collective labor disputes in Latin America, arbitration was the central feature of the system. Since conciliation was virtually reduced to a mere formality and other means of settlement were not held in high esteem, most countries meticulously regulated arbitration. Many commentators who stressed that arbitration was expeditious and led to a final solution indicated that these features were fundamental to satisfactory labor relations.[1]

The reasons for this trend were probably that the government had little confidence in the parties' ability to reach agreements by collective bargaining or conciliation, and wanted to introduce effective systems for settling labor disputes and thereby reduce the risk of strikes and lockouts to a minimum. Some countries also wanted to strengthen the trade union organizations then coming into being, and to encourage the development of labor relations. However, the former objective was taken into account only in Colombia, Mexico, and Panama, while the latter found little reflection in practice. Only Argentina, Chile, and Uruguay, which had long known inflation, occasionally considered using arbitration to further government incomes policy when settling disputes, particularly wage claims. Other countries ignored this possibility until much later, when the center of gravity had already shifted toward conciliation.

In spite of the importance initially ascribed to it and all the regulations made about it, arbitration was not widely accepted in Latin American practice. More and more conciliation meetings were held in nearly all countries, but the number of arbitration cases followed a downward trend. In some countries the number of awards every year did not even reach double digits. In Guatemala arbitration, especially voluntary arbitration, has fallen into almost total disuse.[2] In Chile only three cases of arbitration were registered in 1979–82; even in undertakings in which the right to strike was not recognized, the parties preferred to settle their differences by conciliation. In the Dominican Republic one author states that arbitration is a legal institution very little applied in practice.[3] In Colombia only 20 arbitration awards were registered in 1980.[4]

In countries that have suspended negotiation for some periods or have restricted it, the result has not generally been more arbitration but rather the promulgation of laws or decrees setting wage rates, freezing labor conditions, and otherwise regulating the provisions of collective agreements.

However, arbitration is still important in Brazil, Nicaragua, and Peru, and plays a certain role in Ecuador and Mexico. In Brazil collective awards are in fact a substitute for collective agreements. In Nicaragua the 1981 procedure for the settlement of disputes provides for the appointment of an arbitration tribunal whose ruling will be binding on the parties for the period specified (between one and three years). In Peru about 40 percent of all labor disputes are settled by decision of the administrative labor authorities. The situation is somewhat different in Mexico, where the special conciliation and arbitration boards sometimes make more than 1,000 awards every year, but access to arbitration is really a last step in the peaceful channeling of disputes.[5] Although the system in Ecuador provides in general terms for arbitration, only between 12 and 15 percent of collective disputes are settled by an award made before or after appeal.

The limited spread of arbitration in Latin America has been explained in various ways. In disputes over interests the workers are said to be reluctant to accept any procedure that might lead to the loss or gradual erosion of the right to strike. The workers' organizations have always attached so much importance to militancy and to pressing their claims in a dispute that it has been no easy matter to persuade them to support any settlement procedure that in general attempts to preclude the availability of direct action.[6] The employers also resist delegating the task of fixing labor conditions in their undertaking to a third party, because this would affect their prestige and limit their management rights.

These reasons were particularly important in the first stages of labor relations. More recently the decline of arbitration should more properly be ascribed to the trend toward voluntarism, which has strengthened collective bargaining and settlement of disputes by direct negotiation and conciliation, but has also made the parties less willing to hand over the responsibility of settling conditions of work to a third party. The rise of these more direct forms of settling disputes at the expense of arbitration reflects the greater maturity of the parties and the natural evolution of the labor relations system, which seeks to strike a balance between autonomy and dependence, conflict and cooperation. The idea has been gaining ground that arbitration is a useful way of settling disputes, provided it is used only exceptionally, for disputes that would be especially hard to settle otherwise. Credence has also been given to the view that general and frequent use of arbitration accustoms the parties to depend on intervention by a third party and may cause an atrophy of the system.

The decline in arbitration has thus been a healthy sign in Latin America, even though it has been due mainly to the practice that has grown up among the parties and was neither prescribed nor desired by the legislatures. The legislatures nevertheless involuntarily hastened the decay of arbitration by adopting a structure appropriate for the settlement of disputes over interests—the preference for tripartite boards—whereas the prescribed procedure appeared better suited to settling disputes over rights. This discrepancy between the structure and the operation of arbitration doubtless made it less efficient, so that the parties were further disinclined to use it.

Scope

In principle arbitration may be used to settle any kind of labor dispute, whether individual or collective, economic or legal, but in some countries the legislation restricts its use; in Panama, for example, it covers only economic disputes or disputes over interests. Although in a few other countries the legislation regulates only the arbitration procedure applicable in economic disputes, this does not necessarily rule out the parties' agreeing to submit their individual or collective disputes over rights to arbitration. In this matter the overriding considerations are usually pragmatic ones in which the maintenance of production and industrial peace[7] takes precedence over legal interpretations.

The nature of arbitration changes with the kind of dispute. It may happen that settlement of an individual labor dispute or a collective dispute over rights is subject to the decisions of an arbitration body, because the parties have so agreed, because the law so requires, or, as is most usual, because the relevant collective agreement contains arbitration clauses. In any of these cases the labor arbitrator performs a judicial or quasi-judicial function. In these circumstances, even when the arbitrator is not subject to the procedural regulations binding a judge, he proceeds, like a judge, to lay down the settlement legally applicable to the disagreement between the parties, whether this is an individual or a collective dispute over the application or interpretation of an existing legal rule, or of a clause in a collective agreement. In these cases the arbitrator's final decision is binding, like that of a court of law.

In collective economic disputes the arbitrator's decision is not judicial but standard-setting; he is not called upon to give a decision based on an existing provision, but to establish a new standard to settle the dispute raised by the parties' contrasting claims as to terms and conditions of employment. It is at such times that arbitration takes on its full importance and becomes a specific procedure forming part of labor relations. In such cases the arbitrator's decision does not have formal force of law but the effect of an agreement. Once certain requirements are complied with, it may therefore be revised to adjust its contents to changes in material conditions since the time of the decision.

In Latin American labor law the extension of the arbitrator's powers is usually limited by the notion of public policy in labor matters, which is prominent in most legislation. In ordinary law the parties may submit their disputes to the decision of arbitrators, who may judge according to their conscience, irrespective of what the law prescribes. Similarly, in labor law arbitrators have great freedom of decision, but their decisions may not prejudice the inalienable and unrenounceable rights granted to the worker by labor legislation or collective agreement.

In other words, arbitrators must bear in mind that labor standards, whether those of legislation or of a collective agreement, are matters of public policy—that is, they must uphold rights and prerogatives of which the worker may not be deprived of even if he voluntarily renounces them. Consequently arbitrators are obliged to respect these rights and prerogatives; they may not be impaired by an arbitrator's award and constitute a limit beyond which it cannot go. In Colombia, the Dominican Republic, Honduras, Mexico, and Panama the labor codes expressly sanction this principle, which may be regarded as implicit in the legislation of the other countries of the region.

Arbitration has been used almost solely in the private sector. Its use in public service disputes has been regarded as incompatible with the statutory character generally attributed to civil service employment and with the government's prerogatives as a sovereign body. There are, however, many cases of arbitration in public undertakings, especially in Chile, Honduras, Peru, and Venezuela. Since workers in these undertakings are subject to many restrictions on the right to strike, recourse to arbitration is particularly valuable and generally welcomed by them.

Kinds of Arbitration

The usual kinds of arbitration are private or official, according to the part played in their establishment by agreements or legislation; individual or collegiate, according to the numbers of arbitrators involved; and ad hoc or permanent, according to the nature of the arbitrating body. More important is the distinction between voluntary and compulsory arbitration. This distinction has a number of peculiarities in Latin America, and has a twofold dimension according to whether it refers to submission to arbitration procedure or to the effects of the award. In principle this two-fold quality should produce four different kinds of arbitration, as shown below.

In Terms of Submission to Arbitration	In Terms of the Effects of the Award
Voluntary	Voluntary
Voluntary	Compulsory
Compulsory	Voluntary
Compulsory	Compulsory

In the practice of many industrialized and developing countries, however, voluntary submission to arbitration is supposed to entail the parties' obligation to accept the award, and compulsory submission of a dispute to the arbitrating body normally ends in an award of mandatory effect. This virtually eliminates the first and third classifications of arbitration shown above.

The situation is different in Latin America, where examples of each category can be found. The first exists, for example, in the Dominican Republic, where the parties may decide on their own to submit a dispute to arbitration while reserving the right to accept or reject the arbitrator's award. More often, however, their voluntary decision to submit to arbitration implies acceptance of the award. For example, in many countries collective agreements contain arbitration clauses obliging the parties to settle all their disputes, or only individual and collective disputes over rights, by arbitration. This kind of arbitration, which, like the collective agreement, is the result of a voluntary act, is considered to entail the decision to accept the award. The third kind of arbitration is provided for in Bolivian law, which states that if conciliation fails, the parties must necessarily submit to arbitration, though they retain the right to accept or reject the award unless it relates to an essential service. This is a special kind of arbitration and has been called "indicative arbitration." The fourth kind of arbitration appears in all countries prescribing compulsory systems for the settlement of disputes in public or essential services.

There is another Latin American variety of arbitration that combines voluntary and compulsory arbitration, the combination depending on the decision of one of the parties to the dispute. In Colombia, Mexico, and Panama workers may by a majority decision demand that the dispute be submitted to arbitration; the workers may not then go on strike, and the employers may neither refuse to accept arbitration nor disregard the award. In other words, arbitration is still voluntary for the workers and may not be made compulsory for them, but can be regarded as compulsory for the employers once the workers apply for arbitration.

In practice this system signifies that the workers may voluntarily substitute recourse to arbitration for the exercise of their right to strike. This option enables trade unions that are financially weak, or unwilling to run the risk of a strike, to pass responsibility for settlement of a dispute to an arbitrator. While the system appears to place the employers at a disadvantage, it reflects the legislators' express wish to extend the principle of protection to collective relations. It may be better comprehended in light of the fact that in these countries, lockouts are not as fully accepted as strikes. However, neither in Panama nor in Mexico have the workers often applied for a dispute to be submitted to arbitration. Some use was initially made of this option in Colombia, but legal difficulties led to its virtual abandonment.

Voluntary Arbitration

Save in the exceptional cases mentioned above, voluntary arbitration has the same meaning as in other countries: a system of arbitration carried out according to the wish of the parties, who are free to choose whether to go to arbitration. In spite of its advantages, arbitration of this kind has been little used in Latin America.

Besides the reasons already given for the scanty use made of arbitration in general, there are others that specifically affect the spread of voluntary arbitration. The essential condition for voluntary arbitration is that there should be a roster of arbitrators whose impartiality and ability inspire confidence. However, most Latin American countries have not yet built up a professional corps of independent arbitrators deserving the employers' and workers' confidence. Existing arbitrators are only occasional ones, and arbitration is for them only a secondary activity, generally regarded as unimportant. Only recently have lists of persons unconnected with the government or the parties, and also qualified to act as arbitrators, been drawn up in Colombia and Chile, and very little use is made of them. As arbitrators, officials of the department of labor are generally considered to be conversant with the problems involved, but their impartiality is often challenged by one of the parties. The reverse occurs with members of the judiciary or people unconnected with the government, who might be considered to be impartial but not to know much about labor affairs.

Nevertheless, voluntary arbitration has been growing in importance in connection with disputes over the interpretation or application of collective agreements. For dealing with grievances many agreements provide only for an internal conciliatory procedure that, in case of failure, leads to the labor courts, but some also provide that in the last resort the dispute shall be referred to an arbitration body. In Argentina there are joint committees, chaired by officials of the Department of Labor with the power to vote in case of disagreement, to settle disputes arising over the interpretation and application of collective agreements. In Venezuela many collective agreements extend the competence of the tripartite committees set up to deal with dismissals to any question of interpretation of the agreement, and to any disputes about its application. Under other agreements, such as those of the telephone company, the Social Security Institute, and the iron and steel industry, a tripartite arbitration committee has been set up with a chairman appointed by mutual agreement or through the drawing from among the five names of lawyers on the lists prepared by each of the parties. In Mexico the agreements for the sugar, alcoholic beverages, and similar industries set up joint factory councils and joint field councils, and a National Sugar Committee chaired by a representative of the Department of Labor, and empowers these committees to issue decisions in individual or collective disputes that might lead to a strike.

As indicated before, submission of a labor dispute to voluntary arbitration is contingent on the agreement of the parties. Their agreement may have been given in advance in a collective agreement, and an ad hoc commitment will not then be necessary. Otherwise, the usual practice is to sign an undertaking that sets out the terms on which they agree to submit to arbitration.

In most of the Latin American countries where a voluntary arbitration system has been set up, rules have been issued on the undertaking to submit to arbitration. In El Salvador a written undertaking is not necessary. In Argentina, Colombia, Costa Rica, Chile, the Dominican Republic, Guatemala, Honduras, Panama, and Venezuela a specific arbitration clause or written undertaking is required. In Argentina, Panama, and Venezuela this undertaking is generally prepared with the assistance of conciliation officers; in the Dominican Republic and Mexico it takes the form of a petition or application to the labor authority, while in Colombia and Honduras the arbitration clause may appear in an individual contract, collective agreement, or any subsequent document. In Argentina, Chile, the Dominican Republic, and Guatemala the content of the undertaking to resort to arbitration is prescribed by law. Generally, in these and the other countries the undertaking contains an agreement to submit to arbitration, a statement of the points on which arbitration is required, and rules for the appointment of the arbitrators. It may also contain procedural regulations, as appears to be essential in Chile, Ecuador, and Uruguay, where the legislation does not lay down rules of procedure for voluntary arbitration.

Compulsory Arbitration

Compulsory arbitration systems appeared in Latin America for three reasons. The first was the need for efficient and continuous operation of the public services. The second related to the government's more general concern at the frequency of strikes and other forms of direct action, and the widespread number of strikes. The third was the government's desire to protect the infant trade union movement and give it the right to choose between strikes and arbitration, provided that arbitration then became compulsory for both parties.

These reasons are reflected in the principal kinds of compulsory arbitration in force in the region. In most countries compulsory arbitration is still connected with the government's desire to protect the operation of the public services, although there have been some changes in the meaning given to "public services." In Brazil, Ecuador, Nicaragua, Paraguay, and Peru, the scope of compulsory arbitration is wider and aims at reducing the number of strikes in general, although strikes are not explicitly forbidden by law. In Colombia, Mexico, and Panama compulsory arbitration takes effect when the workers apply for it to the authorities in charge of labor matters.

Besides these principal kinds of compulsory arbitration there are other varieties that are peculiar to certain countries—for example, the one existing in Colombia regarding a strike lasting more than 40 days, or that in Guatemala when the work stoppage is supported by more than half but less than two-thirds of the workers concerned, or that in Venezuela with regard to disputes over interests arising from discussion of an industry-wide collective agreement.

Public Services

The use of compulsory arbitration in the public services makes it necessary to define "public services." Their definition has undergone considerable change, and can even be said to have been replaced by broader concepts. The original intention in many countries was to restrict compulsory arbitration to essential public services or public utilities—that is, services provided by the central administration of the state or a decentralized authority or local concessionnaire to meet the population's basic needs, such as electricity, gas, water, hospitals, transport, and telecommunications. The concept was later extended to cover essential services, in whatever form they were provided to the community. Venezuela in 1966 introduced the idea of services whose interruption would endanger public health or the economic or social well-being of the population. Later, Argentina extended compulsory arbitration to disputes that by their nature could adversely affect national productivity, development, or progress.[8]

Even in the countries that continue to use the concept of essential public services, that concept tends to be extended in three different ways. First, the list of such services often includes activities of lesser importance, such as charitable and philanthropic institutions in Honduras, agricultural and stock-breeding research in Ecuador, milk-processing plants, slaughterhouses, and saltworks in Colombia, and the retailing of food. In some countries case law has also helped to broaden the concept of essential public services: in Guatemala it was ruled that a dispute in a bank seriously affected the national economy.[9] Second, in some countries the undertakings to be regarded as public services were not specified but more or less general definitions were laid down; the final decision was left to the discretion of the classifying authority. Finally, in several countries a list of public services was laid down by law, with a final formula that left the door open to the inclusion of other activities that, in the government's view, could affect public safety or health or the economic and social well-being of the community.

Application by the Workers

Although compulsory arbitration on application by the workers appears to be based on the advisability of giving them a prior choice between a strike and arbitration, only in Colombia is the matter regarded in that way. In Mexico the workers may submit a dispute to the arbitration board even if a strike has already been called, and in Panama the workers are entitled to apply for arbitration by the Department of Labor or its area office "before or during the strike."

Perhaps because of this approach, in Colombia the proceedings are more strictly regulated; they require that the choice between a strike and application for arbitration shall be made through a secret ballot by an absolute majority of the workers in the undertaking, or by a general meeting of the trade union or unions to which at least half of the workers belong. The labor authorities must be given advance notice of the meeting, so that they may attend it and monitor its proceedings. In Mexico the lack of regulations in this respect has raised doubts as to who may call for arbitration. Some experts take the view that only the strikers may decide to submit the dispute to arbitration, while others feel that all the workers affected by the dispute, even if nonunionized, should take part in that decision.[10]

In practice this arbitration procedure, which is binding on both parties but depends on the workers' willingness to resort to it, has been little used by the workers. Either the long-standing traditions of militancy make it difficult for a trade union to take the formal decision not to call a strike, or this is yet another example of the workers' reluctance to allow a third party to decide a dispute over interests. In either case the workers often prefer to continue the dispute until an agreement is reached by direct negotiation or conciliation.

In regard to compulsory arbitration provided for in a collective agreement, Uruguayan courts reject its overall and a priori validity, on the ground that the trade union organization concerned might not be sufficiently strong and representative. In a case concerning the banks the courts ruled that since there was no strong and unified trade union movement, it was inadvisable to stipulate that recourse to ordinary jurisdiction should be relinquished.[11]

Systems of General Application

In the countries in which systems of compulsory arbitration are generally applicable (Brazil, the Dominican Republic, Ecuador, Nicaragua, Paraguay, and Peru), compulsory arbitration is not confined to public utilities or essential services, nor is it related to the attitude adopted by the workers. In principle any dispute in those countries, whatever the sector and irrespective of the workers' position, is referred to compulsory arbitration once direct negotiation and conciliation fail, in order to give full protection to production interests and extend government responsibility to the settlement of all disputes. While the rationale of this form of compulsory arbitration could have included the need to reach development targets, the fact is that when the legislatures provided for this kind of arbitration, they were probably less concerned with development than with the maintenance of order.

There have been no detailed studies so far on the effects of compulsory arbitration on collective bargaining, but it may be significant that some of the countries that have made compulsory arbitration general are those in which bargaining is less advanced. There are of course various reasons for the limited spread of bilateral discussions in those countries, but when the parties know that disputes inevitably go to arbitration in the event of disagreement, they are no doubt less interested in prolonged bargaining and are discouraged from trying to arrive at a collective agreement.

These remarks do not, however, always apply. In the Dominican Republic and Ecuador, for instance, compulsory arbitration is not institutionalized and is far from being an effective alternative to strikes. The relevant laws or codes have foreseen compulsory arbitration, but it coexists with the right to strike, it has not been systematically developed (as it has in Australia and New Zealand), or it is not widely used, particularly when the dispute does not affect a public utility or seems unlikely to cause a breach of the peace.

Composition of Arbitration Bodies

In Latin America there has traditionally been an inclination toward collegiate forms of arbitration that at times has mingled with forms of conciliation, thus giving rise to the system of conciliation and arbitration boards or courts. There are, however, important exceptions. Argentina has always preferred individual officials of the Department of Labor as arbitrators; Chile has recently opted for individual arbitrators; and in Peru collective disputes are settled by administrative officials belonging to the collective bargaining unit of the Department of Labor. Some countries allow the parties to choose either settlement by one arbitrator or by several arbitrators.

The choice between one and several arbitrators has not always been offered in a proper form. Experience shows that the use of an individual arbitrator is more practical and expeditious in disputes over rights, while arbitration boards may be considered more suitable for disputes over interests. When the labor codes were adopted, however, no such distinction was made, because the idea of using arbitration to settle legal disputes (then believed to be a matter for the labor courts) was not widely held. Consequently the settlement procedure laid down in the codes appeared to refer solely to disputes over interests. Because such disputes involve factual and nonlegal aspects, and sometimes have multidisciplinary implications that exceed the competence of a sole arbitrator, their settlement may benefit from the experience of board members representing sectoral interests.

In countries where the system originally conceived was one of permanent boards, specially appointed boards are in practice set up for each case. In other countries distinctions have been made between permanent boards with general jurisdiction and special boards dealing with disputes in a particularly important sector (as in the Chilean copper mining industry), in branches of industry or activities determined by the department of labor, or in certain geographical areas (as in Mexico with the Federal Conciliation and Arbitration Board's special boards in each of the 31 territorial divisions of the country).

The structure of Latin American arbitration systems varies in accordance with the number of appeals permitted. In some countries there is no appeal of arbitration awards; in others appeals are handled by the ordinary courts or the labor courts; and in yet others the arbitration system allows appeal to a higher authority (in Ecuador the Conciliation and Arbitration Appeals Tribunal, in Peru the regional directorate of labor, and in Guatemala a labor court appeals section). The higher body is occasionally decentralized, as in Ecuador, which has tribunals in Quito, Guayaquil, and Cuenca. The higher body may also be required to standardize the decisions of the lower-level boards or courts.

The composition of the arbitration body depends on whether it is permanent or ad hoc. The permanent bodies comprise representatives of employers' and workers' organizations at the national or the sectoral level, who, together with the chairman, are appointed for a fixed period. Ad hoc boards may include such members, but generally comprise the parties' representatives and a chairman who may be a senior official or specialist in the department of labor, a member of the judiciary, a labor inspector, or an arbitrator chosen from a standing list. It is unusual in Latin America for the board to include other government representatives appointed by the department of economic affairs or other departments, or independent members appointed to represent general interests, but a few compulsory arbitration systems do provide for this.

The arbitrator who will act as chairman of the board is generally appointed directly by the government (the executive or judicial branch), but has occasionally been appointed by the arbitrators named by the parties, or by the parties directly (again with the reservation that if they fail to agree, the government will appoint him); recently there has been a tendency to appoint him from a standing list. In Colombia the Department of Labor has drawn up a list of 200 independent persons, mainly lawyers or professors, that has to be approved by the Supreme Court of Justice. In Chile there is a list of arbitrators for the entire country, whose number is fixed by the president of the republic, and the parties may by mutual agreement appoint one of the candidates on that list as their arbitrator. If they cannot agree, they must state their order of preference for the various candidates, and the Labor Inspection Service then appoints the candidate nearest to both parties' preferences.

Opinions differ as to the value of the contribution expected from the nongovernment members or assessors. The general opinion is that the members appointed by the parties are of little use in spite of any requirement that they shall have no direct, material interest in the case. In Ecuador, for example, some writers observe that their short-term appointment to the arbitration body affects the atmosphere of security, impartiality, and continuity that should surround arbitration, and gives the arbitration body a temporary and ephemeral character.[12] In Brazil, where the assessors are appointed for fairly long periods, some experts believe that they can contribute practical knowledge and be an excellent way to democratize justice;[13] others feel that these advantages apply to the settlement of disputes over interests and that the presence of the advisers in handling technical and legal disputes might be undesirable.

Procedure

In most Latin American countries the procedure is the same for voluntary arbitration and (where it occurs) compulsory arbitration. In some countries the rules relate only to voluntary arbitration, but are also used, with some amendments, in compulsory arbitration. These amendments obviously refer to the mandatory character of the proceedings, the method of initiating them, and the powers of the arbitration body. In general the intention is to submit arbitration to a formalistic procedure containing many principles of ordinary law that are apparently more appropriate to disputes over rights. This has caused arbitration of disputes over interests gradually to lose its special character in some countries and to become "a merely formal and legalistic settlement."[14]

In some countries it is expressly stated that the voluntary arbitration procedure laid down in the labor codes is applicable only where collective agreements do not provide for different procedures. Other countries implicitly recognize the right of the parties to agree freely on a procedure differing from that prescribed by law. In either case departure from the statutory procedure is assumed to be valid only if the principle of equal treatment of the parties is guaranteed and the arrangements are not contrary to public order. Such an option does not apply to compulsory arbitration, in which the parties have to follow the procedure prescribed by law.

There are also differences with regard to the start of proceedings, which in compulsory arbitration is by decision of the labor authorities, who convene the parties and fix a date and place for arbitration. Arbitration is not generally resorted to until attempts at direct arrangement and conciliation have failed.

In regard to the stage at which voluntary arbitration is used, there are two procedures. In Chile, El Salvador, Guatemala, and Honduras, the legislation states that the parties may submit a dispute to voluntary arbitration at any stage. In Argentina, Bolivia, Costa Rica, Panama, and Venezuela, the legislation requires previous resort to conciliation, and only if conciliation fails may the parties agree to submit to arbitration. In some of these countries conciliators who fail to reach a compromise on the dispute are required to recommend that the parties submit it to arbitration. In countries where prior conciliation is not compulsory, the intention was perhaps to speed up settlement procedures by relieving the parties of the obligation to resort to prior conciliation when they had already agreed to arbitration. In the other group of countries it was deemed preferable to oblige the parties to exhaust the conciliation procedure, possibly in the belief that settlement by conciliation was more satisfactory than settlement by arbitration. This also avoids premature submissions to arbitration, which might be interpreted as equivalent to renouncing the right to strike.

In most Latin American countries the conduct of the arbitration proceedings relies largely on the application of the parties in voluntary arbitration, whereas compulsory arbitration confers greater powers of intervention on the department of labor and on the chairman of the court. There are no fundamental differences in regard to the effect of the procedure on the exercise of direct action. Compulsory arbitration generally rules out the exercise of the right to strike or to lock out. Many laws also state that submission of a dispute to voluntary arbitration generally entails ceasing all collective stoppages of work. Latin American legislatures apparently regard it as illogical to continue a strike or lockout once the parties agree that their differences should be settled by an arbitrator. There are specific requirements to this effect in Bolivia, Chile, Colombia, Costa Rica, the Dominican Republic, Ecuador, Guatemala, and Honduras.

Once an arbitration court is formed, it usually holds a hearing at which the parties state their cases and indicate what evidence they wish to submit; conciliation is usually attempted at this stage. After this hearing there is a (generally short) period during which the parties present and substantiate their evidence and the arbitrators make such investigations as they deem fit by questioning witnesses, visiting the work place, requesting information from public and private bodies, or calling expert witnesses. In many countries the law expressly grants wide investigatory powers to arbitration bodies, and in some cases stipulates that it is the express duty of persons in positions of authority, including officials of the department of labor, to lend their assistance.

Nearly everywhere a short period is allowed to complete the investigation—four days (renewable for another four) in Ecuador, seven in Bolivia, and ten in the Dominican Republic. In the Dominican Republic the arbitrators are required to make a written report that sets out the results obtained and proposes what they believe to be the best way of ending the dispute and preventing its recurrence. The parties are later summoned to a final hearing at which they can submit their observations. Under the compulsory arbitration procedure of some countries, there is less time to submit or examine evidence, but the arbitration body is empowered to take whatever additional steps it may consider necessary to ascertain the facts of the dispute.

Everywhere the legislature has been at pains to fix a reasonable time for the arbitrators to come to their decision after the period allotted for investigation and evidence: they must make their award within 3 days in

Ecuador; 10 in Argentina, Nicaragua, and Panama; 15 in Costa Rica, Guatemala, and Mexico; and 22 in Bolivia. In some cases the award must be made within a period starting from the date on which the arbitration court is formed—for example, 10 days in Colombia and Honduras (although the parties may extend it) and 30 in Chile, El Salvador, and Venezuela.

Effects of the Award

Since arbitration is governed by a single legal text generally referring to disputes over interests (but really more suitable for disputes over rights), it has not been possible to draw proper distinctions between arbitration based on law and arbitration based on equity. This is particularly evident in the award ending the arbitration process (or *sentencia colectiva*, as some countries prefer to call it) and the principles it is required to follow. In some countries (such as Colombia and Honduras) the code states that the award "must as far as possible follow the lines of the judgments made by judges in labor lawsuits." Something similar happens in the Dominican Republic, where awards must be based on the same principles as in labor court proceedings. In Costa Rica and Guatemala the court must point out the omissions or defects in the applicable law or regulations; while it is the responsibility of the employers' and workers' representatives to establish the points of fact, the consequent exposition of the law is the duty of the presiding judge. If the parties cannot agree on the facts, the presiding judge must settle their disagreement.

Equitable arbitration, applicable in principle to disputes over interests, is more clearly seen in countries that prescribe that arbitrators shall settle the dispute in accordance with their conscience and equity. In Panama, for example, it is clearly stated that the arbitration court shall make its award in accordance with facts and known truth, without following the rules for assessing evidence, and shall examine the facts for their technical relevance and in accordance with the dictates of conscience. Other countries (such as Costa Rica, Guatemala, and Nicaragua) distinguish petitions on points of law from petitions containing economic or social demands, and state that the board may settle the latter with complete freedom and according to its conscience, rejecting or granting all or part of the demands and even conceding matters not requested. It must, however, make a special reference in the award to the main causes of the dispute and to the court's recommendations to eliminate them and prevent the recurrence of similar disputes in future.

Arbitrators in disputes over interests should, then, be allowed quite a wide margin of discretion and some flexibility. Nevertheless, different systems under which the arbitration body's judgment is subordinated to preestablished criteria have been adopted in three countries. In Chile the

1979 Labor Plan introduced, for the first time in Latin America, a "final offer" arbitration system of the whole package variety. According to the plan, the arbitration court is obliged to decide in favor of one of the two final proposals made by the parties when the case was submitted to arbitration; it may not decide in favor of any other course, nor may its award contain proposals from the other party. The plan requires the court to give reasons for its award and mentions as criteria that it must bear in mind the level of employment and wages, the degree of specialization and experience, and the increased productivity obtained. In Peru the arbitration authority must obtain a technical opinion from the Department of Labor's Wages Bureau; this opinion must consider how much the demands would cost, the undertaking's ability to pay, and the effect of demands on the industry and on the national economy. In Brazil labor courts' decisions that do not respect the standards fixed by the government's wage policy may be annulled. Other countries empower the arbitration body to apply to the department of labor for a technical economic opinion, generally at the arbitrators' discretion.

A similar confusion between arbitration according to law and arbitration according to equity can be seen in some countries in connection with assessment of the effects of the award. In Haiti and Honduras the law provides that the award shall be final and have force of law, which seems inappropriate if the award relates to a dispute over interests. In most Latin American countries the law more perceptively states that the award shall have the effect of a collective agreement. The Dominican Republic's draft labor code correctly distinguishes between the collective agreement effects and the effects that can be assimilated to a final decision by referring to the kind of dispute involved.

In many countries the legislation fixes the period of validity of arbitration awards in disputes over interests. In Argentina, Bolivia, Costa Rica, Nicaragua, and Venezuela the award must be valid for at least six months, in Guatemala and Paraguay for one year, and in Chile for two years. In Panama its duration may not be less than two years nor more than four. In El Salvador the law states that its duration shall be three years. In Colombia and Honduras its maximum duration is two years.

In Bolivia, El Salvador, Mexico, and Venezuela there is no appeal of an award after voluntary arbitration. In Argentina the decision taken in a dispute over interests is final, but an appeal for annulment is allowed on the grounds that the award covered matters not included in the submission for arbitration or submitted outside the agreed term. An appeal for annulment may also be made in Panama, and extends to cases in which the submission was null and void or ineffective, or where the award adversely affects existing labor conditions. In Costa Rica, the Dominican Republic, Guatemala, and Nicaragua there is a remedy through the appellate labor court. In Colombia and Honduras there is a right of appeal that may lead the competent local court to annul the award if it does not conform to the terms of the submission or arbitration clause, or affects the rights or prerogatives granted to the parties by the constitution, the law, or existing agreements. In regard to the substance of arbitration cases, the experience of Ecuador and Peru shows that appeals usually lead to an increase in the level of benefits granted to workers by the lower body.

In most cases, once the award is final and during its validity, no new dispute is allowed on the points covered by the award. This is expressly stated in the legislation of Bolivia, Colombia, Guatemala, and Honduras. In Costa Rica the law states that as long as the other party is not involved in a breach of the arbitration award, there must be no disputes on the subjects it covers unless a rise in the cost of living, a fall in the value of the currency, or similar factors (to be assessed by the appropriate bodies in each case) appreciably worsen the economic conditions existing at the time of the award.

The award being binding on both workers and employers, they will be deemed responsible under the rules applicable to the observance of contracts if they fail to comply with it. In Costa Rica, Guatemala, and Venezuela there are specific penalties for contempt of arbitration awards.

Notes

1. See, for instance, Héctor Palacios Piña, *La solución de los conflictos colectivos en la doctrina y en la legislación chilena* (Concepción: Universidad de Concepción, 1963), p. 49; and the conclusions of the Sixth Latin-American Congress of Labour Law and Social Security, Caracas, 1977. (mimeographed.)

2. M. López Larrave, "El arbitraje en Centroamérica," in Universidad Católica Andrés Bello, *Estudios sobre derecho laboral: Homenaje a Rafael Caldera* (Caracas: Editorial Sucre, 1977), vol. II, p. 1274.

3. Porfirio Hernández Quesada, "La huelga y el arbitraje en la legislación dominicana," in *Primeras jornadas iberoaméricanas de derecho del trabajo* (Santiago de los Caballeros: Mater et Magistra University, 1979), p. 423.

4. Ministerio del Trabajo y Seguridad Social, *Memoria 1980* (Bogotá: the Ministry, 1981), p. 20.

5. See Secretaría del Trabajo y Previsión Social de México, *Informe de labores, diciembre de 1978–noviembre de 1979* (Mexico City: the Secretariat, 1979), p. 42.

6. See Héctor Hugo Barbagelata, *Introduction aux institutions de droit du travail en Amérique latine* (Louvain: Presses Universitaires de Louvain, 1980), pp. 263–64.

7. Ernesto Krotoschin, *Instituciones de derecho del trabajo*, 2nd ed. (Buenos Aires: Ediciones Depalma, 1968), p. 638.

8. Law no. 16936 of 1966.

9. López Larrave, "El arbitraje en Centroamérica," p. 1280.

10. Néstor de Buen, *Derecho del trabajo* (Mexico City: Editorial Porrúa, 1974), vol. II, p. 778.

11. See Américo Pla Rodríguez, "Arbitraje y papel de los tribunales del trabajo: Administración de la justicia en el derecho del trabajo," in *Reports and Proceedings, International Society for Labour Law and Social Security, Ninth International Congress* (Heidelberg: Verlagsgesellschaft Recht und Wirtschaft, 1978), vol. II/1, p. 398.

12. Hugo Valencia Haro, *Legislación ecuatoriana del trabajo* (Quito: Editorial Universitaria, 1979), p. 438.

13. Coqueijo Costa, "Arbitration and the Role of Courts. . . ," in *Reports and Proceedings, International Society for Labour Law and Social Security, Ninth Annual Congress* (Heidelberg, Verlagsgesellschaft Recht und Wirtschaft, 1979), vol. II/1, p. 37.

14. Buen, *Derecho del trabajo*, p. 777.

12

Labor Courts

by
Efrén Córdova

Strictly speaking, a "labor court" is a court of law with specialized jurisdiction in disputes over rights in labor matters. This strict definition was that of a time when it appeared that the dichotomy between labor courts and conciliation and arbitration bodies reflected in the first resolutions of the conferences of American states members of the ILO[1] would be universally adopted. A clear distinction was then established between legal and economic disputes—that is, between disputes over the interpretation or application of a preexisting standard and disputes over the introduction of a new standard or amendment of an existing one—labor courts being set up to settle the former, and conciliation and arbitration bodies for the latter.

Variety of Modern Approaches

In modern labor relations, however, in some countries nonjudicial bodies lay down the law, and in other countries certain legal tribunals or courts settle or compose disputes over interests as well as disputes over rights. The nature and composition of the body or tribunal or court vary widely; it may belong to the judicial or executive branch of government, or be regarded as an autonomous body with quasi-judicial functions, and be composed both of members of the judiciary and of lay judges, or only of lay judges, or only of members of the judiciary.

This lack of uniformity is especially common in collective disputes over rights, and is all the more disconcerting because the original formula appeared to be technically correct. It mattered little whether the dispute over rights was individual or collective; in principle it was always dealt with by a court of justice for labor affairs. It was accepted that only a qualified judge, versed in the law and a member of the bench, should be empowered to interpret and apply the law. At the same time labor law developed so independently, and its problems were so different from those that arise in ordinary litigation, that it was necessary for that judge to belong to a specialized body able to follow a procedure different from that of ordinary law. Any other approach was initially regarded in Latin America as transgressing the system of separation of powers, and as a failure to attend to the particular requirements of labor relations.

It is therefore not surprising that this solution was at first adopted by the great majority of Latin American countries. As early as 1949 an ILO report mentioned that there were labor courts in 13 countries of the region.[2] (In some countries they were set up at the beginning of the century; in Guatemala, for example, the agricultural judges who dealt with disputes between landowners and day laborers appeared in 1907.) This is still the legal position in Argentina, Bolivia, Colombia, the Dominican Republic, Ecuador, Guatemala, Haiti, Honduras, Panama, Uruguay, and Venezuela. In most of these countries the labor court has, if minor variants are disregarded, basically the following characteristics: it is a court of law—that is, it deals with disputes over the application or interpretation of legal provisions; it is a court competent to deal solely and exclusively with labor matters; it is a court of jurisdictional authority—that is, it is established by law, its function is to declare the law (jurisdictio), and its judgments are enforceable; and its procedure should be simple, expeditious, and inexpensive.

Because of the economic difficulties that often prevent the formation and staffing of new bodies, some countries expressly stated that where there are no labor courts, collective disputes over rights should be heard by ordinary civil courts. This tended to preserve the judiciary's right to hear and decide labor disputes on the interpretation, application, or declaration of nullity of the provisions contained in law or in collective agreements. In addition, it was recognized that ordinary courts of law were entitled to hear civil actions arising out of labor disputes, and civil liability claims against department of labor officials or employees for violation of relevant regulations.

The Current Latin American Practice

The above-mentioned scheme appeared to be logical and in conformity with constitutional theory, but it could not cope with the dynamics inherent in the labor relations system. In practice many problems arose and there were delays, frustration, and protests. In time the pressure of events burst the bonds of doctrine, and practice diverged from the provisions of legislation. Thus new bodies and procedures grew up, leading to sui generis or out-of-court modes of settlement. Meanwhile, the law in some countries abandoned the dichotomy between labor courts and conciliation and arbitration boards, giving one or the other wide powers to settle disputes of all kinds.

There were several reasons for this change. First, there were many grievances and few courts. Second, the courts could not settle disputes quickly, simply, or without charge. Jurisdictional bodies are essentially circumspect, slow, and formalistic, and are not easily persuaded to change their habits. Third, relations between the parties were maturing, so that they were able to set up their own organization for settling disputes along lines other than those prescribed by law. Formal legalism gave way to practical, expeditious settlements that led to the appearance of a variety of new systems.

The first of these is the Mexican system of conciliation and arbitration boards, which has existed for nearly 60 years. The boards do not confine themselves to settling disputes over interests; their jurisdiction extends to hearing and settling all labor disputes between workers and employers arising out of labor relations or closely related matters. The boards are not part of the judiciary, and consist of a government representative and workers' and employers' representatives appointed for each industry. Besides interpreting the law, the boards actually formulate the law, in the sense that their rulings have the force of law in disputes over interests; they also have administrative functions, particularly in regard to registration of trade unions. The Mexican system combines the boards' action with the judicial organization, since the boards' decisions are subject to appeal to the Supreme Court by means of a petition of relief. The Supreme Court has no direct labor jurisdiction but only ascertains whether awards are constitutional; lower courts are even bound to act as auxiliaries to the boards[3] within their respective spheres of competence.

A variant of the Mexican system of tripartite boards or committees obtains in Panama and Venezuela, where they are used only for a special category of disputes. In Panama there are conciliation and decision boards to deal with unfair dismissals and other legal issues outside the scope of the sectional labor courts;[4] they are tripartite and are considered to form part of the special labor jurisdiction. In Venezuela the tripartite committees are concerned mainly with dismissals, are chaired by Department of Labor officials, and are not judicial bodies, although their decisions may be revised in certain circumstances by the courts.

Besides the boards, there is also substantial juridical action in these countries by the department of labor, which attempts to settle collective disputes over rights by conciliation.[5] Reference has already been made to the importance of this conciliation arrangement, which in Costa Rica and Panama, for example, settles about 75 percent of the legal disputes submitted to it. Still more marked is the action taken in other countries where department of labor officials are competent to deal with complaints on non-observance of labor agreements or the law, to attempt conciliation, and to issue decisions that end the dispute. Peru is perhaps the country in which the labor courts have most obviously been replaced by the administrative authorities, who are empowered to intervene and settle all labor disputes except those arising when an employment contract is terminated. The Peruvian Department of Labor has thus been arrogating to itself powers that are clearly those of a court of law, and issuing administrative decisions that even have force of law. This has caused "an invasion by administrative bodies of the sphere proper to the magistracy" and the appearance of what is in effect an administrative labor court.[6]

This intervention by the administrative authorities in grievances and complaints constituting disputes over rights is also found in other countries, where powers conferred by the law for the enforcement of labor standards have encouraged the issuance of administrative decisions that in reality dispense justice and make the law. In some cases this decision-making power is limited by law to specified problems—as in Venezuela, with respect to the special protection afforded to trade union officials. There are also administrative bodies required by law to administer justice in a specific sector, such as the National Domestic Labor Tribunal in Argentina. Everywhere, however, it is becoming more common for administrative bodies to take over the work previously assigned to labor courts.

Besides the rise of conciliation boards in Mexico and administrative bodies in Peru, there is the more general and recent emergence of the administration of justice by a private system of direct arrangement and arbitration (grievance procedure). This system was introduced into Latin America by the U.S. multinational companies or by trade unions having close links with the North American labor movement. Although it does not always lead to an arbitration award, its operation has been steadily improved and it now takes a growing number of matters away from the labor courts.

Argentina is the country in which this system is most firmly rooted and has been able to take on characteristics of its own; at the undertaking level many individual and collective disputes over rights are settled by "internal committees," while problems of job classification and interpretation, and application of industrywide collective agreements are submitted to "joint committees." Only rarely are the courts called upon by appeal to revise the decisions of a joint committee in a collective dispute. In general, only individual disputes are brought before labor courts, and the joint committees, even when formed in accordance with collective agreements, enjoy a semiofficial status in settling collective legal disputes.

A special situation that further complicates the variety of approaches has arisen in Chile, where the government decided in 1981 to abolish the labor courts and turn them into civil high courts, handing over labor matters to ordinary courts. Labor courts had appeared in Chile in 1927 in the form of administrative courts attached to the Department of Labor, and in 1955 they were incorporated into the judicial branch of government. Labor courts operated for a quarter of a century, and the 1981 decision is equivalent to a return to the pre-1927 position. Curiously, the decision to abolish labor courts was taken on the grounds that the civilian courts had too heavy a workload compared with the relatively few disputes handled by labor judges and labor courts of appeal.

The situation in Chile, the growing use of conciliation and arbitration boards in Mexico and a number of Central American countries, and the combined effect of the private grievance procedure and prior administrative settlement systems in others have greatly reduced the importance of the labor courts. In some countries they have practically ceased to take part in settling collective disputes over rights; elsewhere their competence has become merely derivative or subsidiary; only if a dispute is not settled by the grievance committee or the administrative authorities, is recourse to the courts possible.

This does not mean that there is no longer any reason for labor courts to exist anywhere. Although in some countries their powers are now restricted, they are still courts of last resort, hearing appeals against administrative decisions or arbitration awards, or attempting a settlement where conciliation has failed.

While in some countries the importance of the labor courts was being reduced, they became more important in Brazil. The Brazilian labor courts, which go back to 1940, have retained full powers to hear and decide disputes over rights, and also have standard-setting powers regarding disputes over interests that exceed the normal ones of a judicial authority. Thus Brazil and Mexico, although proceeding from different basic principles regarding the composition of the body concerned, have both set out to abolish the distinction between the labor court and the conciliation and arbitration board. In Brazil the court has absorbed the board; in Mexico the board has absorbed the court. Similarly, while in Mexico the proceedings of the boards are preceded or supplemented by administrative action or by private systems for dispute settlement, in Brazil the role of administrative action and the internal grievance procedure is little more than marginal. In fact, about 90 percent of all disputes, including simple and routine cases, are submitted to the courts in Brazil.

The Brazilian approach is a product of a formerly paternalistic and corporatist society that differs considerably from the present level of development in several regions of the country. In 1940 Getúlio Vargas feared direct bargaining between capital and labor, and designed as an alternative the present system, which aims at the "absorption" of conflict. Labor courts conditioned the parties to channel their claims and grievances through the system, prevented them from adjusting their disputes directly, and nearly monopolized the functioning of labor relations.

In the last few years the strongest trade unions in Brazil have been pressing for more negotiation and less judicial intervention, but the weaker trade unions and the old bureaucratized union leaders (*pelegos*) continue to prefer the labor courts, and both sides have in general adapted themselves to their operation. The decisions settling disputes over interests, and thereby establishing conditions of work, attempt to extend to all workers in the category concerned the conditions obtained by the strongest trade unions; the result is that the courts are regarded as a moderating factor capable of acting to protect the weaker groups in the labor field. Since the trade union movement is relatively weak in Brazil, negotiation is not widespread, and there is no effective machinery for representing workers in the undertaking, the labor courts have played an important role that extends beyond their own range of functions to others normally belonging to grievance committees and conciliation and arbitration boards.

Labor Court Organization

How the courts are organized depends primarily on a decision of principle: whether they are to belong to the judicial branch of government. In most countries it has been decided that they shall so belong, but in some cases their separate organization has been preferred. When they are included in the judicial branch and when they follow models closely approximating the latter, the courts' internal organization normally depends on several basic factors: the size and level of development of the country, the number of steps foreseen in the rules of procedure, the character of the sectors in which the dispute arises, and the pressure of work caused by the number of cases submitted to the court. These factors are in turn influenced by the cost of setting up a full-fledged system of labor courts and the country's economic ability to pay for it.

The geographical factor explains why labor jurisdiction is most complicated in the largest countries. In Argentina there are labor courts in the federal capital, all the provinces, and some provincial territorial subdivisions. In Brazil the distinction is between local courts (*juntas de conciliação e julgamento*), regional courts (at present nine in number), and the Supreme Labor Court in Brasília; in Mexico there are local and state conciliation boards and federal conciliation and arbitration boards. This rather large-scale and costly organization contrasts with that of, for instance, the

Dominican Republic, where labor courts operate only in Santo Domingo and Santiago de los Caballeros, and of Uruguay, where for many years there was only one labor court in Montevideo and there now is only one court of appeal for the whole country.

The formation and number of labor courts also depends on demographic and economic considerations, especially industrial concentration. Brazil offers a conclusive example of this, as may be seen from the fact that since 1970 local courts have been set up only in areas with a worker population of over 12,000 where it can be proved that there have been more than 240 labor disputes for three consecutive years. At the beginning of the 1980s there were more than 30 such local courts in the city of São Paulo. In Colombia and Venezuela labor courts have been opened only in the main industrial centers, and in the Dominican Republic their formation has been postponed for many years in spite of the requirements of the labor code. Bolivia has taken a line of its own by setting up a National Labor Court in La Paz whose members are, however, obliged to live in what are industrially the most important districts of the country: Oruro, Cochabamba, Santa Cruz, Potosí, Sucre, and Tarija.

One important consequence of these economic restrictions is the need to provide for resort to ordinary courts of law where there are no labor courts. The ordinary courts thus become a substitute jurisdiction to deal with labor disputes arising in places where the labor force is too small to justify the appointment of labor courts. In Colombia, for example, the law expressly makes civil judges competent where there are no labor judges. A similar situation is found in many other countries where labor jurisdiction is mixed, including both ordinary and labor jurisdiction.

The recognition of the right to appeal leads to the appearance of the various levels of labor jurisdiction. Procedure in labor matters tends to be as simple and prompt as possible, and such levels should therefore generally be few, but account has to be taken of the litigious spirit and love of legalistic settlements still prevalent in certain countries. In Argentina, for example, it was estimated in 1978 that over 50 percent of the judgments given by the courts of first instance are appealed;[7] in Uruguay the proportion in that year was 90 percent.[8]

The result of this varied situation is that in some countries of Latin America proceedings may take place at one, two, and even three levels. Examples of a single level (as in the provinces of Buenos Aires and Córdoba in Argentina) are few, and the two-level system of Bolivia, Panama, Venezuela, and other countries seems to be the most common. In Brazil there is a two-level system for collective disputes and a three-level system for individual disputes. In Colombia there are labor courts at three levels: first instance (the labor judge), court of appeal (the labor section of the district high court), and high court of cassation or revision of judgments (the Labor Section of the Supreme Court of Justice). It is, however, more usual to have labor court proceedings in the ordinary sense at only two levels, and to go to the Supreme Court of ordinary jurisdiction to have a judgment quashed on legal or procedural points only.

In general the court of first instance in Latin America is an individual judge, except in Brazil and Mexico, which use tripartite bodies in collective disputes.[9] In Venezuela, on application by the parties, a court may be formed comprising a labor judge and two lay members proposed by the litigants, but in practice this provision is little used. The second level is always a court of several members that in some cases has national jurisdiction (as in Bolivia and Peru) and in others departmental or provincial jurisdiction (as in Colombia, Ecuador, and Venezuela). Not all these countries allow cassation; some of them, such as Colombia and Venezuela, allow it only for some applications, depending on the importance of the case, while others, such as Peru, reject it almost totally.

For reasons arising from the kind of sector in which the dispute occurs, a distinction has been drawn between the labor courts with jurisdiction over the entire economy and those with jurisdiction limited to the private or public sector. In Latin America it is supposed that labor jurisdiction functions only in regard to the private sector, and in some cases in regard to public undertakings and wage earners employed on public works, but does not cover the civil service, which is governed by its own administrative procedures. In Mexico, however, besides the system of state and federal boards there is the Federal Conciliation and Arbitration Tribunal to deal with disputes between the federal government and its employees; it comprises a representative of the federal government, a representative of the public employees who is appointed by the Federation of Trade Unions of Government Employees, and a third member appointed by the two others.

Besides these factors pressure of work has led to various kinds of administrative arrangements. If too many cases are brought before a court, it may have to be subdivided into various sections—in Brazil the three or four *turmas* of each regional court—or institutional changes may become necessary. In Mexico, for example, it was this practical reason, together with the wish to settle disputes as nearly as possible in their place of origin, that led to "deconcentration" of federal labor courts and the consequent formation in 1978 of 31 special boards dealing with individual and collective disputes in which the federal authorities were competent. In other countries the labor court may travel to places other than its headquarters, or members of a higher court may deal with, and make awards in, important labor cases tried in a court of first instance.

Composition of the Courts

There are no uniform criteria for the composition of labor courts. In Brazil, Costa Rica, the Dominican Republic, Ecuador, Mexico, and Panama it is preferred that they should be tripartite; in Argentina, Peru, Uruguay, and Venezuela the orthodox system of career judges is preferred. In both groups there are countries that have established tripartite semilegal or administrative bodies with powers of decision in a given sector. In Ecuador and Mexico the constitution recognizes the tripartite composition of the bodies formed to settle collective disputes; in other countries the matter is dealt with by laws or regulations. Perhaps the only point on which there is unanimity is the rejection of joint courts resembling the *conseils de prud'hommes* (lay judges appointed by employers' and workers' organizations and not assisted by a neutral third party) of France and some cantons of Switzerland.

Tripartite composition—a career judge together with other members representing employers and workers—spread initially in Latin America in accordance with the example of the Mexican boards and the model of the first labor courts set up in Germany and the Scandinavian countries. In defense of the system it was said that these judges brought to the court practical knowledge facilitating understanding and settlement of the dispute; that they favored settlements according to equity; and that they had a closer relationship with the parties (in contrast with the occasionally cold and distant attitude of the judges coming from the judiciary) and could more easily win their confidence. The first argument appears more applicable to semijudicial bodies and disputes over interests, in which a thorough knowledge of the economic circumstances and characteristics of the industry or undertaking may facilitate a satisfactory settlement. But it is hard to see how these lay judges can help to settle a dispute over rights that turns on the interpretation and observance of a legal precept or a clause in an agreement. Interestingly, the two countries in which the tripartite principle has been most widely followed in the composition of labor courts, Brazil and Mexico, are the very countries in which one and the same body has been called upon to settle disputes over interests as well as disputes over rights.

The other arguments are valid but, in our opinion, not fundamental. There is nothing to stop a career judge or a court of judges with a legal background from trying to establish a closer relationship with the parties and win their confidence—which may also be won by the prestige of the position of judge and the conviction that the judge or court will act with independence and impartiality.

The experience of some Latin American countries also shows that frequently the presence of employers' and workers' representatives is unnecessary and becomes a mere formality, since they systematically vote for the party they represent. This was shown a few years ago in Argentina, in the administrative court for the banking sector, and is frequently seen in Panama and Venezuela. Some authors in Brazil and Mexico still defend tripartite courts on the grounds that they have educational value and are a means of democratizing justice and encouraging participation; but even in those countries it has been said that the representatives of the parties should refrain from interfering in technical matters and in the internal proceedings of the court.[10] Generally speaking, it is also said that unless it is possible to inculcate in them a high-principled sense of social responsibility, the presence of the workers' and employers' representatives would introduce a spirit of class struggle into the court.

The tripartite principle also raises a number of practical problems regarding the method of appointment, term of office, and technical ability of the workers' and employers' representatives acting as lay judges. Several methods of appointment are possible, the two most used in Latin America being election and appointment by the authorities on the proposal of the most representative employers' and workers' organizations. The first system is used mainly in Mexico. The second is used in Venezuela for the tripartite committees on dismissals. In Brazil both systems are combined as workers' and employers' organizations of the first, second, or third grade (according to the kind of court) hold elections and submit a list of three candidates to the authorities, who choose the representatives from it.

Latin American experience shows that in practice the difficulties arising from the term of office are linked with payment for it. In countries where the post is an honorary one, there is a shortage of qualified persons willing to do the work. Many employers' representatives are unwilling to have their names put forward as candidates, and the only worker members who show any interest have retired from the occupation or are trade union leaders overburdened with other duties. The reverse happens in Brazil and Mexico, where the post carries with it payment on an appreciable scale; in Brazil the lay representatives are elected for three years and generally reelected twice; this affects rotation and makes for bureaucracy.[11]

Qualifications for the post differ in accordance with the jurisdiction of the court: whether it has power to settle disputes over interests or disputes over rights. For the former it would perhaps be sufficient to require a minimum standard of general knowledge or knowledge of the industry concerned, as in Mexico, where candidates must have completed their compulsory education, and in Brazil, where the requirement is at least two years' experience in the occupation or industry. Where the court is to settle disputes over rights, it is hard to see what kind of experience or training the lay judges should be required to have.

It follows that it would seem more appropriate to have courts composed solely of independent judges who are members of the judiciary when those courts are concerned mainly with the settlement of disputes over rights. According to some Latin American authors, justice should be administered solely by impartial persons with specialized legal training, whereas employers' and workers' representatives will inevitably reflect the interests of those they represent. In the Latin American countries that have adopted this point of view, the labor courts are composed of career magistrates, sometimes specialists in labor law who are appointed, like the other members of the judiciary, by competitive examination and are entitled to the same prerogatives, particularly irremovability from office and life tenure. In Venezuela members of labor courts are appointed by a legal council (*consejo de la judicatura*) for five years, but in practice hold their posts for an indefinite period.

In Brazil the position is similar in regard to the career judges composing the labor courts; they belong to the judiciary, enter the profession through a competition, and enjoy the guarantees laid down in the constitution. In Brazil labor courts are generally regarded as being efficient (in regard to rights disputes) and have won considerable prestige.

The practical disadvantages of courts consisting exclusively of career judges are their lack of social conscience, their insistence on applying the letter of the law to the detriment of equity, their love of precedents, and their tendency to settle disputes and controversies by dispassionate examination of the documents and papers submitted to them.

Procedures

Parallel with the establishment of specialized courts, many countries introduced special procedures. Both were intended to provide fair and prompt settlement of disputes. It was not enough to appoint a labor magistracy; if it had to follow the old, complicated, slow, and costly procedure, the administration of justice would suffer. The intention was therefore to simplify and rationalize procedure, adapt it to the parties' needs, and make it as prompt and flexible as the importance of labor in society required.

In Latin America, as elsewhere, it was hoped to achieve this by introducing into legislation on procedure for the settlement of labor disputes the three fundamental principles that it should be simple, speedy, and free of charge. The first principle resulted in greater efforts to make procedure accessible and intelligible, a general desire to encourage oral instead of written proceedings, and above all an effort to get rid of the formality and ritual of civil procedure. Thus, under Mexican law it was forbidden to require a fixed procedure for hearings, submission of documents, and pleadings; and in the Dominican Republic the Labor Code stated that no decision should be quashed on procedural grounds and the Court of Cassation declared that any omission from procedure may be made good.[12] These directions were supplemented by provisions to facilitate the worker's access to the court as well as the submission and examination of evidence, and by requiring the case to be settled on its merits. In some countries the requirement that the parties should be assisted by lawyers has been abolished for the sake of simplicity, and in others emphasis has been laid on the need to give the workers' side full explanations about the course of proceedings.

An attempt was also made to speed up the procedure by limiting the number of instances, motions, and remedies, making time limits short, and providing for privileged handling of certain matters. In the last connection the Dominican Republic Labor Code provides that all matters relating to the application of collective agreements and arbitration awards on disputes over interests shall be subject to summary procedure. In Panama proceedings concerning labor disputes cannot be interrupted, even when preliminary questions have been raised on points of law. In these and other countries notification by letter or telegram has been allowed and considered duly made one day after it is handed in at the post office. Official acceleration of the court's action, and the judge's participation in the submission and examination of evidence (which are explicitly recognized in various countries), were introduced to speed up procedure and show that it was not left entirely to the parties.

The principle that the labor courts' services are free of charge means primarily that the parties do not have to pay the courts' operating expenses, since they are regarded as existing to serve the parties and for the benefit of society. This principle was established in all countries except Brazil and Chile, where the costs of the action are payable by the losing party. In Panama the law states that the worker party may not be sentenced to pay costs, that the paper used in legal action in labor proceedings shall not be subject to stamp tax, that such proceedings shall not be liable to taxes or dues, and that files, applications, and other records shall be processed free of charge.

The principle of service free of charge might also be regarded as covering the provision in some countries, such as Brazil and the Dominican Republic, that the assistance of lawyers is not compulsory. On this point requirements vary, since other countries require the presence of a lawyer and regard "free of charge" as meaning the provision of free legal assistance to workers. In Mexico this assistance takes the form of the government Labor Defense Agency; in Argentina, Panama, Peru, and various Central American countries, that of free legal service by department of labor lawyers; in other countries, a general offer for the defense of indigent persons. There is no lack of judicial assistance services provided by a number of bar associations and law faculties for the benefit of indigent workers. In the Dominican Republic free legal assistance may be extended to employers whose financial circumstances prevent them from exercising their rights as plaintiffs or defendants.

All these systems differ substantially from the public labor attorneys' offices that exist in Argentina and Brazil. Thus, while the Mexican Labor Defense Agency, for example, represents or advises workers and their trade unions on request, in Argentina and Brazil the public attorney's office defends legal order and the commonweal, and has therefore to take an impartial attitude in lawsuits.[13] While in many cases trade unions are also in a position to represent and sponsor the worker, only the wealthier trade unions can give sustained and effective aid. This explains why defense of the workers is a matter of special concern to public attorneys' offices and often appears on the agenda of labor congresses.

The grant of special powers to the labor judge is closely linked to the above principles. The object of these powers is to enforce the principles and increase the equity that must imbue all the operations of the labor courts. They may take the form of setting in motion court action by official order, or of the judge's powers to promote conciliation at any time, or examine such evidence as he deems fit and assess it freely. As laid down by the courts in the Dominican Republic, "labor judges are in duty bound to try to establish the truth by any means of proof acceptable to law."[14] In some countries these special powers include that of granting benefits not claimed by the plaintiff or greater than those claimed. This means that the classic principle of concord between the plaintiff's demands and the terms of the court's decision is no longer applied.

Besides these basic principles, some more recent legislation has sanctioned the principles of concentration (in the sense that the stages of the legal process should follow each other without undue interruption), immediacy (direct contact between the parties and the judge, and the judge's personal presence at the stages of pleading and evidence), and unity of instance (which implies that appeal against the judgment does not completely reopen discussion and examination of the dispute, but simply leads to verification that the final settlement being appealed is in accordance with the law). The Mexican federal labor law, revised in 1980, contains an article that to some extent summarized these principles when it indicated that labor court proceedings must be "public, free of charge, immediate, predominantly oral, and acting on the application of one of the parties. Judges shall be in duty bound to do the necessary to conduct the lawsuit with the utmost economy, concentration, and simplicity."[15]

The dispute settlement procedure is everywhere marked by its emphasis on conciliation. In Brazil there must be an attempt at conciliation before the formal start of judicial proceedings and before the court gives judgment. In Uruguay a conciliation meeting is compulsory before recourse to the court, and may be required by the judge before judgment is given. In the Dominican Republic the representatives of both sides serving as members of the court hold a conciliation hearing at which they are required "to make to the parties such observations as they see fit and try to persuade them to come to a compromise agreement."[16] In some countries, however, the attempt at conciliation is in no way compulsory, and even gives rise to objections in disputes over rights, because it is thought that it might affect the inalienability of the worker's rights. Nevertheless, conciliation is becoming increasingly common, especially when the administrative authorities are the ones attempting to settle the dispute. In Peru the Department of Labor has set up an office for consultation and free legal assistance, one of whose functions is to attempt to bring about a conciliation agreement between the parties before they resort to the courts or to the administrative procedure in force. As mentioned in Chapter 10, similar offices in other countries have been remarkably successful. Experience shows that conciliation is less effective when carried out by a labor judge or labor court or by the entire tripartite body.

Although labor codes and laws of procedure thus sanction the basic principles of dispute settlement procedure, and many authors and judgments highlight the significance and importance of these principles in detail, in many countries there is a gap between principle and practice. In spite of the regulations for prompt and expeditious handling, labor court proceedings still drag on interminably: eight to ten months' average in courts of first instance in Uruguay,[17] one year in Argentina,[18] and several years in judgments relating to dismissals in the Dominican Republic, Peru, and Venezuela. In Chile important collective disputes over rights concerning public undertakings have lasted for long periods in courts of first instance without judgment being given.[19] Some progress has, however, been made in Brazil, where the labor courts deal with about 500,000 cases every year and can nevertheless come to a decision (in disputes over rights) in a little over a year. In Mexico, where at the end of 1977 there was a backlog of over 26,000 cases,[20] the reforms of 1980 tried to speed up procedure by eliminating some of its stages, excessively long postponements, and procedural requirements that have no effect whatsoever on the parties' equality before the law.[21]

Although many laws more or less explicitly require concentration and immediacy, the examination of witnesses and evidence and the maintenance of direct contact with the parties are still left to secretaries and auxiliaries, instead of the judge.[22] In spite of the emphasis on conciliation hearings, these often become an exercise in futility and red tape, and, like the above procedures, are delegated to minor officials. Although oral procedure is often required, there are only a few countries (Brazil, Colombia, Ecuador, and Venezuela) where petitions may be made orally, and in practice this is rare. Panama allows oral evidence, but the rules governing the procedure for dispute settlement constantly refer to the parties' documents, to the file, to the copies of the complaint and of the rejoinder thereto, and to written submission of appeals. As far as legal assistance is concerned, little progress has been made by prohibiting assistance by lawyers completely or authorizing it only in certain cases; the aim should, rather, have been to make procedure so simple that legal assistance became unnecessary.

Admittedly, some principles of the procedure for dispute settlement set out in legal theory and given statutory endorsement do appear somewhat ambitious and theoretical. The principle of oral proceedings, for example, can never be fully applied in practice. Nowhere are proceedings entirely oral; at most, all that could be aimed at is that proceedings should be mainly verbal, in reaction against "the excessive formalism and emphasis on written records characteristic of civil procedure."[23] Neither can extreme "promptitude" in substantiating complaints be hoped for, so long as their number exceeds the capacity to handle them of the few courts that can be set up in a developing country.

Notes

1. See especially the Mexico resolution concerning voluntary conciliation and arbitration (1946) and the Montevideo resolution concerning labor courts (1949) in ILO, *International Standards and Guiding Principles, 1944–1973* (Geneva: ILO, 1975), pp. 96–97, 99–102.

2. ILO, *Labor Courts in Latin America* (Geneva: ILO, 1949), p. 18.

3. See Porfirio Marquet Guerrero, "Integración y funciones de los tribunales del trabajo," communication submitted at the International Meeting of Experts on Labor Law, Mexico City, September 1977.

4. See Arturo Hoyos and Victoria Romero, *Las juntas de conciliación y decisión* (Panama City: 1976), p. 32.

5. See Héctor Hugo Barbagelata, *Introduction aux institutions du droit du travail en Amérique latine* (Louvain: Presses Universitaires de Louvain, 1980), p. 263.

6. Mario Pasco, "Desaparición del fuero administrativo de denuncias laborales," in *Análisis laboral* (Lima), July 1980, p. 3.

7. José I. Somaré, "Arbitraje y papel de los tribunales del trabajo: Administración de la justicia en el derecho del trabajo," in International Society for Labour Law and Social Security, Ninth International Congress, *Informes y debates*, op. cit. p. 2.

8. Américo Pla Rodríguez, "Arbitraje y papel de los tribunales del trabajo: Administración de la justicia en el derecho del trabajo," p. 401.

9. See Ch. 10, sec. "Characteristics of Conciliation in Latin America," for Panama and Venezuela.

10. Coqueijo Costa, "Arbitration and the Role of Courts . . . ," in *Reports and Proceedings, International Society for Labour Law and Social Security, Ninth Annual Congress* (Heidelberg: Verlagsgesellschaft Recht und Wirtschaft, 1978), vol. II/1, p. 37.

11. Coqueijo Costa, *Direito judiciário do trabalho* (Rio de Janeiro: Forense, 1978), p. 637.

12. Judgment of July 15, 1966, *Boletín judicial* no. 668, p. 8.

13. Enrique Fernández Gianotti, "La defensa social," in Academia Mexicana de Derecho del Trabajo y de la Previsión Social, *Ponencias, Congreso internacional de derecho del trabajo del 21 al 24 de julio de 1980* (Mexico City: the Academy, 1980), pp. 12–13.

14. See Lupo Hernández Rueda, "El proceso del trabajo y sus peculiaridades," in Universidad Católica Andrés Bello, *Estudios sobre el derecho laboral: Homenaje a Rafael Caldera* (Caracas: Editorial Sucre, 1977), vol. II, p. 1623.

15. Art. 685.

16. Labor Code, art. 486.

17. Pla Rodríguez, "Arbitraje y papel de los tribunales del trabajo," loc. cit.

18. Somaré, "Arbitraje y papel de los tribunales del trabajo," loc. cit. p. 24.

19. Francisco Walker E., "Una idea para perfeccionar leyes del Plan laboral," in *El Mercurio* (Santiago de Chile), Dec. 18, 1980.

20. Secretaría del Trabajo y Previsión Social de México, *Informe de labores, diciembre de 1976–noviembre de 1977* (Mexico City: the Secretariat, 1977), p. 45.

21. See *Gaceta* (Academia Mexicana de Derecho Procesal del Trabajo), spec. iss., Feb. 1980, p. 36.

22. See "Juicio crítico de los tribunales del trabajo," *El Mercurio* (Santiago de Chile), Jan. 27, 1980, p. C-3.

23. A. Montoya Melgar, *Derecho del trabajo* (Madrid: Editorial Tecnos, 1979), p. 615.

13

Strikes and Lockouts

by
Efrén Córdova and Emilio Morgado

Typology of Latin American Strikes

Industrial relations theory views strikes and lockouts as forms of direct action normally used to obtain acceptance of the workers' or employers' demands in connection with disputes over interests. In Latin American practice, strikes also are often used to compel observance of labor standards contained in agreements, arbitration awards, or legislation, as well as in individual disputes. Such disputes should, however, be satisfactorily and promptly settled by the procedure prescribed by law, without any need for pressure techniques. Also, there are frequent protest strikes for political or other reasons that do not fall within the scope of labor relations in the strict sense. Sympathy strikes have been a feature of the early trade union history of some countries.

Resort to strikes for reasons not altogether corresponding to their primary justification, and their use as an offensive weapon by revolutionary syndicalism, have given them an aura of polemics and mysticism, and partly explain the restrictive attitude toward them still found in the legislation of many countries.

This legal inflexibility influences the nature of strikes. It was stated in Chapter 9 that in Latin America there are many disputes but relatively few legal strikes. This is due partly to the severe and formalistic tenor of the law, and partly to the decentralized system of negotiation, which carries in itself the seeds of innumerable disagreements and at the enterprise level reflects the basic weakness of trade unions compared with the employer. In Mexico, for example, numerous strike notices are issued every year, but work stoppages actually occur in only 3 or 4 percent of those cases. In Panama only 4.5 percent of the lists of workers' demands presented in 1979 and 1980 led to a strike.[1]

243

Judging by the statistics of many countries, illegal strikes are not very frequent; in the four largest countries of the region, the total number of strikes declared every year is relatively small. In greater Buenos Aires, between 1960 and 1970 there were only 216 strikes and 552 other kinds of concerted cessations of work such as slowdowns. The number of strikes in Brazil has recently risen (400 strikes were called in 1979 and 1980), but this rise must be regarded as exceptional, since in 1978 it was estimated that the number of strikes was insignificant.[2] There are not many strikes in Colombia; between 1977 and 1979 the total number of man-hours lost by strikes was only 72,499. Data on Venezuela and other countries tend to confirm this general impression that direct action is relatively infrequent.

Nevertheless, statistics are not always an accurate record of illegal strikes; the very fact that they are illegal, and that the department of labor or the courts do not always intervene, means that some of them do not find their way into statistics. Moreover, a careful examination of the daily press for the last few years would show that the number of illegal strikes has risen appreciably.

Closer examination will also show that the causes of illegal strikes are complex and varied. Although in several countries various factors are still simultaneously operating and are closely interrelated, certain specific causes can be identified as being of primary importance at separate stages of labor relations.

At the first stage, in which labor relations accounted for most of the social agitation in Latin America, illegal strikes occurred because the procedural and substantial requirements for calling a legal strike were exceedingly rigid. The conditions laid down by law were so complex and time-consuming that it was hard for a trade union to call a strike at the time it wished to or with the effects desired. Many trade unions were accordingly obliged to break the law and suspend work before legal formalities were exhausted. As already stated, numerous strikes were also the result of distortion of the labor relations system, which by making the government the regulator, moderator, composer, and arbitrator of labor relations made it important to attract government attention and bring about prompt settlement of the dispute.[3] While the procedure still in force in many countries is more or less stringent, it does not account for the total number of illegal strikes.

The second stage was that of quantitative increase in unionization and growing realization of the desire to negotiate. Trade unions felt stronger and looked to negotiation as a means of satisfying pressures from the shop floor. However, negotiations at the undertaking level could not lead to satisfaction of all labor demands, which frequently concerned social services or wages policies, and this created discontent among the rank and file. Neither the government nor the trade unions perceived the need to coordinate collective bargaining in the strict sense of the term with the political bargaining carried out at the top levels of the trade union movement; consequently illegal stoppages of work occurred.

At a third stage illegal strikes become more general both inside and outside the labor relations system, as acts in defiance of the system. Some are called by small trade unions whose weakness and scanty bargaining power drive them to act in extralegal ways; others are protest manifestations resulting from temporary coalitions between the most radical sectors of the workers' movement and extremist groups in society at large. Various forms of social protest (such as street demonstrations and the occupation of buildings) not necessarily entailing stoppages of work in particular undertakings are sometimes included in this category. In all these cases a new social force can be seen that is not yet one of the main parties to the labor relations system: the underemployed or unemployed urban proletariat, increasingly numerous and militant, a product of urbanization without industrialization and liable to be mobilized in time of crisis or social conflict. Such movements have been observed more frequently since the recession of 1973 and the application of labor policies that seek to arrest its consequences by controlling wages. Their effects have been particularly severe in the Andean and Central American countries, where, according to some authors, trade unions have often acted as "spokesmen of popular discontent."[4]

As a result there is a noticeable trend toward a rise in the number of illegal strikes compared with legal strikes. This rise is not, however, always accompanied by a proportionate increase in the number of workers taking part in the strike, as will be seen from Table 13.1.

Table 13.1.   Legal and Illegal Strikes in Colombia, Chile, and Venezuela

	Colombia (1977–79)	Chile (Jan. 1961– Sept. 1973)	Venezuela (1980)
Legal strikes	108	3,144	4
Illegal strikes	612	16,252	185
Average number of workers taking part in each strike			
Legal strikes	348*	161	127
Illegal strikes	145*	283	352

*The average was higher in 1977 and lower in 1979.
Sources: Respective departments of labor records and reports.

Although many strikes, particularly in industry, are no more than a peaceful stoppage of work, many others are accompanied by backup action or take special forms. More or less violent backup action including sabotage was a feature of many strikes in the first stages of labor relations. Until a few years ago Argentina, Uruguay, and other countries in which labor relations are undergoing change experienced every available means of exerting pressure on the employer: picketing, working to rule, occupation of the work place and boycott.[5] Boycott has, however, proved ineffective in these and other countries of the region, while picketing would appear to be unnecessary in a legal strike. It is now more usual to employ disguised or "irregular" forms of strike, such as slowdowns, which in Bolivia comprised 57 percent of all work stoppages in the period 1970–75. Staggered strikes and working to rule were used in the great railway disputes in Argentina and Mexico that took place in the 1970s.

Nowadays backup action is less important to the success of a strike than the publicity and agitation that aims at mobilizing public opinion in support of a strike or putting the government in an embarrassing position. The strikers' primary objectives are to attract the attention of the mass media and to provoke government intervention. The economic pressure brought to bear on the employer is important, but still more important is the impact of the publicity obtained by a strike; hence the occasional occupation of workplaces, government offices, embassies, and churches, and the barricades raised to block streets, roads, and bridges. Recently the intention of making the strike more effective has led to resort to other means of publicity, such as sequestration of executives or technicians of the employing undertaking. In some countries during the 1970s general strikes, normally short, were attempted in order to put pressure on the public authorities to take certain action in the general interest, or as a protest against the effects of inflation and anti-inflation policies.

Direct and Indirect Causes of Strikes

Statistics on the causes of strikes usually do no more than record their direct apparent causes; only rarely do they allude to the underlying social and political reasons leading sooner or later to strikes. For example, differences of opinion between employers and the trade unions on what constitutes fair income distribution are a fairly widespread indirect cause of strikes that is seldom reflected in the statistics. These differences may take on the magnitude of a dispute in times of economic crisis caused by contingencies, such as inflation or recession, that erode the workers' purchasing power and adversely affect employment security.

Developments in Latin American political systems also influence the nature and frequency of strikes. Strikes do not take place on imaginary islands or in isolated subsystems, but in very real political circumstances whose character, complexion, and vicissitudes do much to bring about an attitude of acceptance or rejection in which strikes often occur.

To return to labor relations, some strikes are caused because established procedures for collective bargaining and for preventing or settling disputes are ineffective. At the undertaking level another cause is the general lack of channels of communication and means of participation whereby the parties can identify and settle difficulties arising in individual and collective labor relations. Unsettled problems accumulate and create tension and frustration that break out in collective bargaining or when a demand goes unsatisfied. Numerous strikes are caused merely by a dismissal or by poor human relations, all matters that could have been settled by proper personnel management. In circumstances like these, strikes act as a substitute for personnel management and are in themselves a way of settling disputes.

If we now look more closely into labor relations and direct causes of disputes, we see a trend toward more strikes caused by deadlocks in the process of concluding or revising agreements, and relatively fewer strikes caused by the nonobservance of a collective agreement or by individual disputes. The trend is particularly marked in Mexico and Venezuela, where the difficulty of reaching agreement in wage bargaining is identifiable as the main factor in the dispute. As collective relations mature, the parties tend to improve their machinery for administering the agreement and to avoid the harm done by work stoppages called on issues that could be settled peacefully.

This trend is also seen in other countries and has been gaining ground in the last few years. As is seen in Table 13.2, wages were the cause of more than 50 percent of strikes in all the countries listed in the table, except Peru. Disputes over wages obviously acquired greater importance in times of inflationary pressures, since workers then attach a sense of urgency to wage demands and trade unions give more priority to such demands than to claims relating to other working conditions or relations between the undertaking and the trade unions. The general strike declared in Ecuador in 1983 and a recent major walkout staged in Mexico (probably the largest since the early 1960s) were organized in connection with demands for wage increases prompted by cost of living problems. In four of the countries included in the table the second main cause is still nonobservance of statutory provisions or of collective agreements. The table also shows the lingering significance of sympathy strikes in the Andean countries, and the large number of strikes called in Peru to get managers or labor authorities dismissed; the latter circumstance points to the high degree of distrust that still characterizes labor–management relations in certain countries. In Brazil a considerable number of recent strikes appear to have been touched off by fear of closure and workers' concern for their job security and income protection.[6]

Table 13.2. Causes of Strikes in Seven Countries (percent)

Causes	Brazil (1979)	Colombia (1977)	Chile (1961–73)	Ecuador (1979)	Mexico (1978)	Panama (1970–80)	Peru (1978–79)
Wage demands	62	51	53	71	61	54	35
Demands for better working conditions	9		12				3
Nonobservance of collective agreements or legislation	18	11			39	46	32
Dismissals or transfers		3	8	16			10
Trade union relations	8		10				
Sympathy strikes	1	1	5	5			9
Employer's economic and financial policy							1
Expropriation			5				
Other causes	2	34[a]	7	8			10[b]

[a]Including a "national civic strike."
[b]Including 7 strikes to oblige the dismissal of labor authorities and 28 strikes to oblige the dismissal of other authorities, 19 protest strikes against the rise in the cost of living, 5 strikes for regional reasons, and 36 strikes for unspecified reasons.
Source: Annual reports of the department of labor.

The Legal Aspects of Strikes

Legislative Trends

Both strikes and lockouts entail an element of coercion that raises problems of legal recognition. In Latin America (as elsewhere) it was strikes that raised the greatest problems, and these were aggravated by the frequent use of more or less violent backup methods, some of which, such as sabotage, are still proscribed under penal as well as labor law.

Some Latin American countries regulated the right to strike almost as soon as the first collective disputes began to arise, whereas others continued for a long time to regard strikes as illegal. In either case there was practically no period of toleration, as there was in other parts of the world.[7] Legal regulation of strikes was accordingly influenced by the violent revolutionary strikes typical of the first stages of labor relations.

The first regulations appeared at the beginning of the century (Argentina, 1910; Peru, 1913; and Colombia, 1918 and 1919); they were concerned mainly with policing strike action and taking care that strikes did not threaten property rights or the maintenance of law and order. Some years later other measures began to be adopted that sought to make the exercise of the right to strike conditional on previous exhaustion of the procedure for peaceful settlement of disputes. At this point governments began to regard strikes as a normal part of the labor relations system, however rudimentary and restrictive their recognition of them; their policy seemed to be one of institutionalizing resort to strikes and getting them to exercise a certain function in the labor relations system. However, this was only partly possible; strikes could be incorporated into the legal system only with reservations and by hedging them round with strict requirements and formalities.

Some authors believe that the real object of labor policy was to absorb and defuse the dispute.[8] This was done by combining consensus with coercion, and using procedural as well as substantive methods. At times the procedural methods did more to hinder exercise of the right to strike than to direct it into appropriate channels; the substantive measures were designed to concede advantages and benefits to individual workers so as to lessen the likelihood of collective disputes and resort to strikes.

Constitutional Recognition

A somewhat equivocal situation was thus built up that culminated in official recognition of the right to strike by the national constitution. While the government's attitude continued to be ambiguous and some strike movements were in practice repressed, many countries decided to give the right to strike top-level recognition by conferring constitutional rank on it. As of 1983, 15 countries of Latin America have included the right to strike in their constitutions: Argentina (the 1853 Constitution, as amended), Bolivia (1967), Brazil (1967), Colombia (the 1866 Constitution, as amended), Costa Rica (1949), the Dominican Republic (1966), Ecuador (1979), El Salvador (1962), Guatemala (1965), Honduras (1965), Mexico (1917), Panama (1972), Peru (1979), Uruguay (1966), and Venezuela (1961).

Constitutional recognition of the right to strike raised two important problems in nearly all the countries of the region. The first problem was whether to include lockouts as a right of the employers—that is, whether to put this technique of exerting pressure on the same plane as the right to strike, or to take the view that the intrinsic power of employers and the aims of lockouts were such that they were unworthy of sanction by the constitution. In Costa Rica, the Dominican Republic, Ecuador, El Salvador, Guatemala, Honduras, and Mexico lockouts have been included; but in Mexico and Honduras the constitution states that lockouts shall be legal only where excess production makes it necessary to suspend work in order to keep prices within economic limits, after approval by the Conciliation and Arbitration Board. In Argentina, Bolivia, Colombia, Panama, Peru, Uruguay, and Venezuela, on the contrary, only the workers' right to strike has been recognized; but although lockouts are not recognized by the constitution, this does not prevent them from being regulated by law or resorted to in practice.[9]

The second problem concerns the equivocal situation and the fear that recognition of the right to strike could lead to its unrestricted use. Constitutions, therefore, were careful to introduce limitations on the right to strike. They prohibited strikes in public services and public utilities as well as coercive or violent action. Constitutional provisions also specified what socioeconomic aims strikes might pursue, or indicated that recognition was subject to the regulation of strikes by law.

The constitution's concern to regulate strikes is reflected in the labor laws; in most Latin American countries strikes are regulated by an abundance of detailed statutory provisions. These are mainly concerned with the definition of the right to strike and the limits within which it may be exercised, the conditions to be complied with for a strike to be legal, the legal effects of striking, the duration of a strike, and settlement procedures. In general the purpose of these constitutional and legal requirements was to give specific treatment to the right to strike, in view of its economic and political effects as well as its significant role in labor relations.

Work stoppages were originally frowned upon because of their effects on the incomes of the workers and undertakings concerned, the supply of goods and services to other undertakings and the community at large, the state's revenue from taxation, and the success of national and sectoral development plans. Moreover, if such stoppages were excessively frequent, they were regarded as potentially harmful events that left unhealed wounds in the quality of labor relations in the undertaking, undermined the efficacy of methods of peaceful settlement of labor disputes, discouraged investments, and might even signify that the very basis of the country's political regime was in question.

As well as representing the sovereignty of the people and holding police powers, Latin American governments still view themselves as the planners and directors of economic and social policy, and therefore take care that their development programs are not adversely affected by the behavior of economic sectors and units. The problem is, accordingly, to reconcile the right to strike, and the right to declare a lockout, with the socioeconomic and political aims contained in development plans and overall public policies. Only recently have many governments begun to realize that open or latent labor disputes are part and parcel of the labor relations system of modern pluralistic societies.

Definitions and Limitations

In most countries the legislation contains definitions of a strike that refer to what are usually the four basic elements of the strike concept: stoppage of work, temporary character, participation of a group or plurality of workers, and the aim of improving or protecting economic or occupational interests. Some countries seek to elaborate on these factors and add further requirements. In Colombia and Costa Rica, for example, stoppages of work must be peaceful. In Costa Rica and Panama the law specifies the minimum number of workers (respectively three and five) who must take part in the decision to stop work. Other countries, including El Salvador and Mexico, prefer to allude to a plurality or coalition of workers. Colombia defines the aims of the strike as "economic and occupational," and Costa Rica relates them to "the intention of defending or improving occupational or socioeconomic interests."

Some legislation establishes permanent general restrictions on the right to strike, either including them in definitions or inserting them in other legal texts. In Ecuador and Peru there are compulsory arbitration systems that appear to make exercise of the right to strike incompatible with implementation of the arbitration award. However, there are now relatively few such awards, and in Ecuador it is permissible to strike before the award is made. In Chile the 1979 Labor Plan excludes a number of undertakings of "strategic" importance to the economy, or providing essential services, from exercise of the right to strike; the government makes an annual list of such undertakings, which in 1980 comprised 28 work places. In other countries, such as Argentina, there are general but temporary restrictions expressly designed to cope with economic or political emergencies. In Brazil, the Dominican Republic, and Uruguay the system in force for the settlement of collective disputes makes exercise of the right to strike virtually impossible or very difficult. In Nicaragua the right to strike has been suspended during the period of economic and social emergency. In other countries there are restrictions on certain categories of workers, such as civil servants, workers in public utilities and state undertakings, the armed forces, and the police.

Legal restrictions on the right to strike, although exceptional, usually can be extensively applied, being couched in terms that go beyond the declared intention of limiting the right to strike. As stated in Chapter 11, where strikes in the public services are prohibited, statements and enumerations are sometimes resorted to that enable the prohibition to be widely applied and to include activities in which the phrase "public service" is not beyond doubt identical with "essential service." In Panama a 1981 provision submitted labor disputes in public enterprises to compulsory arbitration and gave central and regional labor directorates a discretionary power to prohibit strikes in such cases. In some countries the restrictions in force have been described as distorting the relationship between labor discontent and the number of strikes.[10]

In spite of the legal restrictions and the socioeconomic limitations, the strike weapon is substantially used in Latin American industries. This is shown, for example, by the repeated strikes in the civil service and public utilities of nearly all the countries of the region, and the recent strikes in the automobile industries of Argentina and Brazil, some "essential" undertakings in Chile, and public transport in the Dominican Republic.

Requirements, Time Limits, and Prior Warnings

In most countries of the region the procedure for the peaceful settlement of disputes must be exhausted before a strike may be called. Since the procedure is not always designed to lead to a prompt settlement, the outcome of such provisions is in practice of dilatory effect and doubtful value. At the same time the lack of appropriate procedures for the conduct of negotiations may also mean that the need for a strike sometimes takes the place of the right to strike. It is no rare thing for a strike to be in practice the best way of compelling collective bargaining and obliging the authorities to attend to the dispute(s) at hand. This reversal of the normal sequence of events places the strike at the beginning of the process, thus aggravating the effect of subsequent deadlocks in the discussions and making settlement more difficult. Settlement is primarily concerned to end the situation caused by the work stoppage, and may put off any consideration of the substance of the dispute. As a result the dispute is still latent, and may flare up again at any moment. The same thing happens where the conciliation or mediation procedure is not as adequate or impartial as it should be, or is so bureaucratic that its full and timely exercise is difficult.

In most countries the legislation requires that an absolute majority (50 percent plus one) of the workers concerned agrees to the strike, but a greater majority is sometimes required: 60 percent in Costa Rica and the Dominican Republic, and 75 percent in Bolivia and Paraguay. Voting on the proposal to go on strike must take place at a special meeting, the convening of which is regulated in most cases by legislation, some of which requires a notary public or an official from the department of labor to attend, in order to verify that the meeting was conducted according to law. In some countries, including Chile, El Salvador, and Paraguay, voting must be by secret ballot.

In several countries the legislation stipulates the period of notice to be given before a strike may start. These waiting periods between the date on which the strike is announced and its actual commencement are intended, inter alia, to enable the parties to make new efforts to arrive at a peaceful settlement, and especially to give the department of labor an opportunity to intervene in the dispute. Its intervention is of course subsequent to the one that may have taken place during the negotiations for a peaceful settlement.

In view of the supposed imminence of the strike at this stage, such notice is generally short: 72 hours in Costa Rica, Chile, and Peru; 120 hours in Venezuela; 5 days in Bolivia, Colombia, and Panama; 6 days in Mexico; 7 days in El Salvador; and 10 days in Ecuador. Maximum periods are sometimes specified at whose expiry the strike may not take place. In Colombia it may not take place once 30 days have elapsed after the date of the strike notice; in Panama the strike notice must be given within the 20 days following the end of the conciliation procedure, and the strike must start within the 3 working days following the expiry of that period.

Effects

The effects of the strike differ greatly according to whether the strike is legal or illegal, and are regulated by law. If a strike is illegal, the legislation in most countries recognizes the employer's right to terminate employment contracts, and also lays down a procedure for resumption of work. Some legislation also lays down rules concerning the civil or criminal liability of persons involved in an illegal strike.

Generally speaking, legal strikes entail stoppage of work, nonpayment of wages during the stoppage, and suspension of other ancillary rights.

Stoppage of Work

In most countries the legislation lays down rules to ensure that the stoppage of work takes place in a peaceful manner, that it occurs without violence against persons or property, and that the establishments affected do in fact suspend their operations; the recruitment of new personnel to take the place of strikers, and the entry of workers opposed to the strike who want to go on working, are forbidden.

These two aspects of the most important effect of the strike are further evidence of how equivocal the official position is. The law prohibits any action apt to cause disorder or destroy working material, instruments, and equipment, and it forbids physical or moral violence against the employer or the workers; but it also clearly prescribes that a legal strike shall close the establishment or business, that new workers may not be recruited to take the place of the strikers, and that the minority groups of workers who wish to go on working may not enter the premises. Protection of legal strikes is greatest in Ecuador, where strikers are entitled to occupy their factory, workshop, or work place for the duration of the strike. Admittedly the occupation must be supervised by the police, but the police are also bound to "guarantee the parties' rights and prohibit the entry to work places of agitators or strikebreakers."

To understand this feature of Latin American labor law, reference must be made to the origins of collective labor relations. There was generally an element of violence in the first strikes, because industry, then in its early stages, employed few skilled workers and the strikers were generally workers with little training, for whom substitutes could easily be found.[11] It was in answer to that state of affairs and to prevent violence that the law of many countries prohibited the use of "blacklegs" or strike breakers. At the same time this provision made picketing (now mentioned only in the Panama Labor Code) unnecessary and reflected the state's primary concern with maintaining order. Problems still arise in some countries because protection of the right to strike and the consequent prohibition of the use of strikebreakers apply only to legal strikes; since most strikes do not comply with legal requirements, the protection afforded by law is practically irrelevant.

Legislation on work stoppages usually authorizes the continuance of work regarded as essential. In Colombia, for instance, the employer may not conclude new employment contracts for the resumption of the suspended services except in departments whose operation is essential, and then only if the strikers do not allow the staff of those departments to work. In Mexico the law provides that before work is stopped, the Conciliation and Arbitration Board shall, after consulting the parties, fix the minimum number of workers necessary to continue work whose interruption would seriously prejudice the safety and preservation of the premises, machinery, and raw materials or the resumption of work. It is also prescribed that strikers must continue to work on ships, aircraft, trains, buses, and other transport vehicles on a journey until they reach their destination. Similarly, strikers must continue their work in hospitals, sanatoriums, clinics, and similar establishments until all the inpatients who were in them when the strike was declared are transferred to another establishment. In all these cases the employer may use other workers if strikers refuse to do the necessary work, and the Conciliation and Arbitration Board may, where necessary, call in the police so that such workers may do the work in question.

In Panama there is a similar provision applying to ships and aircraft, and it is prescribed that in other public services, strikers must inform the labor authorities of the emergency shifts in the centers affected by the strike, in order that these centers shall not be put completely out of action. The emergency shifts must comprise between 20 and 30 percent of all the workers in those services, and the labor authorities may increase the number of workers on these shifts to up to 30 percent if they consider the lower percentage fixed by the strikers to be insufficient. There are similar prescriptions in the legislation of Chile, the Dominican Republic, Ecuador, and Paraguay.

Stoppage of work is also affected where legislation requires resumption of work, as in Chile, where the president of the republic may decree resumption of work for 90 days if the strike, by reason of its characteristics, timing, or duration, causes serious harm to public health or supplies, or to the economy or safety of the nation. In such cases a mediator is appointed and the duration of the strike allowed by law is suspended. Work is resumed on the conditions in force when the draft collective agreement was submitted. The legislation of Panama states that if a strike takes place in a public utility, the government may take over its direction and administration for the minimum time necessary to prevent prejudice to the community. In Venezuela, in strikes in undertakings or services where a stoppage imperils public health or the national economy, the government may order work to be resumed on such conditions as the general interest may require, by issuing a special decree stating its reasons. In such cases the necessary staff may not be recruited on conditions worse than those laid down in a report issued by the Conciliation Board or its chairman.

Nonpayment of Wages

One of the legal effects of a strike is nonpayment of wages for its duration. This is the general principle applied in nearly every part of the world; its basis is that, because of the nature of the employment contract, if the services contracted for are not performed, their counterpart, wages or salary, ceases to be payable. In a sense this principle also responds to the nature and rationale of strikes as trials of strength; both parties should feel the effects of the stoppage—the employer by ceasing to produce and the workers by ceasing to draw their wages. There are, however, exceptions to this principle. In Ecuador and Panama workers engaged in a legal strike other than a sympathy strike are entitled to draw their full wages throughout the strike; in Panama the strike must also have been caused by the employer, and in Ecuador the right may be enforced unless the Conciliation and Arbitration Board unanimously decides otherwise or totally rejects the demands made, or if the workers call a strike without following legal requirements. In Costa Rica, if the labor courts declare that the employer is responsible for a legal strike—by non-observance of a collective agreement, unjustified refusal to conclude a collective agreement, or maltreatment of or violence to workers—he shall pay wages for the duration of the strike. In Mexico, if the Conciliation and Arbitration Board declares in its award that the employer is responsible for the strike, the employer shall pay wages for the duration of the strike.

There are, in our opinion, two reasons for these provisions. The first is the desire for social justice that has inspired the legislators of many Latin American countries who have guaranteed the right to strike and carried this recognition to its logical conclusion. In the view of these legislators, if the workers' demands are reasonable and the workers' organizations are right in taking strike action, their interests should not suffer from the strike and it would be unfair to deprive the weak and innocent party of its only means of subsistence for the days on which it exercised a right conferred by the law and the constitution.

The second reason is a more practical one. It is assumed in other industrial relations systems that loss of wages during the strike will be compensated by an indemnity paid from the strike fund formed by the trade unions. In Latin America there are, to all intents and purposes, no strike funds, or they are very limited because it is the nature of trade unions at the undertaking level to be financially weak, particularly in countries where union dues are low or irregularly paid; nor are there unemployment insurance schemes or any form of similar compensation available. It was therefore considered necessary to make some other provision for the livelihood of striking workers.

Duration

A strike is by definition temporary—that is, it must not be equivalent to a permanent termination of work. In some countries (Colombia, for instance) the legislation empowers the state to intervene in long strikes, but it is exceptional to regulate the period for which a strike may last, as is done in Chile and Panama.

In Chile, once 60 days have elapsed from the start of the strike, workers who maintain their decision not to go to work are considered to have resigned of their own free will; this cause of termination of contract has the same effects as the worker's resignation, but the right to severance pay subsists. Needless to say, this approach tends to distort the nature of a strike and places an unjustifiable burden on the workers (though in practice not many work stoppages last more than a few days or weeks).

In Panama the law states that the strike may be declared either for a definite or an indefinite period, provided that in the latter case, stoppage of work is temporary. If the duration of the strike is unspecified, it is considered to have been declared for an indefinite period.

In practice the duration of the great majority of strikes declared in Latin America does not exceed 50 days, and a high proportion of them last only one day or from one to ten days. The longest stikes in the history of Brazil (Belo Horizonte, 1982) and Costa Rica (Banana Development Corporation, 1982) lasted 117 and 63 days, respectively; while there have been longer ones in Argentina, Colombia, and Mexico, these are very exceptional cases. Table 13.3 gives details of the duration of strikes in six countries of the region.

The duration of the strike appears to depend more on how promptly the government intervenes to settle it, either because of its economic or political effects or in answer to pressure brought upon it to intervene, than upon either party's ability to hold out. Another important factor is whether the strike is legal or illegal; legal strikes tend to last much longer than illegal ones. For example, in Colombia in 1977, 51 percent of all illegal strikes lasted from 1 to 5 days and 25 percent only 1 day, whereas 61 percent of all legal strikes lasted between 11 and 50 days, and 26 percent over 90 days.

Propensity to Strike

In Latin America the socioeconomic background is not particularly favorable to strikes. There are also other factors concerning political

Table 13.3. Duration of Strikes

Number of Strikes, by Duration

Colombia (1977)		Ecuador (1979)		Panama (1979–80)	
Duration (days)	*No. of Strikes*	*Duration (days)*	*No. of Strikes*	*Duration (days)*	*No. of Strikes*
Under 1	69	1–2	1	1	8
1–5	150	3–10	17	2–10	10
6–10	11	11–50	17	11–20	7
11–15	21	51–100	1	21–31	3
16–30	35	101 and over	1		
31–50	13				
51–70	3				
71–90	3				
91–130	5				
131–180	4				
181–240	3				

Changes in Duration of Strikes

Average Duration (days)	Costa Rica (1972–80)	Chile (1979–80)	Peru (1967–76)
2	1973		
3	1972 and 1975		1969
5			1967 and 1968
6	1974		1970
7	1978		1976
9	1976 and 1979		1971 and 1972
10	1980		
11			1974
12			1975
14			1973
18		16/8/80–12/11/80	
20	1977	16/8/79–30/6/80	

Sources: Respective departments of labor records and reports.

forces and the strength of the parties to the labor relations system that condition the exercise of the right to strike and may in practice make it less frequent.

Obviously, where unemployment and underemployment are high, strikes may be called less often, especially if they are illegal, because participation in an illegal strike invalidates the statutory protection of the workers' job security. Another conditioning factor is the political atmosphere prevailing in each country. If that atmosphere is not propitious to trade union activity, strikes are tacitly restricted; and if a strike does take place, it either tends to be labeled political, and therefore not entitled to recognition under labor legislation, or the public authorities responsible for settling labor disputes tend to lack the neutrality and objectivity required to bring about a proper settlement. It may be noted, in this respect, that in Chile during the first two years of implementation of the 1979 Labor Plan, strikes were declared in 3 percent of the total number of negotiations;[12] this percentage does not differ substantially from the one in Mexico.[13]

A third factor is the labor relations system in the country, economic sector, or undertaking concerned; where there is a tradition of bargaining, and of regarding strikes as a last resort to be used only when direct or indirect negotiation has broken down, its effects are necessarily different from those in a tradition of confrontation. A fourth conditioning factor is trade union organization and finance; it is difficult (though not impossible) to call and conduct strikes in work places or sectors where there is no trade union, where the union's powers are limited, or where workers' organizations cannot afford the direct or indirect cost of a strike. Statistics clearly show this. In Colombia in 1977, 67.7 percent of the workers in undertakings affected by strikes (67.1 percent in manufacturing industry), and 52.1 percent of the strikers (51.9 percent in manufacturing industry), were unionized. In Ecuador works councils took part in 32.4 percent of the strikes in 1979. This relation between unionized labor and strikes does not signify that the exercise of the right to organize is in itself a major cause of the propensity to strike; it merely provides the necessary organizational infrastructure.

A fifth conditioning factor is the ideological position of the trade union movement. If, for strategic reasons suiting that position, the strike weapon is useful, the propensity to strike will be greater. On the other hand, certain strategic interests usually lessen the propensity to strike of trade union organizations that by and large support national social policy or decide to coexist peacefully with it though having different aims. For example, the propensity to strike is not the same in the "insurgent" or radical trade unions of Mexico City as in the "independent" or autonomous trade unions of Monterrey.

Table 13.4. Frequency of Strikes in Eleven Countries, 1970–80

	1970	1971	1972	1973	1974	1975	1976
Argentina	5	16	12		543	1,266	
Bolivia				350	420	551	
Costa Rica				14	8	18	14
Chile	1,819	2,696	3,325	2,050			
Ecuador					61	61	58
El Salvador		12	23	6	6	14	2
Guatemala	36	1	4	16	53	7	16
Mexico	206	204	207	211	742	236	547
Panama	6	280		11	3	6	15
Peru	345	377	409	788	570	779	440
Venezuela	64	106	172	250	116	100	171

	1977	1978	1979	1980	Total No. of Strikes	Annual Average
Argentina					1,842	368
Bolivia					1,321	440
Costa Rica	10	14	20	61	159	20
Chile					9,890	2,473
Ecuador	9	7	37	75	308	44
El Salvador	19	29	103	95	249	31
Guatemala	9	229	7	51	429	39
Mexico	476	758	795		4,382	438
Panama	4	3	10	18	356	36
Peru	234	364	653	739	5,698	518
Venezuela	214	190	145	195	1,673	157

Source: Based on ILO, *Year Book of Labour Statistics, 1980* (Geneva: ILO, 1981), supplemented for Bolivia and Ecuador by data from department of labor records.

As will be seen from Table 13.4, the number of strikes varies greatly from country to country and year to year. If Chile is left out of account, the average number of strikes was appreciably higher in Bolivia and Peru than elsewhere. In Peru 1970–78 was a period of intense social mobilization, but other factors also made for the greater propensity to strike.[14] The annual averages of Mexico (438) and Venezuela (152) reflect the great volume of bargaining in those countries and do not appear at all excessive.

The greatest variation over time is observable in Argentina, where very few strikes were called during the years of military government from 1970 to 1973 and there was subsequently a marked increase during the Perón regime. The table also shows the large number of strikes during the Allende government in Chile. Both situations highlight the importance of the political factor and the presence of legal provisions restricting or favoring the right to strike. The political situation and the deterioration of the general social climate of the country are also shown in the sharp increase of strikes in Guatemala in 1978 and El Salvador in 1979.

The number of strikes is an indicator of the propensity to call strikes but gives no general idea of their impact on society. In Argentina in 1972, a total of 61,259 workers took part in the 12 strikes called, an average of 5,105 workers for each strike, probably because the strikes affected undertakings in the same industry. In Ecuador, where bargaining is at the undertaking level, the average number of workers taking part in strikes between 1975 and 1979 was 195 in 1975, 164 in 1976, 89 in 1977, 77 in 1978, and 65 in 1979. In the same period the average number of strikers was higher in Peru, where it was 793 in 1975, 581 in 1976, 1,693 in 1977, and 3,568 in 1978; this suggests that many strikers were called as social protests and had nothing to do with the bargaining level. As is shown in Table 13.5, Chile under Allende and Peru throughout the 1970s were the only countries in which the total number of workers participating in strikes constantly reached at least six figures. Their annual averages of workers taking part in strikes are certainly far above those of the other countries. In 1981 Peru reached its highest record of strikes (871) and workers involved (856,910).[15]

Incidence

By combining the data on the number of strikes with the data on their duration and number of strikers, we arrive at the number of man-hours lost by strikes—that is, their incidence. From the data in Table 13.5 it is clear that, except for Chile under the Allende government, Peru tops the list of Latin American countries for total man-days lost by strikes and man-days lost in a single year (over 2.2 million in 1980, and almost 2.5 million in 1981).

Table 13.5. Number of Workers Participating and Man-Days Lost by Strikes in Ten Countries, 1970–80

		1970	1971	1972	1973	1974	1975
Argentina	WP	2912	68632	61259		271697	
	DL	32849	159277	153047		651555	
Costa Rica	WP				8303	15300	11500
	DL				17913	328922	47252
Chile	WP	656170	298677	393954	711028		
	DL	2804517	1387517	1678124	2503356		
Ecuador	WP					5948	11913
	DL					105380	418230
El Salvador	WP		10614	3919	618	37406	2902
	DL		196595	42021	7118		39059
Guatemala	WP	27067	92	4868	22711	43934	8336
	DL	50934	460	33240	257089	562593	53476
Mexico	WP	14329	9299	2684	8395	17863	9680
	DL						
Panama	WP	7510	15606		1414	232	
	DL	13148				1063	
Peru	WP	110990	161415	130643	416251	362737	617120
	DL	722732	1360244	791377	1961086	1676630	2533676
Venezuela	WP	23934	39094	24654	45508	17463	25752
	DL	234349	519919	146186	144671	129978	100662

Strikes generally take place in the urban centers in which economic activity and trade union organization are most concentrated. In Brazil, 87.5 percent of the strikes in 1978 and 40 percent of strikes in 1979 occurred in the state of São Paulo (in 1978, 83.1 percent of the strikes were in greater São Paulo and 6.6 percent in the rest of that state). In Colombia 29 percent of illegal strikes and 33 percent of legal strikes in the period 1977–79 were in the territorial division of Cundinamarca-Bogotá and involved 26 and 25 percent, respectively, of the 126,412 workers taking part in illegal and legal strikes. No less than 44 percent of all working hours lost through illegal strikes during this period were lost in that territorial division; the Cundinamarca-Bogotá area also accounted for 3.5 percent of the

		1976	1977	1978	1979	1980
Argentina	WP					
	DL					
Costa Rica	WP		10592	20168	25671	24750
	DL		74121	176780	275130	427350
Chile	WP					
	DL					
Ecuador	WP	7016	802	538	2387	16065
	DL	265110	43282	17394	60012	508170
El Salvador	WP	25300	32879	7169	29432	12110
	DL	601800	154792	72962	292280	44217
Guatemala	WP	5757	8670	144956	42170	68683
	DL	167831	60641	1479246		817300
Mexico	WP	23684	13411	4976	17264	
	DL					
Panama	WP	2080	205	867	1161	2438
	DL	18939	915	3003	44292	158740
Peru	WP	258101	1315400	1398387	841140	481480
	DL	852778	1726300	4518092	1676300	2239900
Venezuela	WP	33932	63923	25340	23270	67960
	DL	91267	86000	39840	50020	315310

WP = workers participating.
DL = man-days lost.
Source: ILO, *Year Book of Labor Statistics, 1981* (Geneva: ILO, 1982).

total time lost in legal strikes. In the same period the figures for the Valle del Cauca territorial division, in which the city of Cali is situated, were 12 percent of all legal and illegal strikes, 11 percent of the total number of strikers, and 16 percent of all working hours lost by legal and illegal strikes. In Costa Rica between January 1, 1972, and August 31, 1980, 6 of the 163 strikes were national ones and 41 took place in San José.

Available statistics also show a connection between strikes and the sector of economic activity in which they took place. The extent of unionization and the nature of labor relations in those sectors partly explain these connections. Table 13.6 gives relevant information for ten countries in the region, from which it will be seen that in most countries strikes were mainly in manufacturing industry. This was so in Colombia (45 percent of strikes in 1977), Ecuador (38 percent of strikes in 1979), El Salvador (72 percent of strikes in 1978), Peru (44 percent of strikes in 1979 and 1980), Mexico (76 percent of strikes in undertakings under federal jurisdiction between 1971 and 1978), and Venezuela (64 percent of strikes in 1977). The preponderance of strikes in this sector is confirmed by the fact that most strikers in Colombia, Ecuador, Peru, and Venezuela were workers in manufacturing industry. Also, in Colombia, Peru, and Venezuela most of the man-hours lost by strikes were in manufacturing industry.

There are, however, important variations that may be due both to the economic structure of the countries concerned and to changing circumstances. In Costa Rica 46 percent of strikes between 1972 and 1980 were in agriculture, followed by 28.2 percent in the services sector and 12.9 percent in manufacturing industry. In Guatemala in 1978, strikes were mainly in the services sector (85 percent), followed by transport, storage, and communications (4.4 percent), agriculture (3 percent), and banking (2.6 percent); strikes in manufacturing industry accounted for 2.2 percent of the total number in that year. In Panama strikes in manufacturing industry accounted for 11.4 percent of all strikes between 1976 and 1980, less than in commerce, restaurants, and hotels (38.6 percent), construction (27.3 percent), and transport, storage, and communications (13.6 percent).

Lockouts

A lockout is a temporary stoppage of work and plant shutdown by an employer or group of employers to compel workers to agree to the conditions of work offered them. Such conditions may be those already in force in the undertaking(s), or consist of amendments due to changes in the circumstances governing those conditions.

In Latin America the legislation either accepts the substance of the above definition or regards a lockout as a suspension (which may be temporary or permanent, partial or total) of the activities of one or more undertakings for economic, financial or technical reasons, resulting in the amendent, suspension, or termination of the contract of the workers affected. In the latter event a lockout is in fact a mass layoff and ceases to be a means of pressure in the industrial relations context, but its effects are nevertheless such that it is usually treated as a labor dispute.

Table 13.6. Strikes in Ten Countries, by Branch of Economic Activity

	Colombia	Costa Rica	Chile	Ecuador	El Salvador	Guatemala	Mexico[1]	Panama	Peru	Venezuela
	1977	1972–80	1961–73	1979	1978	1978	1971–78	1976–80	1979–80	1977
Agriculture, forestry, hunting, fishing	3	75	4,818	3		7		2	27	16
Mining, quarrying	2	21	1,693	1	1	1	15	2	197	2
Manufacturing	144		4,118	15	21	5	753	5	615	136
Electricity, gas, water	1		354	1	1	5			58	1
Construction		8	1,988	2	5			12	12	24
Wholesale and retail trade, restaurants, hotels	4		555					17	245[2]	10
Transport, storage, communications	17	5	1,750	1	1	10		6	66	6
Financial institutions, insurance, real estate, business services	63	3				6				
Community, social, and personal services	83	46	3,993[3]	11		194	36		149	10
Activities not adequately described		5	127[4]				190[5]		23	19

[1]Strikes in undertakings under federal jurisdiction, Sept. 1971-Nov. 1978.

[2]Including strikes in banks.

[3]Including 3,579 strikes in the public sector.

[4]Including 65 general strikes.

[5]Comprising 15 strikes in decentralized agencies and undertakings with state participation, 160 strikes in undertakings operating under federal contracts or concessions and allied industries, 8 strikes in undertakings carrying out work in federal areas or territorial waters, and 7 strikes in activities not adequately described.

Source: Annual reports of the department of labor.

Legislation of the first kind includes that of Bolivia, Colombia, Costa Rica, and Venezuela, and the second that of Ecuador, Mexico, Panama, and Peru. The countries in which a lockout is recognized as a legitimate means of pressure in a collective dispute also fall into two groups, according to whether the lockout is used for both offensive and defensive purposes, or only for defensive purposes. Examples of the groups are Venezuela and Chile, respectively. In Venezuela a lockout may be used to make the workers accept certain conditions of work; in Chile it may be used only where a strike has already been declared that affects over 50 percent of the workers or leads to interruption of activities essential to the operation of the undertaking. The Argentine theory of labor law accepts only a defensive lockout, on the grounds that any other form of lockout would authorize the employer to deprive his workers of the benefits and conditions already enjoyed by them and guaranteed by law.[16]

The common denominator of legislation in the countries where lockouts are accepted as a means of pressure includes the following: conciliation and arbitration procedure must first be exhausted; prior notice must be given; stoppage of work must be peaceful—that is, without coercion or violence; lockouts in the public services are prohibited or must comply with special conditions. Curiously, one of the countries permitting lockouts in the public services is Colombia, although it prohibits strikes in that sector.

Whereas in Bolivia and Costa Rica legislation assumes that several employers are involved, in Colombia and Venezuela a single employer may exercise the right to lock out. There are also differences in regard to the duration of the lockout, which may not exceed 30 days in Chile and may go on indefinitely in other countries.

As for the effects of a lockout, the law generally prescribes that a legal lockout shall suspend contracts of employment. If the undertaking resumes work within a certain time, the employer must give the dismissed workers priority in employment, on conditions not worse than those they enjoyed at the start of the lockout. Illegal lockouts give the workers the right to demand immediate reemployment with payment of unpaid wages, or to regard their contracts of employment as terminated and draw the appropriate legal indemnities and benefits.

In general, lockouts are not as meticulously regulated by law as strikes are in most countries. This is partly because there are so few of them: there were only two cases in Chile in 1979–82 (in spite of the increased importance given to the lockout in the Labor Plan), a few in Colombia and Venezuela in the last few years, and none in the Dominican Republic and Ecuador in the several decades for which labor legislation has been in force. Not even the attenuated form of lockout allowed by the Mexican Constitution appears to have been put into practice.

Notes

1. Unless otherwise stated, the statistics in this chapter have been taken from annual department of labor reports. Publications of the Institute of Economic and Social Planning of Brazil and of the Departamento de Relaciones del Trabajo y Desarrollo Organizacional (DERTO) of the University of Chile have also been consulted.

2. See A. F. Cesarino, Jr., and Marly A. Cardone, "Brazil," in R. Blanpain, ed., *International Encyclopaedia for Labor Law and Industrial Relations*, (Deventer, Netherlands: Kluwer, 1978), p. 146.

3. See Ch. 7, sec. "Union Security Clauses."

4. Danilo Jiménez Veiga, *El sindicalismo en Centroamérica y la intervención del estado en la década de 1980* (Mexico City: Instituto Nacional de Estudios del Trabajo, 1981), p. 46.

5. See A. Vázquez Vialard, *Derecho del trabajo y seguridad social*, (Buenos Aires: Editorial Astrea, 1978), p. 570; and Héctor Hugo Barbagelata, "El derecho del trabajo del Uruguay," in *El derecho del trabajo latinoamérica* (Mexico City: Univsidad Nacional Autónoma de México, 1974), p. 501.

6. *Social and Labour Bulletin* no. 4 (Dec. 1982): 459.

7. Ignacio Escobar Uribe, *Los conflictos colectivos de trabajo en Colombia* (Bogotá: Editorial Temis, 1975), p. 87.

8. See Jorge Santistevan, *El derecho de huelga en el Perú* (Lima: CEDYS, 1981), passim.

9. See, for instance, A. J. Ruprecht, "Argentina," in R. Blanpain, ed., *International Encyclopaedia*, vol. II *for Labour Law...*, p. 165.

10. "Evolución reciente de las huelgas," in *Análisis laboral* (Lima) June 1981, p. 16.

11. See Miguel Urrutia, *Historia del sindicalismo en Colombia* (Bogotá: Ediciones Universidad de los Andes, 1969), p. 96.

12. M. Barrera and T. Selamé, "Caracterización del Plan laboral y sus consecuencias para el sindicalismo chileno," *Documento* (Santiago de Chile) no. 8 (June 1982): 29.

13. See Ch. 10, sec. "Current Problems."

14. See Denis Sulmont, "Conflictos laborales y movilización popular: Perú, 1968-76," *Revista mexicana de sociología*, Apr.-June 1978, pp. 685 ff.

15. ILO, *Year Book of Labour Statistics*, 1982 (Geneva: ILO, 1983), p. 677.

16. See Ruprecht, "Argentina," loc. cit.

INDEX

About the Editor

Born in Havana, Cuba, and an American citizen since 1966, Efrén Córdova holds a Doctor of Law degree from the University of Havana and a Ph.D. in industrial and labor relations from Cornell University. He taught labor law and labor relations at the universities of Havana and Puerto Rico (Río Piedras). In 1967 he joined the ILO, where he has been chief of the Labor Law and Labor Relations Branch for several years. Dr. Córdova has written extensively on labor relations in general and Latin America in particular. A member of various professional organizations, he is the secretary of the International Industrial Relations Association.